"It Still Beats Working!"

"It Still Beats Working!"

My Forty Years of Motor Racing Fun

Eoin Young

First published in Great Britain in 2003 by
Transport Bookman Publications Limited
8 South Street,
Isleworth,
Middlesex. TW7 7DH

© Eoin S.Young 2003

ISBN 0 85184 069 8

Jacket design and layout by Peter Renn Photography.

Printed and bound in Great Britain by
Butler & Tanner Ltd, Frome and London

Contents

Foreword

Quite where and when I first met Eoin Young is lost now in the mists of time, but with some confidence I can say he had a smile on his face and a glass in his hand. When I first joined the Formula 1 press corps, in 1971, Eoin had already been on the scene for many years, and I remember being vastly impressed that he seemed to know everybody - and even more so that they seemed to know him.

This was to serve me very well, because Eoin had all the contacts I then lacked. In those days you didn't arrange interviews with drivers or team owners through a barrage of PR people; you simply went up to the person with whom you wished to speak, and arranged a time. It was that simple.

Or it should have been. For me, though, it wasn't, because all my life I had looked upon these people – these *Formula 1* people – as gods, and introducing myself to them was about as easy as sticking my hand in a fire.

ESY had no such inhibitions – indeed if he has inhibitions of any kind they have never been apparent to me – and in those early days he did much to smooth my path, not only introducing me to half the paddock, but also suggesting outlets for my stories, and putting me in touch with the right people.

Freelance journalism is like freelance anything, in that it tends to be dog-eat-dog, but Eoin was not only good enough to share his contacts with me, and others, he was also sufficiently confident to do it, well aware of his standing in the racing community.

Colleagues will tell you, as I, that we all aspired one day to be in Eoin's position, able to write a story quickly and easily, then to syndicate it to magazines across the world, and wait for the cheques to come in. This, we agreed, was an operator *sans pareil*.

It was the same when he went into the memorabilia business. I once wrote that Eoin was the kind of bloke who would pass you in a revolving door, and it's true that he is a genius when it comes to doing deals, thinking on his feet.

I remember vividly (and not without pain) an occasion in Paris some years ago, when we were rooting through miscellaneous 'racing stuff' in a backstreet shop specialising in sporting ephemera. I came across a newspaper, a special edition commemorating the race from Paris to Rouen in 1894, this the very first motoring competition of any kind.

Given its age, it appeared in good condition, and the price – about 12 quid – seemed remarkably modest; having no interest in it myself, I drew it to Mr Young's attention. He foamed at the mouth.

Actually, he didn't, but still his excitement was evident. This was held in check while he swiftly settled up with the dealer for a mound of material, after which he summoned a cab, and instructed the driver – in English, of course – to proceed to our hotel with all possible dispatch.

Once there, he dialled a number in California. "It's Eoin Young, calling from Paris. I've got something here you may feel you have to own..." After describing the item, he asked the hapless client what sort of money he would prepared to pay for it. The man came up with an improbably high figure. "Isn't that amazing?" the vendor murmured. "The very figure I had in mind..."

As I recall, we dined well that evening.

If I had to pick one adjective to describe Eoin, it would be 'laconic'. He is easily bored, and not always successful at concealing it, as more than one earnest PR has discovered over time. "Excuse me," he will say, "I think you're confusing me with someone who cares..."

Something about which he does care is books. "Why write them?" he has said to me a time or two. "There's much more money in selling them." But that's the throwaway remark – he has, after all, written many himself, and is an avid reader, with catholic tastes.

When it comes to his own writing, Eoin's hallmarks are fluency and ease. It goes without saying that he is a great raconteur, and he writes as he speaks – when I read one his articles, I can hear the words. In many ways, the most difficult aspect of writing is to make it seem effortless, and this quality has always characterised an article by Eoin Young. He is 'a natural'.

My colleagues and I hold him in great regard and affection, recalling not only the countless dinners, the verbal sparring, the droll one-liners, but also his kindness on so many occasions. Truth is, Eoin is far less hard-boiled than he might have you believe, a close friend for so many years, and among the writers I have most admired in this capricious world of Formula 1.

I raise a glass to him. He'll like that.

Nigel Roebuck
9 October 2003

Dedication

I dedicate this book to my good friend, Euan Sarginson, in New Zealand. We met when he was photographing the Tasman Series and I was working with Bruce McLaren's team back in the 'sixties. For the following four decades we have kept in touch and when I am in New Zealand I often enjoy the comfort of the west wing in 'Sarginson Towers' overlooking Governor's Bay. It was Euan who met Denis Jenkinson at the Barley Mow and startled him with an observation that you will read about later in this book. He survived a major cancer op late in 2003 and it is now my professional calling to ensure that his fluid levels are maintained while I am visiting. His chances of coming out the right end of the operation were nothing I felt like putting money on, and if I don't tell him now he may never know that I wrote what I considered to be a superb eulogy which I've now had to put on hold. Jenks used to say that it should be compulsory for people to read their obituaries before they passed over – and he would certainly have been impressed with his. Euan is well known for his carefully crafted and delivered eulogies and I said in mine on him that I would have preferred him to be reading mine, than me reading his. So that's one chore he's saved me. What are friends for...

Acknowledgement

My thanks to Peter Foubister at Haymarket Publications for his permission to borrow back quotes from my columns in *Autocar* and to soliloquise on Denis Jenkinson's words in *Motor Sport*. Thanks are also due to the editors of *Classic Cars* in the UK and *New Zealand Classic Car* for allowing me to re-process words from early columns and features. My partner, rally photographer Gail Barwood has provided photographs from her archives recalling our various activities in motorsport, Peter Renn has crafted the cover design and Milan Fistonic is due praise for his instant ability to access reference on just about any subject I wing to him.

I am delighted to be able to work at last with Clive Stroud and Transport Bookman, having discussed book projects with his father, Frank, before his untimely death. I had imagined that our ideas might have died with Dad, but Clive has been an enthusiastic supporter of this second edition of my autobiography, and we talk of it being the beginning rather than the end of our co-operation in the world of words.

Last, but by no means least, I want to thank Eddie Borowski at Chaters motoring bookshop in Isleworth, for his time, skill and patience in reading this manuscript with a studied expert eye and drawing attention to my various batterings of the English language that might have been better expressed his way...

Introduction

I sometimes think that church mice are probably better fixed for funds than I am these days but I doubt that they enjoy life as much. This book is a collection of my motor racing memories of brave men, fast cars, and dangerous races. There are features and columns that I've thoroughly enjoyed writing and now that I am going back through my files of four decades I'm finding tales of the times that I had totally forgotten. I've enjoyed going back down memory lane, so I hope you do too. In addition to all the yesterdays, I have included a chapter called Classic Summer which covers the top old car events at Vintage Prescott, the Goodwood Circuit Revival races, the Beaulieu Autojumble and the classic Alpenfahrt rally in the Austrian mountains – on consecutive weekends during the summer of 2003, just to prove that there is a world of motorsport outside Formula 1.

"It Beats Working" had scarcely hit the bookshop shelves back in 1996 before I was being asked why I hadn't told the story about so-and-so and it soon became apparent that there were more Barley Mow after-lunch tales that weren't included than were between the covers of what has now become the first volume of my autobiography.

Since then I have moved on from Formula 1 to a more relaxed style of motor sport, concentrating on classic events such as those splendid events that Lord March stages with such style twice a summer at Goodwood and the leisurely classic series of summer races in New Zealand. This is something of a bonus for having spent 35 years covering Formula 1 which in that time went from being almost an amateur sport to a professional business. When I first arrived from New Zealand in 1961 the Grand Prix 'circus' moved around the world as a group of mates and it only got serious every second Sunday. Now the Grand Prix circus works inside high fences and even the drivers on the back of the grid are millionaires with managers to keep them that way. In 1961 there were perhaps 60 journalists and photographers at each race. Now there are over 600. I'm not saying that this is a bad situation, just a mark of professional progress orchestrated by Bernie Ecclestone, but I am pleased not to be of their number.

I was rewarded with official confirmation that my time was up when I applied for a media credential to cover the 2003 British Grand Prix, having worked out that I had covered 449 GPs and this would be celebrating my 450th. And out. But, like Sir Jackie Stewart, I was unable to take part in my last Grand Prix. My media application was accepted and I motored from Bookham to Silverstone to sign on and receive the pass which would give me access to the paddock and the media room. No problem there, then. But on my way back down the M40 my mobile rang and it was the Press Officer who had just signed me in to say that the FIA Press functionary who had originally cleared my credential, had now cancelled it. So forget my 450th Grand Prix. Far from being an embarrassment and an annoyance, I took it as a clear signal that there was more to motor racing than the monster formula 1 has become. Time to move on and enjoy racing as it was in the good old days and I have to say that it is a pleasure not to be trailing F1 races around the world. I've done all that to the point where it was a chore to climb on the next plane and check in at the next hotel. I was suffering *déjà vu* in spades.

What a luxury to be able to watch Saturday qualifying and the Sunday races from the comfort of my own armchair and to be able to stroll the 47 seconds down the High Street to the Royal Oak in Bookham when the race is over and the TV pundits have explained what I have just been watching.

I covered the 100th anniversary of the Gordon Bennett race run on the Athy circuit near Dublin in 1903 and it was a revelation. There were Mercedes entries from Germany, but nary a sign of a motorhome or a McLaren media centre, just motorsport people enjoying a brand of motorsport that would totally mystify managers in the Formula 1 paddock. Enjoy? What sort of word is that? Where's the profit margin? Can we conceptualise enjoyment? Get someone on to it... Don't laugh. That's what happens.

I keep saying that I am enjoying my motorsport now so I hope you don't think I am over-playing the word. I am finding that my sort of motorsport now is just like it was in the Good Old Days for Formula 1 in the 'sixties.

There is a whole world of motorsport outside the fences of Formula 1. When Lord March decided to launch his Revival meetings on the Goodwood race circuit he called me and asked if I would arrange a press lunch for him at the Barley Mow in West Horsley. Here we speak of a man with a stately home, race courses for horses and cars and a pub of his own, but he said more of the motorsport media knew about 'mine'. We booked out the dining room and it was an enthusiastic lunch. Lord March stood to outline his ideas for the new event that included a collar-and-tie minimum dress code in the paddock. I was moved to suggest that Charles was perhaps making a joke. He wasn't. The dress code was an integral part of the whole scene and while you still see chaps whose necks are not a normal setting for a tie, Sir Stirling Moss has remarked on the success of the move to bring a period sense of style back to the sport, to the point where the paying public are now also making the effort and turning out in their 'fifties best. It has become a hugely successful international motorsport happening

Nigel Roebuck captured the surging success of the Goodwoods when he wrote in his "Autosport" column that some wag at the Festival hillclimb had called out to Jenson Button "Hey Jenson! What's it like to be competing in front of a big crowd?"

This is not so much as a second volume of autobiography, but a collection of memories and anecdotes and features and columns that I have enjoyed recording over the years. My page in *Autocar* ran for over 30 years before it was terminated in a manner that was never explained in any way that I understood. *Straight from the Grid* had run each week on a long-time basis that set new records in the oldest-established motoring magazine in Britain.

In fact I began writing a weekly column on motorsport in the late 1950s in *The Timaru Herald* in my New Zealand hometown and when I started working with Bruce McLaren in 1962, we penned his columns together for *Autosport* and a syndicate of overseas magazines. The *Autocar* page started on January 5, 1967, and the first one featured a photograph of Jim Clark trying out the Lycoming Special. The caption read: 'Don't tell Colin Chapman...Jim Clark tries a piece of local ironmongery at Teretonga, New Zealand, during the Tasman series last season. The car has a flat-four Lycoming aero engine, turned upside down, converted to dry sump, and fitted with fuel injection.' Can you see Michael Schumacher doing that now? Yeah, right. It was surprise enough that Jimmy had done it then!

I have never pretended to know about the mechanics of a motorcar but I could tell the sort of tales about the people involved that always complemented the actual race report, which was the main reason that Peter Garnier, then Sports Editor, had hired me. In that debut page, I previewed the Tasman Series that was about to begin and wrote about Mario Andretti having THINK CHARGE taped across the steering wheel of his Lola T70 at Nassau. 'Mario was offered a quarter of a million dollars (near enough £90,000) if he would switch his personal racing contract from Firestone to Goodyear! And that – in case you're still counting the noughts – is an awful lot of money to pay one man for doing anything!' And it was, in those days. I also told about Denny Hulme's drive at Indianapolis in one of Dan Gurney's Eagles. 'Denny said he had to concentrate on the fact that the Eagle's clutch pedal was mounted up above the steering column and out of the way, and the brake pedal was on the left. The Eagle being a 2-pedal machine with low to get started and high for everything else, didn't require more than a couple of stabs at the clutch, so for economy of cockpit room, the clutch pedal was tucked upstairs. This also meant a change in driving style to go-kart fashion with the right foot for 'go' and the left foot for 'stop'.'

That was the way it was going to be for the next three decades and I have always sort of dated the start of my diaries from 1967 but I recently discovered a tatty incomplete run of the short-lived *Auto News* that appeared in the summer of 1966 from the same stable as the hugely successful *Motorcycle News* with the hopes that the same success would follow. It didn't. But it was fun while it lasted and to gather the feel of what motor racing life was like back then, this seems a good place to start the second volume of the book of my career which if it does nothing else, brings back memories of how extremely fortunate I have been to know the many and varied characters in international racing and to be part of a scene that was too leisurely to survive. There are some who point out that this season will be the Good Old Days five years from now, but I don't subscribe to that theory.

In fact it was an early editor of *Auto News*, hired from a Fleet Street daily, who made the point that the mark of a good journalist in a paper like ours was to entertain first and inform second. I have been pleased to follow that dictum ever since and I hope you agree that it works.

My year now revolves around old-car happenings with the Southern Festival of Speed, four races in the South Island of New Zealand in February and when I arrived back in Britain I was heading straight to Ireland for the anniversaries of the Gordon Bennett race near Dublin and a fortnight later in the Tourist Trophy races on the Ards course near Belfast. Join me for those two weekends as this book gets under way...

In Dublin a Century after the Gordon Bennett Race

I doubt if it gets much better than this. I was in Ireland, immersed in the incredible centenary of the Gordon Bennett races that ran on the Athy road course near Dublin, and I was actually driving the factory Napier that Charles Jarrott had raced on that very stretch of Irish road a 100 years before. It wasn't virtual reality. This was the real thing. We were sitting high, stark in the 60mph air-stream that felt like a hurricane and I was more than a tad aware that Jarrott had somersaulted this very car in this very race when the steering broke... I've almost got an eagle's view over the flat bonnet and the tall narrow front tyres. The engine is a huge monobloc 7.5-litre 4-cylinder with copper manifolding, a polished mechanical antique. Under way, it seems to be firing at every lamp-post.

John Bentley is the Napier's minder and ten years before he had driven me down the mountain on the Isle of Man in this same car, taking me beyond the edge of fear as we reached around 70mph downhill with brakes that wouldn't have done much for our pensions if they'd been required for any sort of emergency retardation. This time I was doing the driving and frightening myself. John sat impassively alongside, probably wondering why I was driving so slowly. It's all an aspect thing. Depends which seat you're sitting in. The gear lever was tucked tight against my right thigh on a quadrant. Pull away to clear the stop, back for first, and forward through neutral to second and top. It was incredibly long-legged, loping along effortlessly in top gear. The brakes on the rear wheels only, were operated by a foot pedal and abetted by the push-forward handbrake. I am acutely aware that I am nominally in control of the most

6

valuable historic British racing car and suddenly we are on the entrance to the Killashee Hotel, headquarters of the event, and I am down-shifting and trying to indicate a last-minute right-turn while all the while remembering that John had warned against sudden braking in case the rear wheels locked. Lord Montagu had just been driving the car which has a permanent place in the National Motor Museum at Beaulieu. It was his grandfather who had pushed the bill through parliament in London all those years ago that would give permission for the road race in Ireland. Driving the Napier topped out an amazing week of Irish racing memories.

James Gordon Bennett was the American Bernie Ecclestone who established a form of order in the chaos that was motor racing at the turn of the century, sponsoring an international series of races for teams of three from each country, cars to be chosen from national eliminating trials. Son of the owner of the New York *Herald Tribune,* he had spent his youth in Paris, then returned to work with his father in the newspaper office. He was a wealthy and wild sporting businessman who drove a coach and four into Manhattan stark naked, won a $90,000 bet by skippering his 190-ton yacht *Henrietta* across the Atlantic in a match race, and fought a duel with his former fiancee's brother after he had arrived drunk at a society reception in Baltimore and pissed in the grand piano. While it was being played. Consider the engagement instantly annulled. Legend has it that the immediately estranged relation fired his pistol into the air as gentlemen then did; Gordon Bennett aimed his shot but missed. Such behaviour may have contributed to his return to France to run the Paris office of the newspaper and he continued his flamboyant ways. Ken Purdy described him as 'one of the great pioneer journalists of the pistol-and-horsewhip school'. He sent Stanley to Africa in 1869 to search for and find the explorer David Livingstone (remember the famous quote – *Dr Livingston, I presume?*) and he pioneered weather forecasting in his paper and the use of wireless telegraphy to speed the news. He used a specially fitted 80hp Mercedes to cut distribution time of his papers in Paris.

In Europe 'GB' cruised his superyacht, the 2000-ton *Lysistrata,* around the Mediterranean on a regular basis. "Toulon, Villefranche, Cannes and Monaco reaped a rich harvest from supplies furnished for the owner's guests and the crew of 62 hands," Montague Grahame-White noted at the time. Towards the end of the 1800s "He took up a permanent residence in France and besides owning a magnificent mansion in the most fashionable quarter of the Gay City, he had a palatial *demesne* at Versailles, a few kilometres away, at both of which he entertained his numerous friends in the most lavish style imaginable." He was renowned for the drawer of expensive pocket watches kept in his desk which he gifted as favours to friends or in return for exceptional services.

He had watched the first city to city motor races starting from Paris in the late 1890s and realising the potential for publicity he announced his *Coupe Internationale,* an international automobile competition with rules stipulating every part of the car had to be manufactured in the country of origin. National colours were announced: green for Britain, blue for France, white for Germany and red for the USA. Britain's emerald green was thought to be in tribute to Ireland hosting the event, after the race had been refused a venue in mainland Britain where the speed limit was 12mph, but arguments about the origin of 'British Racing Green' still simmer.

The irony was that Gordon Bennett never drove a car, showed no interest in general motoring and never attended one of his contests. He would later sponsor similar international contests for balloon racing, aeroplane and yachting competitions.

After Gordon Bennett's name had become famous in motoring circles, G.B. plates were devised for British cars touring abroad. This led to a correspondent to the *New York Herald* to ask how many motor vehicles were owned by the proprietor of the paper. It was well known that Gordon Bennett had a plate at the front and back of his cars bearing his initials, so that messenger boys sent for his chauffeur at restaurant parking places, could find him. When G.B. plates appeared quite frequently on the Continent, Gordon Bennett was often reported as having dined the same night at three or four different restaurants in the next morning's newspapers. . . The colourful G.B. legend ended when he died in 1918.

The first Gordon Bennett race was a 353-mile race from Paris to Lyons in 1900 won by Panhard for France the marque which also won the second race from Paris to Bordeaux in 1901. Regulations stated that the winning nation had to host the next race so there was a measure of embarrassment when Selwyn Francis Edge won the 1902 Gordon Bennett category in the Paris-Vienna race in a British Napier. Motor racing was banned on public highways in Britain but a solution was found by bending the regulations and running the race in Ireland on July 2nd 1903. The French had tried to ban Edge from the 1902 results claiming outside assistance when he inadvertently dropped his Napier into a riverbed but they failed. Ironically, if they had succeeded the 1903 race wouldn't have been run because racing was briefly banned in France after the Paris Madrid debacle a month before the Gordon Bennett race in Ireland.

A hundred years down the road and again there were three Napiers representing 'the green' on a peculiar figure-of-8 dual circuit of 45 miles and 58 miles based on Athy (say it Ath-eye) near Dublin, but only one was in the original race.

I had hitched a ride out to the Gordon Bennett monument on the old course with Nigel Stennett-Cox in his claret 1926 Speed Model 3-litre Bentley with *Rumbleguts* lettered on the bonnet. He stands out from the old-car crowd with a long black ponytail and sandals but he had bought a couple of large cans of Guinness, that famous local Irish speciality, so he can't be all bad. Then he takes his cap off and the ponytail goes with it. When he gives me his card at the end of an adventurous day, topped when we both got to drive the Napier, I find that he is a psychologist with a string of degrees! I ask how he rates me after a day in his company and he says it will cost me ten guineas consultancy fee to find out... Not your average vintagent.

At the monument stone we are soon rewarded when wealthy German collector Berthold Ruckwarth arrives at some pace in his 1903 Mercedes 60hp, a clone of the '03 race cars, with high-dollar London car dealer, Charles Howard as his passenger. Ruckwarth looks as though he might have raced in 1903. A few minutes later and the icing was on the photo cake when Dutch museum-owner, Evert Louwman thundered in with his 1904 Napier.

Henry Ford was about to start production of his first cars in 1903 but Alexander Winton was already the largest car maker in the USA and he entered two cars in the Irish race, a flat-six for himself and a flat-four for Percy Owen who ran the New York Winton office, held national records for the mile and kilometre and had won the Long Island race in 1902 in Winton cars. Louis Mooers, chief engineer at Peerless drove one of these cars with a curious totally perforated bonnet, prompting one Irish wag to announce it as a 'flying meatsafe' as it took the start. Both Wintons were unusual looking, being literally flat slabs with the driver and mechanic totally exposed. They were also handicapped by having only *one* very long gear... They all failed dismally in the race and never appeared in international racing for some years, during which time the Americans were stripped of their colours and red became for all time the Italian racing hue.

The Mercedes team were handicapped by having no cars! Their three 90 horsepower racers had been destroyed by a fire that razed the Canstatt factory, and they had to borrow a trio of last year's 60 horsepower cars for Belgian drivers Camille Jenatzy and Baron de Caters and the American sportsman Foxhall Keane. There was a dark suggestion after the race that perhaps Mercedes had been able to salvage just one 90hp engine from the fire, and fitted it in Jenatzy's car. Note that there were *no* German drivers in the Mercedes team representing Germany. At one stage Charles Rolls was considered for a place in the team. Jenatzy had looked like taking the honours for Mercedes in the Paris-Madrid but was a last minute retirement with a misfire – caused by a fly in the carburettor. He amused his crew by bringing the errant fly to Ireland in a bottle.

France was represented by Rene de Knyff and Henry Farman on Panhard-Levassors and Fernand Gabriel in the upturned boat-shaped Mors he had driven into the lead in the Paris-Madrid when it was halted at Bordeau. The British team of three Napiers were driven by S.F. Edge, Charles Jarrott and J.W. Stocks, a motorcycle racer having his first race in a car.

In 1903 there were less than 290 cars in all of Ireland but 100 years later for the centenary event sponsored appropriately by Mercedes, there were over 300 entries of pre-1931 vintage cars. To match the Napiers, Tim Scott brought his 1903 Mercedes '60' from Jersey for the re-run and Berthold Ruckwarth brought his 1903 Mercedes-Simplex '60' from Germany. Dieter Dressel was another German entry in his 1904 Mercedes 18/128, which had been a well-known Brooklands car when the track opened in 1907, and was owned by the Sears family in Britain for nearly half a century. Dressel is hosting the 1904 Gordon Bennett happening on the original Bad Homburg course in Germany next year (2004) with sponsorship from Mercedes and German automobile clubs.

In 1903 there were 12 starters and they set off at seven minute intervals. Edge led for Napier on the first lap, but Jenatzy moved ahead on lap two and was never challenged. Edge dropped back with overheating and tyre problems, but Jarrott's Napier crashed after a steering problem sent him out of control and the car somersaulted. Jarrott was thrown clear but his mechanic, Cecil Bianchi, was trapped under the car by a strap round his wrist to stop him being thrown from the car over bumps during the race. Jarrott lifted the heavy car so that a spectator could free Bianchi, then both collapsed. When he tried to lift a similar

Napier the following week, he could not. It was the sheer charge of the moment that had given him the necessary strength. Jarrott came to, to find sheets had been placed over both of them, by spectators who thought they were dead!

Jenatzy won in 6hr 39min at an average of 49.2mph, 10 minutes ahead of De Knyff's Panhard in second place with Farman in the other works Panhard third, Gabriel's Mors fourth and Edge's Napier fifth and last finisher.

100 years later the winner was Ireland as every competitor rated the event highly and the people most enthusiastic.

Ards and the Tourist Trophy 75th Jubilee

A few weeks after the Gordon Bennett excitement in Dublin I was back in Ireland, this time in the north and being hosted by Basil McCoy, who also spends time at both ends of the earth, at home in Ulster and on holiday in New Zealand, following old motor cars. To stitch the Ards TT accurately into the overall fabric of racing history, it is important to note that the first race in 1928 on a thirteen and two thirds mile course of nominally British public roads in Northern Ireland, was run a year before the first Grand Prix around the streets of Monaco. They talked of crowds of half a million watching the early TTs, coming by train from nearby Belfast although that has to be taken with a pinch of Irish salt. But the crowds were huge, to be sure...

The course was a rough triangle from Dundonald to New-townards, Comber and back to Dundonald. Tazio Nuvolari and Rudi Caracciola figured large in the seven-year history of the race, Caracciola winning for Mercedes in 1929 and Nuvolari winning for Alfa Romeo in 1930 and for MG in 1933. E.R. (Eddie) Hall was effectively the last of the Bentley Boys when he persuaded Rolls-Royce to build him a competition version of the latest Bentley specifically to race in the TT. He raced the car in evolving form in 1934, 1935 and 1936 being beaten into second place by the handicapper each year. After that inaugural TT won by Lea Francis, Alfa Romeos, MGs or Rileys always won.

Eddie and his wife Joan, his pit manager in their racing days, were at Ards in 1978 for the 50th anniversary and recounting the ploys they invented in the TTs. How Eddie had come past the pits in the closing stages of the 1936 TT, shaking his fist at the team who had fuel and a change of wheels all ready. "The India tyres people were puzzled because they knew the tyres would last," said Eddie. "But they weren't sure how I was going to last out on fuel. The others were worried because they knew we were OK for fuel but didn't know whether the tyres would last. My wife and I knew that if I was going to run the race through without a stop, I would wave my fist as a signal. What the other teams didn't know was that we had fitted a special 50-gallon tank in the Bentley to run the race without a stop. We had 11 gallons left at the finish...if it hadn't been raining, I think we would have won that year."

The 75th anniversary of the first TT attracted an entry of 175 cars in 2003 'of the type' that ran during the history of the event from 1928 to the final race in 1936 when a fatal accident resulted in the TT being switched to Donington on 'the mainland'. The entry to the jubilee event organised by the Ulster Vintage Car Club in June was so over-subscribed that some of the events were restricted to 'visitors' and local competitors were asked to stand down and become spectators.

Nuvolari's drive in the K3 MG was an event in itself. Whitney Straight, the wealthy young American, had entered the car in 1933 but had to scratch on doctor's orders and offered the drive to Nuvolari instead. He had never even *seen* a Wilson pre-selector gearbox before but he soon grasped the principle. His riding mechanic, Alec Hounslow, dined out on the story of his ride for the rest of his life.

Twentyfive years ago I took part in the celebration of the 50th TT anniversary, driving Rob Walker's Delahaye 135S which had set fastest lap of 135.25kph early in the 1936 race driven by Tom Clarke, but he retired after 22 laps. The lap record would stand in perpetuity at 137.6kph to Frenchman Rene Lebegue in another of the six Delahayes entered. A stirring photograph of a string of Delahayes racing into Comber is in pride of place in the famous McWhinney's butcher's shop on the outside of the tight right-hander exiting the square in Comber (say it *Cumber*). Other racing photographs on the butcher's wall show Tim Birkin's Alfa Romeo shunted nose-first into the sandbags protecting the butcher's door. A lady butcher could recite the circumstance of the crash, for always part of the Ards TT folklore, how Campari and Birkin, both in Alfa Romeos had tried to 'suck each other in' under brakes. Birkin crashed and Campari sailed up the escape road unscathed.

Billy Rockell, who had been Birkin's riding mechanic in that 1931 TT, told me a quarter century ago the 'real' story of the incident. "Campari and Birkin had both stopped for fuel and we were racing for the lead. He would come up alongside us in corners where he had no chance of passing, revving his engine and squealing the brakes – and I mean *squealing* them. I could tell that this was unsettling 'The Guvnor'. As we went into the right-hander at the butcher's shop in Comber (say it Cumber), we were on the inside and Campari comes roaring up the outside revving his engine again and hard on the brakes with the wheels locked, but I'm sure he never had any intention of going round the corner. The 'Guvnor' thought he was being out-braked and misjudged the corner. We went straight into the sandbags while Campari went up the escape road, reversed back into the race and left us there looking at the damage." Was it a deliberate trick by the Italian? "I'm not saying," said the diplomatic Rockell then. "But you must remember that Campari had put Howe into a field in the samerace..."

Anthony Powes-Lybbe was at the Ards 50th anniversary. He had raced an Alvis at Ards in the TTs of 1934 and 1935 but was better known for his exploits in a Monza Alfa Romeo. He told us how he fed and educated four children on the proceeds of his motor racing in the 1930s, what with starting money, prize monies and trade bonuses. "I remember we used to get a bonus from Ferodo although I was never absolutely sure whether we had Ferodo linings in the Monza. I suppose they *might* have been...I bought the car, raced it and sold it again without ever looking at the brake linings."

A 93-year-old lady had asked to stand at a window above the Comber butcher in 2003 to watch the cars make three laps on the Friday evening this year. She had stood there to watch all *nine* TTs when the racing was for real.

Campari had a reputation of being something of a wild man at Ards. The year before, in the 1931 race, there had been 'no-passing' zones indicated at various tight spots, but the Alfa ace ignored these and a contemporary history described him as 'overtaking slower cars on this side, that side, any side and any place, straight or bend.' The stewards demanded that he be called into the pits for a reprimand, and the burly Giuseppe became the first driver in racing history to suffer a 'drive through' penalty. It wasn't meant to be that way. Campari refused to stop and cruised down the pitlane while the Clerk of the Course ran alongside shouting at him, and Campari, not understanding a word, bawled back his own thoughts on the matter and then shot away at high speed.'

In the first race from the Le Mans-type start, the cars had to have their hoods up for two laps and then stop to furl them. The following year crews had to run across the track and put the erected hoods *down* before starting. Photographs of the first race show an amazing spectacle as 44 drivers and 44 mechanics – total 88! – all ran across the track to climb aboard.

Malcolm Campbell stopped to doff the top of his Bugatti in the 1928 race only to have fuel leaking from a specially enlarged tank, explode into a blaze that engulfed the car. A photograph of the incident shows a boy-scout in shorts with 'Pyrex Patrol' on his arm and a baby extinguisher. "He'd have been better off with petrol in it – at least it would have got the fire over faster!" quipped an Irish bystander, studying the old photograph.

Seventyfive years on and in the TT Bar in Comber there are racing photographs everywhere. A special TT anniversary menu this year listed such delicacies as Caracciola Cod, Chicken Lagonda and Rib Eye Riley. Eddie Irvine grew up in a house near the old course. But that's recent Irish racing history. This week we were living in the past.

'Scrap' Thistlethwaite set fastest lap of the first race at

74.39mph in his 6.7-litre SS Mercedes that he had shipped to Ulster on the deck of his private steam yacht which he anchored in Bangor Bay. I could have seen it from my window in the Bangor Bay Inn if I'd been staying there 75 years earlier.

A line of Singers drew in behind Basil McCoy's Alvis 12/60 in a lineup outside Stormont. I asked the driver of the first one if he had checked his steering. The English owner regarded me frostily and said "It's a six cylinder. . ." as though that answered my question. If I'd been up on Singer lore, I suppose it would have. In 1934 three of the four Singers crashed at the same section of the course with identical steering failures. The fourth car was prudently withdrawn.

Tom Delaney, son of Terry Delaney who competed in the fateful 1903 Paris-Madrid race, was driving the Lea Francis that Kaye Don drove to win the first TT in 1928. Tom, now a sprightly 92, bought the car in 1930, led the Irish GP in 1931, sold it a few years later and eventually found it again. He still competes with it and on the Friday evening laps of the old course he broke a half-shaft and reckoned he was out for the rest of the event. At dinner that evening he was telling the story and one of his friends said he could help. He had a spare Lea Francis axle that had been in his garage for fifty years – and Tom was motoring again the next day!

The black long-tailed Riley famously flown over the hedge into a cabbage field by Freddie Dixon in 1932 was back at Ards in 2003 with the matriarchal owner, Mrs Farquhar, in attendance. Shotaro Kobyashi had brought his 1928 Brooklands Riley from Japan, a car with impeccable local credentials having been raced to sixth place in the 1933 TT by Bobby Baird, wealthy owner of *The Belfast Telegraph* newspaper. Clive Doyle had brought his Lagonda LG45R over from the USA. It had been raced in the 1936 TT by Brian Lewis. George Daniels, the grizzled gravel-voiced chronometer-crafter from the Isle of Man, was enjoying his 1932 Alfa Romeo that had been raced by Earl Howe to a class win and 4th overall at Ards in 1932. Markus Kern carried

17

German racing white colours with his massive 1930 Mercedes SS which Malcolm Campbell had raced in the 1930 and 1931 TTs. Dr John Mills had brought his 1927 Austro-Daimler from New Zealand. It was thought that it *might* have been an ex-team car that ran in the 1928 TT but there was no definite confirmation. It still looked a rarity in automotive terms, tended by fellow-Kiwi John Stickney. Something of an internationalist, Mills lives in Nelson and teaches English in Equador...

Tim Ely had entered his Riley Ulster Imp, one of the four cars entered by the works in the 1934 TT. It was made special by the bow tie attached to the radiator grille. Mike Hawthorn had been given the car as a 21st birthday present in 1950. The lanky Englishman, who won the world championship for Ferrari in 1958, wore a bow tie when racing. As one did...

There were endless social events and appearances for entrants and cars as well as three glorious laps of the original course on the Friday evening, and hillclimb runs through the lush grounds of the Belfast Folk Museum grounds on the outskirts of Belfast. Somehow the hillclimbs failed to flatter the gallant old machinery but there was racing nostalgia cloaked around every car at the event in Ulster, remembering a major motor racing event that captured world headlines 75 years ago.

There had been a touching moment with the Delahaye at the earlier anniversary. As we were about to depart from a morning coffee stop, Joan Hall paused at the car and whispered "Eddie could have won easily with this car." Moments later Eddie arrived, surveyed the racing grace of the Delahaye and announced that it was all very well, but it should never have been allowed to race in the TT because "It was a Grand Prix car with mudguards..."

* * *

As an addendum to Nuvolari's classic win in the Ards story, I found a column piece I had written in October 1982, quoting from John Thornley, General Manager of MG who had written the marque bible "Maintaining the Breed" in 1950. He recalled conversations with Alec Hounslow who had been Tazio's riding mechanic in the K3 when they won the TT. "Such fright as he experienced was, it appears, confined entirely to the first practice lap, during which Nuvolari had not got the hang of the self-changing gearbox, selecting third but not kicking the pedal, and in consequence arrived a good deal too fast at most of the hazards. The score on the very first lap was three complete gyrations in the square at Newtownards, a rearward visit to within inches of the famous butcher's shop at Comber, and an excursion up the escape road in the direction of Belfast at the Dundonald Hairpin. Otherwise the lap passed off without untoward incident, ending with a visit to the pit where pit manager McConnell explained that the left-hand pedal did rather more than perform its conventional function of disconnecting the drive.

"Hounslow cannot recall, from the period of the race itself, any perceptible application of the brakes. Even towards the end of the run, when 'the little man' was turning things full on, his braking did not amount to much more than steadying the car, and the fast cornering was achieved by position and timing. All corners were cut extremely fine – Nuvolari had suggested that Hounslow would care to put a coin down in the road and that he would wager to put his front wheel over it on every lap – and on one occasion a rear hub chipped a splinter out of a roadside telegraph pole."

I wonder if Nuvolari and Hounslow thought that it had been a difficult, physically punishing day's work, or did Hounslow have real satisfaction in his body from having gained a lot of pleasure in Nuvolari's continued control of the MG. His average speed for the 1932 TT in the supercharged 1100cc MG was 78.65mph for the 478 mile race in just on six hours over the country road circuit of 13 2/3-miles.

19

Home and Away

The first volume of my autobiography ended with me sitting in the kitchen of my elegant apartment in the Old Rectory in East Horsley, watching the suits hurrying to catch the train for their offices in London and being pleased I didn't have to join them. Seven years on and the Sue I was linked with then was soon elsewhere and I was in New Zealand in 1997 sharing a rented house with a Susan who was, how shall I put it, a turbulent lady. When I was back in Surrey I had a phone call from her in Christchurch shrieking that the house was on fire and the brigade was on its way. Turned out that she had tried to light the open fire with her cigarette lighter, burned her hand, threw the lighter on to the settee...which exploded in flames and set the room ablaze. Just the sort of phone call you need on the other side of the world. Maybe being on the other side of the world was close enough. It wasn't more than an hour later when the phone rang again and it was Susan shrieking down the line again. This time she was in the middle of a road accident on her way to A&E to get her burns tended. "Some f**king woman driver has just tee-boned the Toyota!" It was one of those nights.

An amusing sidelight on life with Susan was when the gardener, who was apparently a motor racing enthusiast and had just read *It Beats Working*, told Susan that he was surprised how quickly she had lost her English accent. Mistaking Sue for Susan. Then there was the night when we had been out late and came home for a bedtime nightcap that neither of us needed but had to have. At some point Susan announced that she hated my hair style. "It looks just like your father's," she said, and I had to admit that what locks I had, did tend towards the traditional Kiwi family side-parting. Next thing I know she has scissors out and is cutting my hair off! The barber the next morning tried hard not to laugh but he rescued it, and if you ever get to read this, Susan, I still quite like your re-style.

Maybe she won't get to read it. I went home one day to find the house empty. No furniture, no clothes, no Susan. The whole house just impeccably clean. Just like she'd never been there. She had moved on. Turbulent lady, as I said.

I always used to stay at the Diplomat Motel on Papanui Road in Christchurch when Rob and Lois Sweney ran it, and looked after me like an extension of their family. Tolerated me, might be a better way of describing it. I usually had the corner unit with the swimming pool at one side and the spa pool at the back. We called it Young's Unit. Both facilities were locked at 9pm so that the tenant in the corner unit would not be bothered by late night water sporting frolics, but since the corner tenant – me – had the keys when I was in residence, I enjoyed what were more or less private facilities.

I had met Gail Barwood at a *Driver* magazine lunch in Auckland the previous year and supplied her with contact numbers for motorsport photographers in the UK because she wanted to further her interest in rallying photography. I had a phone call from her at the end of the UK summer, thanking me for my help, and after she had carefully reminded me who she was, I invited her down for dinner a night or two before she was returning to New Zealand via the Rally of Australia in Perth. We got on well, so I arranged to go back to New Zealand via Perth as well. It would be my first rally.

At that stage I had a permanent Formula 1 credential which, as far as I understood, included international rallies as well so I sent a fax advising the Press Officer of my plan to cover their event. The reply was a forest of forms to complete. Puzzled, I checked with the FIA Press Office in Paris and they confirmed that my F1 credential was good for rallies. "I suggest that you tell them that," said the FIA Press Officer. I suggested that *he* might tell them that. Next morning there was a fax from the

21

Press Office in Perth confirming that, er, perhaps a mistake had been made and forms weren't required to be filled in after all. So no problem there, then.

I met up with Gail in Perth and we went to a rally dinner. We were walking into my first ever rally function and the first person we met was Andrew Cowan, then team manager of Mitsubishi. We had met a long time ago and he said "Eoin, I don't wish to be rude, but what the f**k are you doing here at a *rally*!" I said I wasn't entirely certain.

That night around midnight the phone rang in our hotel room and there was a chap, whose name I didn't catch, saying that he had just come from a dinner with the FIA Stewards and he had been told that I had had a major problem with my credentials. I assured him that it was long sorted and not to worry. He insisted that he *was* worrying and to make up for my perceived hassle, there was a spare seat in the FIA Steward's helicopter and would I like to fly to all the special stages the following day? Gail was less than totally amused at this VIP arrangement for a rally rookie, as I was scheduled to meet the helicopter at 9am and she was scheduled to leave by car with her photographer mates five hours earlier...

Gail lived in the North Island of New Zealand and I had imagined that if Susan was in Christchurch in the South Island, perhaps the twain would never meet. That wasn't quite how either of them saw it, I guess and perhaps this may have had a bearing on Susan's peremptory disappearance. Gail moved down to Christchurch and we went back to the UK at the end of the colonial summer.

The owner of the Old Rectory in Horsley was a property developer eager to develop the Old Rectory and quite anxious to see me not living in the first floor apartment. When Gail came back from New Zealand, he drew my attention to the clause in my rental agreement which stipulated single occupancy so we started looking for alternative accommodation. It was not the work of a moment. Working within my price constraints we

22

looked at flats and small houses but nothing came close to the huge stylish rooms in the Old Rectory. I had imagined that my ideal living quarters would be something the size of a hotel suite and the Old Rectory exactly matched that.

We were looking at the house photographs in an estate agency in Bookham High Street, a village or two away from Horsley, and nothing that I could afford looked worth a visit. Then Gail was pointing out a semi-detached period cottage that for some reason was almost within my house-buying budget. We asked at the Henshaws agency where this little jewel might be and were told that it was right next door in the High Street. It measured up to my goal of a hotel suite in that it was one-down, two-up, built around 1500, with low beams and every sort of attractive period come-on plus the advantage of a bathroom with a modern shower, a fitted kitchen downstairs – and gas fired central heating. It was called Englands House, which was another attraction to a prospective colonial owner. There was a small lawn off the High Street, then you walked through the front door and straight into the beamed lounge. There were two bedrooms upstairs. Our joined-up neighbour was James McCormick, a dentist who converted his larger part of the house into a dental surgery and he suggested that we share the long broad lawns and gardens out the back.

Gail decorated Englands House with a motor racing theme of framed photographs that included a dramatic panoramic shot of the 1955 Grand Prix grid start at Monaco over the old fireplace, a signed portrait of Bruce McLaren, Sir Jackie Stewart and I 'singing in the rain' under an umbrella outside the Tip Top Bar in Monaco after he had won the Grand Prix in 1966 and a host of family frames.

I found a basement to turn into my office close by and I am writing this with a wall of filing cabinets beside me and a wall of books behind me. It is strange to think that a village called Bookham does not have a book shop, so I have made amends by using the basement as the command centre (if that's not too dynamic a description for an office that looks as though an anti-personnel bomb has only recently gone off in it) for my website catalogue of rare motor racing books and memorabilia. Find us on www.eoinyoung.com

Moving from Horsley to Bookham meant switching locals from the Barley Mow to the Royal Oak, always a consideration among pub people the world over. You are one or you aren't and if you aren't, there is no point trying to explain what it means. It isn't just about drinking, it's about congenial company and conversation and a jar of something soothing sort of goes along with it. Drunk doesn't feature. That's for amateurs and losers. When I left home what seems like all those years ago, John Woodiwiss, legendary landlord at the Barley Mow, gave me a room above the pub for as long as I needed. As Sandra observed "I used to tell people that you lived in that pub – and now you *do*."

"Woody" had no interest in motor racing beyond the fact that I had filled the old beamed barn out the back with my huge stock of motor racing books and memorabilia, so I trust he might be amused to look down from above (always assuming he's up there) and know that the current owner of the pub, John Andon, is a dedicated motor racing enthusiast with a collection of Triumphs TRs and AC Cobras which he races in classic events. He runs an automotive powder paint company based in Columbus, Ohio, and in the UK and Europe and has given the historic old pub a motor sporting theme with special attention to the Tyrrell Team that was based nearby.

Back in Bookham, Peter Renn is a photographer but he is also a car person with a Spridget that he has supercharged and an XJ6 Jaguar as his commuter, suitably large and luxurious to accommodate his six-six tallness. He understands computers and has set up my website so that he can service our customers worldwide whichever side of the globe I may be on. He understands that I don't understand any part of computers apart from putting words like this into my laptop...and sometimes being able to get them out again. Andrew Knowles, is another Bookham villager who dreads to hear that I am at the other end of the telephone because he knows it means I've got another problem! When he last made a visit to fix my printer (diagnosed instantly as the plug not homing in the back of the laptop!) he left a typed note on my IBM that read: Work You Bastard. I'm not entirely convinced whether that was his test run for the printer, or firm advice for me... Simon Third suffers the same problem in Christchurch, knowing that if I'm on the phone it's not to ask him if he's going to the next motor race; it's because I'm in dire need of laptop assistance. Between them all, they save me from myself and my electronic word machine.

As if you needed confirmation of my shortfall in the electrical department, I have been asked to recount my purchase of a new kettle out in New Zealand, in fact while I was finishing off *It Beats Working* in 1995. I was running on coffee and the kettle in our beach house had failed, so I made the trip into Kerikeri to buy a new one. There wasn't a cord in the box, so I used the cord from the old kettle short-term and remonstrated with the lady in the electrical shop next time I was in the village. She was puzzled, but raided another new kettle for a cord. I said maybe I was the victim of the last time she did that. A fortnight later, when the manuscript was finally finished, I was becoming aware that the water from the kettle had a strange taste to it. The house out at Opito Bay was on rain water because there were no mains and I must have supposed it might have been something in the water tank. That was when I took the lid off the kettle...and discovered the well-boiled cord of the kettle and the sodden remains of the instructions booklet and guarantee...

Gail's daughter Michelle lives and works in Northampton having been born and brought up in New Zealand, while my daughter Selina, who was born and brought up in Surrey, now lives in Lyttelton New Zealand, where she illustrates children's books for UK publishers and is bringing up my grandson Alfie, who turned four while Selina and he were staying in Surrey with Grandma Sandra in the summer of 2003.

When Selina first went out to live in New Zealand I gave her a *bon voyage* card and wrote in it 'Never forget the fukkit factor.' She asked what it meant and I passed on my life rule that says if it all goes wrong, just say 'f**ck it!' and do something else. Well, it's worked for me. Sort of.

Alfie is a mercurial young man with a manner very much his own. When he and Selina arrived in the Royal Oak for the first time, he walked in as though he belonged, saying to anyone listening "Hi. I'm Alfie and this is Selina." Age 3. Apparently he was asked what he would like to do one afternoon, when the expected reply might have been a visit to the zoo, but he said that he would like to go to the pub and see Grandad.

Life in Bookham and life in Christchurch is remarkably similar as far as I am concerned, even though they are at opposite ends of the earth. In Christchurch my office is conveniently placed a couple of floors above the Fazazz emporium, run by the brothers Bain, Gavin and John and offering everything for the motoring enthusiast. It's a Big Boy's Toyshop with new motoring books and a stock of pre-read titles that often include rarities, models, toys, sales catalogues, art and a selection of interesting vintage and classic cars on always on display for sale. The lift to my office is a refreshingly vintage device with old-fashioned folding doors that clang shut and then it grinds upwards to my New Zealand wordsmithery.

Lunch is usually at the High Street Café, a few minutes walk away, and the company is always convivial, usually including William and Barbara Lee from their *Panache* fashion boutique, my photographer mate Euan Sarginson, Robin Alborn (former printing magnate) and most Fridays we are joined by Dave Moore, motoring editor of the Christchurch *Press* and all-round good chap.

Pubs in New Zealand tend to be drinking barns with not a lot in the way of character but The Brewer's Arms in the upmarket

Merivale suburb of Christchurch has cultivated an atmosphere all of its own which comes as close to character as I have found. A lot of this pub's personality is to do with Debbie, the feistily attractive little landlady. Members of YUB racing tend to meet at 'The Brewers' on a fairly regular basis in the early evenings. You have to know that YUB stands for 'You Useless Bastard' and membership is by invitation only and covers a small group of enthusiasts who race their own elderly Formula Fords at every opportunity. Peter (Baldric) Grant is the YUB obergruppenfuhrer and with Peter Ward, they are often to be found helping to organise racing at the nearby Ruapuna race track which is celebrating its 40th anniversary.

In Surrey I am back in book writing, author mode, while Gail pursues her rally photography and tends her garden.

On ROAD & TRACK

For reasons I can't remember now and couldn't have been particularly clear then, I was invited to Hockenheim close to Christmas in 1969 to be driven and to drive Porsche racing cars. They were using the short stadium course and it was snowing and *freezing* cold. We stayed overnight at a nearby hotel and were milling about in the foyer with everyone asking how we were getting to the track when a loud voice on the stairs said "Iss simple – Ve vill form ranks of three and ve vill *march*." It was Brian Redman sending up his German team. We all thought it was a good deal funnier than Porsche director, Huschke von Hanstein who had just come into the hotel. Wrap up warm and imagine you're with me at Hockenheim in the 3-litre 908 sports-racer that some Porsche person had given me, presumably under the mistaken impression that I knew what to do with it.

The 908 wasn't answering the helm. It was mechanical mutiny. The corner on the short slushy Hockenheim circuit was banked off to the left, but the 3-litre open Porsche works racer wanted to go straight ahead. I didn't have time to wonder how Jo Siffert or Pedro Rodriguez would have handled the situation. Preferring an attempt to take the corner rather than a damp walk back to the pits and explain the miscalculation to team manager Rico Steinemann, I steered in the direction of the road. The sensation that you're about to be passed on the outside by your own tail is rather an embarrassing one. I just knew it was all sweeping round behind me as I steered valiantly in the direction of the spin.

For a few tenths of a second it was a stalemate and we went along sideways while I hoped against hope that (a) it didn't spin, (b) it didn't hit anything and (c) nobody was watching. I groped for another gear – any gear – since if I'd managed to get into a situation like this, the gear I was currently slotted into was obviously the wrong one. Then everything was going slower and I was sort of slithering along at right-angles to the road. A new gear with lots of revs and acceleration and we were back in business with the wind rushing up over the nose of the 908 and trying to lift my helmet off. If this was being a racing driver, Siffert could keep it. I have never had my electric IBM typewriter (It's 1969, remember. Now I use an IBM Thinkpad laptop) sideways on a wet track, so it just goes to show that writing is a whole lot safer than racing.

It made me very pleased that we weren't allowed to drive ourselves in the two 4.5-litre flat-12 Porsche 917s, a spyder and a coupe. I foolishly volunteered for a ride with Brian Redman in the open car. I'm sure I've been more uncomfortable but I can't remember exactly when. The door shut down about three inches from my teeth so that I was sitting with my head sticking out of a not-very-generous cut-out in the tin tonneau cover. The CSI certainly never try the passenger seats for comfort when these things are homologated. Brian complained that it was only firing on nine cylinders, but nine was enough for excitement. A squirt of throttle out of each corner put the car sideways, and on the straight the blast of air-stream over the nose gagged me. It was literally suffocation from too much air; when I tried to turn sideways it was like having all the air sucked from my lungs. It was also freezing cold. And when we came up behind Siffert doing some quiet dicing in the closed 917, the fat garden-roller tyres on the back flung muddy water in my face. It was icy hell.

To make matters worse, when we returned to the pits the owner of the crash helmet tried to tug it off my head without undoing the chin-strap. By comparison, my ride in the closed coupe 917 with Pedro Rodriguez was sublime comfort. The 917 seemed to end at the bottom of the sloping windscreen and the road rushed under us, while Pedro kept his little beady eyes glued on it, maintaining some semblance of direction. After the open car this was like having your feet up in front of the fire, watching the television, except that our lounge doesn't have a wall of engine at the back with a rack of fuel injectors all spitting and sucking away.

As we stopped in the pit-lane, Pedro asked if I'd enjoyed it. I mumbled something that might have been yes. He grinned "The last one, I *speeen* and his eyes, they go *beeeg* like *theees*!" I'll just bet they did.

Brian Redman took me for a couple of laps in a standard 911S and I marvelled at his pace and control. It occurred to me that Porsche either make their road cars like their racing cars or their racing cars like road cars. The 908 transmission had been just as smooth as a road car. You didn't have to grit teeth and gears to take off. Racing drivers always seem to have that edge of perfect balance and control that I can never emulate when I get behind the wheel. It's a similar comparison between the average Porsche and lesser makes. The Porsche does it all with that much better balance and precision.

* * *

My early columns weren't totally racing, in fact some of those that I like reading now were more about general motoring. This one in *Auto News* in May 1966 was headlined **The Law Pulled Me Out of Bed at Dawn**:

'There were only two alternatives really. It could have been the milkman with a bill, or a copper. No-one goes around ringing people's doorbells at eight o'clock on a Saturday morning. I didn't particularly want to pay the milkman even if I did face the prospect of missing my morning pint, but supposing that it was a copper, perhaps I might get dragged off in chains for resisting authority or something by sleeping on while the man wound the doorbell off. So I got up.

He didn't really look like a policeman. Not like Barlow, anyway. More like Dixon. He didn't have a uniform (they've got a plainclothes bloke after me!) and I thought perhaps he *might* have picked up the summons on the floor of the lobby and was just doing me a favour. No such luck.

This was the real thing, and while he went through his regulation speech as though he was handing the royal sceptre to this dishevelled, bleary-eyed citizen, my mind raced through a scintillating defence speech that would have staggered Perry Mason. "Unh, Ummmm. Thanks." Well, perhaps it wouldn't have staggered Perry Mason, but I've yet to meet anyone who can summon big words with ease when they've been de-bedded at dawn by the law.

Anyway, the reason for this servant of the Queen being abroad so early was the serving of a summons which had been hanging about somewhere since last November the 18th, when, according to the cold facts before me, a private motor car, of which I was in charge, was seen parked between an uncontrolled pedestrian crossing and the double line of studs indicating the approach to the crossing.

The mind boggles at the thought of a pedestrian crossing getting out of control... Howsomever. The fact remains that the offence with which I have been charged these six months later requires my licence to be endorsed if I am found guilty and even Perry Mason would take a tumble on this one, notwithstanding the fact that the officer says he was obliged to leave the scene before I returned to the private vehicle of which I was in charge.

So this means that because of a parking offence, under the generous 'three strikes yer out' licence-losing arrangement, I now have only two swings left. Which makes those two infinitely more valuable than perhaps the three were before.

But when you think about it, it's like getting hung for stealing a loaf of bread. But that was all of a hundred years ago. Now we're civilised...'

* * *

The next helping was headlined **Why Such Cold Fish?:**

'Talking about licences and lady drivers and driving instructors (which we weren't), have you ever wondered why the driving test examiner is such a cold fish? Mind you, he bursts out and says "good morning", but apart from stilted instructions for the rest of the run, that's your lot. No interesting side-chat about the thrills of sitting alongside the last prospect for a licence, or even anything as innocuous as the weather. Nothing. And while you fend off a blind mad fool of a cyclist who came rocketing out of a side road that you never saw, you just know that he's writing something on his pad that will cost you your ticket.

I can now tell you that this apparent rude lack of basic conversational manners is probably because his last customer was a member of the fair sex who was sent along by a driving school that was likely to run out of instructors if she stayed on their books. These driving instructors really earn their keep.

Sitting beside the average female motorist is a fairly shattering experience, but the very thought of sitting there when they weren't sure which little pedal was the brake, would surely get an X certificate. The fact that some nerveless James Bond sat there and suffered while his lady customer drove through red lights or stalled when the lights went green in town and had a mental block while being instructed in very basic and polite English on the starting procedure deserves special mention in despatches! And all that tooting can't help their state of mind either.

I suppose driving instructors' wives get a little on the twitchy side too, being woken in the dead of night with their old man screaming "Brake! *BRAKE!*"

I went for a terror trip with a young lady the other day, and of course she never put a wheel wrong. But I *knew* that she hadn't seen the car stopping in front as soon as I did and I had to suppress a sneer when she nearly got a wrong gear once. Well, you've got to find *something* wrong, haven't you? They get so damned superior if they get the idea that you think they're good drivers.

Back in the dark old days BMC (Before Mini Coopers) I happened upon the Nurburgring in company with John Whitmore (now Sir John) and Christabel Carlisle (now Lady somebody) in their racing Minis. Actually I had survived a spine-chilling run down from Denmark with Whitmore in the green 850 Mini that he had cleaned up the British saloon car championship with in 1961. Makes me shiver just thinking about that trip, and he thought it was funny!

Anyway. We made it to the 'Ring where John was to drive with Christabel in her Mini, and as Christabel had never been to the Nurburgring, John had first to show her the way round and then sit with her to make sure that she did it right. There's courage for you! I was driving Whitter's Mini round at a very respectable pace behind them to leap to the rescue, should I see a red Mini sticking out of the scenery.

During all this unofficial lappery, I did several laps with Christabel (after she had learnt the ups and downs and twists and turns to the extent of not lining up for a right-hander than might turn out to be a left!) and I must say she was an exceptionally calm and speedy young lady, even though I suspect she wasn't really sure of anything apart from the necessity to press that little Brick through the Eiffel mountains as fast, and if possible, faster, than Whitmore had done.

Which goes to show that perhaps lady drivers aren't as bad as we'd like to think they are. But I still wouldn't fancy the job of teaching them. That 'L' on the back stands for *Look Out!* in my book. . .

* * *

L for Leather

I had driving test memories of my own that I wrote originally in the 1960s for the long-defunct *Austin Magazine*:

"Remember your own driving test? Aren't you glad that you don't have to go through it again now? My first test was in New Zealand as a 15-year-old farmer's son. You could get your licence at that age in the colonies because so many kids lived beyond the reach of public transport. We had a brand new Austin A40 pick-up and a traffic cop who had to police an area half the size of Surrey. He was regarded as a mixture of local bobby and parish priest, a final figure of outside authority who was always invoked by your mother when 'wait till your father gets home', didn't seem to cut enough ice. His favourite place of entrapment was outside the nearest pub, not so that he could catch you coming out but so that he could slip in conveniently during the baking, thirst-making summer afternoons.

I must have started driving at about age 13, when the A40 arrived. Before that we had a horse and cart and travelled by steam train; the line ran alongside our fence line and the loco driver would stop if you stood by the tracks and signalled.

With two year's experience behind the wheel, I was enjoying a 15-year-old's supreme confidence. For the test, the traffic cop would direct you a few miles around a country block and then start glancing at his watch, impatient to resume vigil outside the local boozer.

That was before he delivered his verbal ear-bashing. He said he knew damned well that I'd been driving on the public highway without a licence, and didn't I know it was against the law? Instead of taking me for a test, he should be writing out a different sort of ticket! My cockiness melted into shivering fright. But that was the extent of it. The lesson was well and truly rammed home and the test was passed.

Ten years later and I was a director of McLaren Racing at our headquarters in a grubby trading estate in Feltham, Middlesex. The insurance company was alarmed that our small colonial clan did not have British driving licences, so though our New Zealand licences were technically legal, it was only through a

34

loophole, and there could be a problem if anyone had an accident. We had to take the British driving test.

We thought it would be a mere formality, a waste of half an hour when we already had perfectly good licences. But that was before we started to ask around. Everyone failed first time, they said. And if you didn't go to a driving instructor first, that was tantamount to a guarantee that you'd fail. Why did we need lessons if we could drive? Because we needed to learn how to pass the test, not how to drive a car. The wisdom ran that these were two quite different things. It didn't make a lot of sense. We had to slip into Sunday driver mode and behave like all the old dodderers we kept falling over in our hurry to get to or from races.

It began to dawn on me that my chances of ever satisfying anyone as sanctimonious as a British driving examiner were minimal in the extreme, so I might as well be amused by it. But I swear that it was by accident, not design that the day of my driving test happened to be the week when I had the works competition Austin-Healey 3000 on a test – a genuine Big Healey, just back from the Targa Florio, where it had been raced by Paul Hawkins and Timo Makinen.

(Mention of Hawkins, the archetypal carved-from-granite Aussie racer, reminds of the piece in *Hawkeye,* a recent biography, where Paul went for his UK driving test in a Ferrari. 'Half way through the test, the examiner baled out, saying "You're f*** ing mad!' before storming off and leaving Hawkins somewhat bemused and perplexed.')

I can only marvel now, at BMC allowing ARX 91B – a works racer – to go out to someone like me for a week when it was obviously in active service, simply between events. The Big Healey was just as it had arrived back from Sicily. Genuine Targa dust coated the wheel-arches and genuine Hawkins last-second brake-dust choked the vents. The huge white roundels on the sides gave clear notice that this was a racer in the unlikely event that you weren't alerted by the noise.

BMC racing modifications brought the power up to 195bhp, quite strong enough for class competition in the 1960s. Indoor furnishings were definitely of the racing kind. Trim was nil and everything was matt black to cut down the glare. The boot was full of petrol tank, so the spare wheel, jack and tools were strapped behind the seats. The driver's seat was a hip-hugging special racing job, designed to keep the hero Hawkins firmly at the helm in the twisty bits. The passenger's seat was an afterthought to appease the scrutineers, definitely not to please the passenger.

Instrumentation was kept to a competition minimum. An oil pressure/water temperature gauge sat in the centre of the facia above a row of labelled switches for wipers, lights, windscreen washers, panel light and key-starter. A defunct speedometer read in kph and the rev counter was set at an angle to give the driver the benefit of the red sector (6000rpm) between the wheel spokes. The wheel was a heavily padded, sprung affair of smallish diameter. In the days when every road car had a slender plastic-rimmed wheel, that padded racy number made me feel I was in a four-wheel-drift just by gripping hold of it.

The body showed signs of road rash at the front, where Hawkins and/or Makinen had borrowed a few extra inches of Sicilian scenery to make up time. The white hardtop had Perspex side-screens. Tweaking the starter produced a shattering roar from the side exhausts beneath the passenger's door. The gearbox was a delight, the gear-knob a fist-sized lump of wood that also housed the overdrive switch. Under acceleration, the 'box made as much noise as the blaring exhaust. Petrol consumption was intimidating. When we collected the car from BMC's Holland Park depot in London, the big tank was showing half full, so we barked and bellowed into a service station to top up. 'Only a few gallons,' I said to the attendant, 'it's half full already.' Snapping open the big filler cap you could hear subterranean gurglings deep in there somewhere. The attendant turned on the pump and began one of those idle conversations of indeterminate length and direction. (In New Zealand every service station attendant asks how your day has been at a time when you want to snarl "What the f**k has it got to do with you?" but seldom do.) We were interrupted abruptly when the pump snapped itself off, having delivered 14 gallons – and the tank *still* wasn't full.

I was bothered that driving a competition car such as this in London traffic would foul the plugs, but I hadn't taken into account the truck-like qualities of the big six, even in racing tune. Once you had become accustomed to the din, and mastered the art of shouted conversation, life was easy. Top gear was quieter than the other three, but by then the trees and walls were coming up fairly rapidly and idle chat was passed over in favour of concentrating on staying on the road and out of Mini boots.

I suppose after a day or two, I came to accept the gross Healey rather in the same way some people grow fond of huge Alsations that bark a threatened hand amputation at anyone brave enough to come close, but indoors are just like pussycats. My state of blissful acceptance of my growling, even indecent pet must have reached slightly mad proportions if I contemplated going for my driving test in it.

But there I was, striding down the footpath in Surbiton, almost running to keep up with the examiner, a John Cleese clone who looked at least nine feet tall. My mind was rapidly filling with horrible visions of that scanty homologation-minimum-specification passenger's seat. All attempts at conversation were obviously going to be wasted, as my lanky, pinstripe-suited examiner folded himself down into the tiny seat and attempted to compose himself with pad and pencil. In a sing-song voice, he started delivering his instructions parrot-fashion, trying not to look as uncomfortable as he must have felt. I suppose his alternative – to run away screaming – would have been bad form.

"Now at the end of the road there is a turn to the left and I want you to turn left." Much exaggerated looking in the mirror (swivel-eyed glances not permitted), down-changing, winkers flashing, arms waving. Full marks. "At the junction I want you to turn right up the hill and stop in your own time at the side of the road." Repeated down-changing, mirror-craning, arm-waving, handbrake on-off-on-off, looking every which way, venturing bravely across a deserted junction and then stopping on the hill with the handbrake firmly, officially on.

Actually, the handbrake didn't work at *all*. The dragging-on of the lever at each stop – especially for the hill start – was performed with a great flourish while my right foot was desperately heel-and-toeing on footbrake and accelerator.

The part I've dined out on ever since, came when my examiner announced that when he tapped his notebook on the dash "like this" – and he whacked his notebook on the top of the fascia to remove all chance of confusion – I was to make an emergency stop "as though a child were crossing the road in front of you". It wasn't hard to spy out of the corner of my eye exactly when the pad started to descend. My foot slammed the brake pedal at the mille-second his pad hit the top of the dash.

The examiner was plucked from his seat of pain by the giant hand of gravity, as the Healey's competition brakes hauled it to a dead stop. There was no provision for a passenger's seat belt in the racer. His head hit the windscreen and as he slumped back into the seat, dazed, he gently disappeared in a drifting cloud of brake dust and rubber smoke coming in through the vents. When he reappeared, he was having no trouble keeping his sense of humour under firm control. Very un-amused, he was.

Then there were the *Highway Code* questions, disposed of easily enough, but he couldn't wait to say, "I am sorry but you haven't passed your test. Here is a booklet which might help you with your next attempt..." He might have been politely sorry that I had failed my

Test, but certainly didn't *look* sorry as he uncurled himself from that cramped passenger's seat.

He didn't say he had failed me because I had brought an extremely silly car for the driving test. He said I had failed because I cut a corner on the deserted junction.

In 1988, daughter Selina passed her driving test first time. She confided that her only bad moment was when she realised they were approaching a roundabout at which she always had a mental block. The examiner wanted her to go left. She feigned misunderstanding, slipped into the first side road left and drove on with all the 17-year-old innocence she could muster. I don't think that sort of family artifice would have helped me with the Healey.

My man had marked me failed as soon as he saw the car. He just let me seal my own fate at that deserted junction.

Two Horses

The Citroen 2CV and I share various characteristics. We're both chaps of a certain style and we both have an adequate performance given our chosen way of life. In 1966 I covered the Paris Salon for *Auto News* and part of the story was to go out to the banked Montlhery circuit and try the new cars. My hotel had a modest room rate but I was asked to pack my clothes and luggage away in the wardrobe each morning. As near as I could understand, Madame at the desk was telling me that some of the local girls worked up there during the day. I wondered at the enterprise of the French, doubling the use of rooms to aid the cause of local business. Years later the centime dropped...

'The spartan little corrugated iron 2CV Citroen has always intrigued me more than somewhat, so I set out on my slowest lap of the day. The Citroen man thought I'd got lost! The gearchange is a push-pull-and-occasional-twist arrangement poking out of the dash which requires some Gallic intuition to know just when to twist or push or pull.

The man explained the system very carefully in French, but

as English is the only language I can speak with reasonable ease it wasn't much use. I found first and staggered out to the track only to bog down in the search for second just a little way down the straight while Matras and other French things went hurtling by at close range.

I managed to find first again, and finally after some twiddling, second reported. Third was to pull it right out and top was to push it right in. Providing that you didn't strike second on the way! The steering was enormously heavy, the acceleration not exactly shattering and the heaving and rolling on corners was something to experience. But all the time it kept four wheels on the deck and generally behaved in a less alarming fashion than its progress from outside suggested.

The banking was great. We bounced on to it somewhere about the middle yellow line and maintained this dashing wall-of-death act until the velocity of this delightful piece of peasant's machinery dwindled in comparison with the steepness of the banking, and lack of courage decided a descent to a lower lane on the banking and a gentle chug-chug back to the pits.'

I have owned a 2CV or *deux* since then and been smitten with them. Sue Lambert, who waitressed at the Barley Mow, arrived at work one day in a splendid 2CV and told me she had bought it from a specialist workshop up on Ranmore Common. And he had another. It was a grey-and-black Charleston and it looked fantastic. It really was low mileage with one old lady owner from new and it drove superbly. I would take it to New Zealand where Christchurch without hills would flatter the modest urge of the Neanderthal Citroen. The 2CV was crammed with luggage as a sort of 4-wheeled corrugated container and shipped to Lyttelton. It had to go through comprehensive technical compliance checks but these would not pose a problem. The car was perfect. The inspector phoned. There was some rust in the chassis. I said I'd have it fixed. He said I'd better come and look at it. Me looking at it with my level of technical expertise was not going to serve any useful purpose so I called in the services of Allan

Stanton, the chassis expert at Auto Restorations who joined me and the inspector under the 2CV on the hoist. I whispered "Is he right about a bit of rust?" Allan thought the man was being generous. And then he poked his ballpoint pen right through the chassis rail! It turned out that the one elderly lady owner had never garaged it and driven it resolutely on the salted roads of the Surrey winter...and the chassis was totally stuffed. End of 2CV. I sold it to an eager chap who wanted to throw money at it and install a new chassis and I'm sure he is another convert to the charm of *Deux Chevaux* ownership. It's a cult. Once bitten, smitten.

* * *

In the days before Political Correctness put a measure on how much you could drink before driving it was said in New Zealand that you would only be judged unfit to conduct a motor vehicle if the policeman opened the door and you fell out. After a party in the wee small hours of an Auckland morning I remember waking up and finding myself at the wheel of my car, carefully parked in front of a rubbish skip on the side of the road. It had a red warning light hanging from the back...and I had apparently gone to sleep waiting for it to change to green...

Then there was the night in Sydney when I went to a party in a wealthy suburb but when it got late enough that I wanted to drive back to our motel at Warwick Farm, my car was well and truly parked in. The party host was a generous fellow and threw me the keys of his new S-Type Bentley parked out on the kerb. He said he'd drive my car out to the circuit the next day. I was half way out to Warwick Farm when an induced weariness overcame me and I turned down a side road for a nap. When I awoke the sun was rising and I realised I was in a very expensive new motorcar. Which refused to start. Nothing. *Nada*. Not a peep. For reasons I don't recall I raised the bonnet and poked about in the engine room, tugging plug leads and prodding

41

other bits. As though this would make any difference. Back behind the wheel I raged at the technical deficiencies of a modern Bentley and in desperation I pushed and pulled everything in reach. And Lo – it whispered into life. Yes, yes, I know it now but I didn't know it then. I was trying to start it with the selector in 'D' for Drive...

* * *

December seemed to be the favourite month for manufacturers to invite journalists to drive their racing cars and in 1982 Renault flew a group of intrepid Formula 1 journalists down to the Paul Ricard circuit in the south of France to try their 500-horsepower turbo Formula 1 car! I have always believed that God has us all scheduled to do certain things in life and if He meant me to be a Grand Prix driver, he would have equipped me with the necessary courage and skill and mentioned something about it before now. A Sign perhaps. There is also the saying that 'Those who can, do. Those who can't, write about it.' So I am quite content to write about other people driving racing cars. I am also aware, however, that some of my colleagues fancy their chances behind the wheel, but after their debut in the cockpit of a full-throated turbo-car, I imagine any hallucinations of Grand Prix stardom will have faded to the point where they are barely discernible to the naked eye.

To minimise the enormous risks involved in letting these writing rookies loose in a racer, Renault had arranged to close the airstrip at Ricard so that no cornering was involved. Just runs straight up and straight back with a hairpin turn at each end. And just one car at a time with a small Formula Renault Martini to accustom oneself to what it was going to be like. I had been fortunate in establishing a role as a non-combatant for the exercise so I felt none of the horror that I am sure flitted through the minds of my fellow-scribes when they arrived up at the airstrip to see team-manager and former Le Mans winner,

Gerard Larrousse, warming-up on a still-wet strip, with the spray flying high behind him, the tail snaking under acceleration and the revs banging off the limiter with wheelspin through puddles. Daunting wasn't quite a man enough word to describe the sensation. It soon became apparent that it wasn't going to be the fear of power and the speed, it was the fear of botching the start and stalling in front of the assembled company which included Formula 1 driver Eddie Cheever who was taking some delight in burying his former critics with well chosen words in coping with what, to him, must have been the most elementary of problems. Like starting off. "You have to think about it like pulling a big heavy trailer with a small car," counselled Cheever. "You don't just drop the clutch with the revs up. You have to build up the revs then e-a-s-e it away." Practice, presumably, makes perfect. I don't imagine Cheever plans to e-a-s-e it away off the grid when he starts his first Grand Prix with the yellow car!

Most people stalled at some time. Cheever would shake his head and say "The problem is they're scared they they'll break the gearbox or blow-up the engine. I tell you there's no one here who can break any part of that car." Some of the crunches from the region of the gearbox seemed about to belie Cheever's faith in the machinery, but he shrugged and said that unless you played the revs and the shift just right you wouldn't get it into the lower cog "not even with both hands..."

There is a certain amount of friendly rivalry extant between Nigel Roebuck of *Autosport* and Alan Henry of *Motoring News* (now Sports Editor at *Autocar*) with much cross-talk during the season about the modest altitude of one, and the girth of the other, and while Henry had driven a Grand Prix car before, Roebuck had not. As the day dragged on and the Austrian and Italian journalists had their runs and their 'moments', Nigel was subject to some 'psyching' to the point where he must have been contemplating a drive with all fingers crossed.

In fact he managed to start correctly and motored out on to

the strip. Back and forth with apparently a minimum of problems and by now the butterflies must have been banished. Power out of the slow turn, a sudden flick of the tail over a damp patch and before he could react, the Renault was plunging off the strip under power! The butterflies had turned into vultures and were devouring the luckless Roebuck as he sat there in the wild thyme and savouring the crushed herbs of Provence, having spun to a stop and stalled.

He later told the story that I was the first to reach his stalled car, and that I had leaned into the cockpit saying 'Thanks very much for that – you've just written my column for me!'

Without skirts and with the new flat-bottom configuration, the car was undamaged and once re-started, Roebuck continued and finished his allotted lappery without further incident. Just the bad dent to his honour, and Alan Henry still to make his run. As I had expected and Nigel had feared, the Henry performance went off without a hitch, despite an intense programme of mental malignment from Roebuck observing at the edge of the strip. I felt I should admonish him for his obvious thoughts and through gritted teeth he admitted as much. "I don't want him to hurt himself...I'd just like him to go off the road and damage the car a little..." But he didn't, and Roebuck retained the honour of being the only driver that day to spin a Grand Prix car in a straight line.

* * *

When Le Mans winner Duncan Hamilton was based in Bagshot, his son Adrian phoned to say that they had bought back the D-Type Jaguar that his Dad had driven to second place at Le Mans in 1954 and would I like to drive it? Of course I would. I drove off into the countryside and the D-Type was bliss, a dream of a car built for a purpose – to win the 24-hour race at Le Mans – and this target was achieved in 1955-56-57. I eventually came back along the bypass and gave it a brief blast before turning off and driving to the Hamilton motorcar emporium. As I was tooling along, a motorcycle cop suddenly appeared with siren screaming and lights flashing – coming the other way. He spotted me in the 'D' and stood the bike on its nose, wheeling round and pulling in behind me on the Hamilton forecourt. He pulled the bike back on its stand, carefully drew his gauntlets off and removed his helmet to announce that I had been doing 120mph on the bypass. I asked how he could possibly have known that since he wasn't there. He said he had *heard* me. I explained that I was testing the car and had, in fact, been in second gear and while it might have *sounded* like 120, it was probably only doing 50. Not at all convinced, he asked if the D-Type was mine. Not mine, I replied. "It's his..." and there was the burly bearded Duncan standing there, looking for all the world like actor, James Robertson Justice. Duncan smoothed the copper, who eventually climbed back on his bike, leaving Duncan chuckling.

In those days Duncan drove an XJ12 Jaguar, a gas-guzzler that was a luxury bargain to buy for that very reason. Duncan had a badge bar on the front bumper with rare badges for Brooklands Track, Brooklands Aero Club, British Racing Drivers' Club and others and I was moved to mention that his badge bar was probably worth more than the motorcar. Months later at the BRDC annual dinner in a posh London hotel, Duncan and I happened to be in neighbouring stalls have a post-prandial pee. "Oh, it's you," he observed. "Do you remember how you told me that my badge bar was worth more than my Jaguar? I thought you were a cheeky young bugger, but I put the badge bar into Christies and it made *four times* what the Jag was worth!"

Duncan's memoirs *Touch Wood*, published in the 1960s were wonderful tales of derring-do but others would suggest that it was a brilliant work of fiction. His description of he and co-driver Tony Rolt being told that they weren't going to be driving the C-Type Jaguar in 1953 and going on a bar-crawl, only to be tracked down on race morning and sobered up by Jaguar team management because the car had been made ready, has gone down in Le Mans legend. Some time after Duncan's death, I was talking to Tony Rolt at Donington and asked him about that tale but he dismissed it as Duncan's fabrication. He said it had never been as dramatic as that but he had gone along with the story while Duncan was alive because he thought it would have been a shame to spoil the aura.

* * *

Ted Walker runs an archive of millions of historic racing negatives, selling 10x8in black-and-white-prints at a fiver a time at classic races and vintage events, and at the Prescott Hillclimb he flourished a print at me, demanding to know what I had been doing with a car that looked alarmingly like a Del-Boy Reliant 3-wheeler. It *was* a Reliant 3-wheeler. It took me a while to remember that I had actually driven the little car on test for the prestigious American monthly *Road & Track* when I was writing a monthly column for them. They had planned a road test on the new Lotus Elan Plus Two and had a colour photograph of the car, presumably a mock-up, scheduled for their cover. I was to drive the car but Lotus kept putting the test date back. And back. And back. To the point where we were nearing deadline and it appeared that the chances of getting a drive in the new car, were nil. This is the gist of the piece that I wrote and which appeared in the magazine:

'The alert reader will notice that the fibreglass-bodied 2+2 in this driving impression is not, in fact, the promised Lotus Elan +2. Inexplicably, cars suddenly became unavailable from Lotus and the editor demanded a last-minute replacement. "Drive some other plastic car, then," he snarled over the Trans-Atlantic phone, "and send me 750 words by Wednesday!" So I've come as close as I could on such short notice and Lynx-eyed readers are asked please not to write to Reliant pointing out the shortage of road wheels on the car, as they assured me that they were quite aware it is a 3-wheeler and that, in fact, they planned it that way all along.

'After being advised to start off in second as first was a stump-puller, I fired up and wobbled somewhat uncertainly out into the traffic. Gaining confidence after a few familiarising swoops and darts, I warmed to the task, rapidly gaining confidence. Finding a clear stretch, I gave the Reliant its head and in practically no time at all we were going 30, 35, 40, 45 and even 50mph! And 50mph *is* speed in a 3-wheeler, believe me!'

A Classic Old Car Summer

As if to prove that there was motorsporting life outside Formula 1, the summer of 2003 became a refreshingly busy succession of weekends of old-car happenings. It all started out pleasantly enough in August, driving a modern Volkswagen Cabriolet top-down to Prescott for the Vintage Sports Car Club hillclimb. The sun shone and all was well with the world, especially the world within the Prescott orchards.

I would have paid just to wander around the amazing vintage machinery on casual display in the public car park, never mind the endless array of heroic old competition cars in the paddock . A giant glistening Blower Bentley was in among the Alvises. A French-registered Type 35 Bugatti was lined up alongside a Rolls Royce Silver Ghost and a Model T Ford speedster. A lady in an elegant 1950s Citroen DS convertible asked the parking marshal if she could have a gap for a picnic table. No problem, madam. This was vintage Prescott and the sun was shining. Picnics were what Prescott was all about.

In the paddock you stepped back in time and you could literally choose your era and marque to stroll around and luxuriate in nostalgia. It always reminds me of Bolster's 'Bloody Mary' special with its gang of motorcycle engines – starting with one, doubling to two, and doubling again to *four* JAPs in a time when it wasn't Japanese, it was J.A. Prestwich.

John Vary Bolster, with his jaunty moustache, deerstalker, twinkling eye and raucous conversation, was the epitome of the British vintagent. It was Bolster who built his famed Bloody Mary in 1929 when he and his brother Richard fitted a 760cc J.A.P. twin of 1914 vintage into an ash-framed chassis with three longitudinal members. "All of the machinery is mounted between the central and left chassis members, the driver occupying a parallel coffin between the central and right longitudinal members," Bolster wrote in *Specials*, a book he was well qualified to pen.

Bolster and his brother each had a vintage special but they were unable to travel together on the road due, John once explained, to a complicated situation vis-à-vis the vehicle licensing department, whereby both cars had the same registration number...

Robin Harcourt-Smith was my Bolster substitute in the 2003 Prescott paddock with his spidery Hornet chain-drive special fitted with a pair of 1926 Harley Davidson 1250cc vee-twins side by side. It was all very much string-and-bobbin engineering and a piece of wood seemed to play an important part in the firing-up of the machine, tensioning a variety of cables until ignition had been made. I never did work that out. Heavy netting served as a cockpit (if there was a cockpit) floor and a protection against loose bits attacking the driver. "I've had two chains break, but the links just fall down on the track..." As opposed to coming *up* and attacking his tender bits. There are two more Harley motors on the way from the States, so another 4-engined special in the spirit of Bloody Mary will soon be in progress. The original Bloody Mary was built in 1929 but the Hornet started life in the 1980s created around vintage bits, a habit that the VSCC encourages providing the car is 'in the spirit' of the vintage era.

Dr Gray's Hardy Special was another motorcycle-engined car that had started life with a 1929 GN chassis and in 1954 it was fitted with a mid-mounted 1000cc J.A.P. vee-twin of 1930 vintage producing 80-90 horsepower with the help of a Centric supercharger and an eye-watering methanol fuel mix. It put all that power through a pre-war Norton motorcycle gearbox but Dr Gray said he tried not to use the clutch, spinning the rear wheels instead on takeoff.

Julian Ghosh, VSCC Duty Director, explained the high and handsome Penny Farthings whistling about on Sunday morning, warming for a vintage cycle race up the hill as honouring their noise curfew until 10am on the Sabbath. In the trade area early on Sunday morning there were bleary survivors of the jazz band the night before and the proximity of the bar. One dealer, Graeme Simpson, was celebrating the new day with smoky barbecued bacon and claret for breakfast and invited me to join him. Bolster would have approved. I did.

For this same VSCC Prescott weekend back in 1963, Bolster had resuscitated Bloody Mary and immersed himself in the weekend, up to his elbows in mending deranged transmission parts. "I am very careful, when making such repairs, not to modernise the car," he wrote. "It would be easy to fit smaller wheels with larger tyres, hydraulic brakes and Weber carburettors. This would probably knock a few seconds off the time, but she wouldn't be a true vintage car any more and one might just as well buy a Lotus and have done with it...I did a fairly safe first run and a 'hairy' second trip, which was faster, perhaps because I had enjoyed a glass of Beaujolais in the interval."

Bolster was a great Francophile and he would have been first to sign the petition at Prescott to help save the Montlhery banked circuit near Paris – France's equivalent to Brooklands – and encourage the French enthusiasts with their petition tent, to start their special Salmson with its clattering 1930s 9-cylinder 2.8-litre radial engine. It drew a crowd every time it started.

When he died of a heart attack in 1984 aged 74, Bolster had been Technical Editor of "Autosport" from its very first issue in 1950. He had been coerced into joining the world's first weekly magazine devoted to motor sport by founding editor, Gregor Grant, while Bolster was still in hospital, swathed in bandages after somersaulting an ERA in the 1949 British Grand Prix at Silverstone. "Gregor reckoned the doctors were making a pretty poor job, and what I needed was a drink. Suffice to say that in the next couple of hours we dealt with a bottle of rum, and Gregor was right, for it was just what I needed." During that two-hour engagement while the rum was applied internally for strictly medicinal purposes, Gregor planted the idea of his new magazine with Bolster, and stressed the pivotal role his recently retired racing driver friend would play.

Bolster lived through an era when drinking was an integral part of daily life, when each day was designed to be enjoyed to the full, far from the politically correctness of life today. Bolster was at Goodwood the weekend that Mike Hawthorn won the main race, flew his Percival Gull back to Fairoaks airfield and then *drove* back to Goodwood so that he wouldn't miss the fun of the traditional pub-crawl home with his mates. Changed days.

Some men have myths created about their achievements but lack the personality to match the myth. When you meet them later in life, you wonder if this can be the man about whom you had read and heard so much. John Bolster was definitely not one of these men. There wasn't a myth made large enough to accommodate the Bolster legend. I had read the first two Bolster books (*Specials* and *Motoring Is My Business*) while I was growing up in New Zealand and from half a world away we knew of the exploits of Bolster and Grant and wondered at their ideal life of racing, fast cars and rowdy parties that they seemed to lead. The fearsome pair didn't disappoint upon eventually meeting. They always appeared to be personalities at least on a par with the people they were writing about and when I first met them in 1961 my illusions remained intact. They *were* just as impressive as the people they were writing about. Bolster was the life of every party – and there were plenty of them back then. He knew every rude song in English and French and would give voice to them all in the later stages of the evening.

They were a great pair. Gregor was famous for his tall stories, his embroidering of the truth in confidential asides in his Scottish burr and Bolster always ribbed him about it. Towards the end of many a convivial dinner, Bolster would stand, tap a glass and announce with his gentle lisp, "Somewhere in the world, at this vewy moment, Gwegor Gwant is telling a lie...!"

Bolster was one of those effervescent people who were never far from the fun...and if there wasn't any, he would create it. Ask John how he was and he would always reply "Oh, pwetty wuff, you know..." and then proceed to last the night out better than any of his younger counterparts at any new car launch. The story is told of Bolster arriving in the "Autosport" offices and announcing "I've just been to lunch with Rolls-Royce....for the last *two days...*"

I recall one hectic evening in Paris in 1964 in the company of Bolster, Jabby Crombac and others at Roger le Grenouilles in the Rue des Grands Agustines, when at one point in the evening it started raining feathers! Bolster had climbed the stairs to a balcony above the table and slit a pillow! A young lady in an angora sweater soon resembled a part-plucked chicken and felt obliged to divest herself of the garment at the dinner table, the easier to remove the feathers, a move which may have been uppermost in Bolster's mind to start with. He used to say that Jabby, ("Autosport" Continental Correspondent from the first issue) was one of the reasons he liked Paris. That night also included a breezy and probably sobering trip through Paris streets with Bolster and me clinging to the roof of Crombac's huge vintage Hispano Suiza. Those sort of escapades always seemed like such good ideas at the time but not quite so humorous when you are trying to explain it to the Gendarmes.

"From the point of view of the *bon viveur*, Paris has two inestimable advantages," Bolster wrote in 1958. "One of these is that the water is undrinkable, and the other is that the telephone service is atrocious. In London, one's meals are interrupted by a string of calls and the sheer brutal efficiency of the telephone renders gracious living impossible." I wonder what he would have made of the mobile phones today?

The germ of the Bolster myth began with Bloody Mary with its big J.A.P. twin which he drove with gusto in hillclimbs and sprints. "The rear cylinder eventually flew past my ear one day,

52

followed by pieces of piston and sundry bits of hot metal, so we lashed out and bought another J.A.P. for 50 shillings." In the winter of 1933 he fitted Bloody Mary with two of these J.A.P. twins running on alcohol fuel and the car survives to this day as do the tales of Bolster's heroic enthusiasm so necessary to conduct 'B.M.' in anger.

"I certainly think it is worth spending a few extra shillings on 'dope' to save many pounds in engine repairs. Anyway, old 'B.M.' seems to enjoy her alcohol as much as her owner does. Morons have called this fuel 'liquid dynamite' which is exactly what it is not. If one thinks of it as gentle stuff which preserves one's motor, one will have a true appreciation of its value."

Then there was the 4-litre special with four J.A.P. engines up front. It was the most extraordinary looking car with Bolster sitting just ahead of the rear wheels with his knees up and the steering wheel almost against his chest in a most ungainly fashion. The engines were in pairs and if the arrangement looked fearsome it had performance to match. "To begin with, a violent vibration period was extremely destructive, but this was cured by the use of flexible mountings at strategic points. It has always been my view that an ounce of rubber is worth a ton of theory and it was certainly borne out in this case." Bolster said he had never experienced anything like the acceleration of the car in those pre-war days – 0-100mph in about 10sec.

Some Englishmen of Bolster's age believed that Britain stopped making decent cider when they stopped making barrels large enough to put Frenchmen in, but Bolster was always an enthusiastic Francophile, revelling in his escapades across the channel, enjoying his food and wine and fast French cars. They didn't have to be fast. His favourite transport at one stage in his career was a tiny rear-engined Renault 750 saloon. He was as familiar with the French world of old cars as he was with the British and he wrote *French Vintage Cars* in 1964. His Brighton Runner was a 1903 Panhard but another love in his life – in addition to his devoted wife, Rosemary – was an absolutely superb 1911 Silver Ghost Rolls-Royce that he maintained in a manner of which Sir Henry Royce would have approved.

Bolster also indulged in more serious forms of racing with an ERA and over the winter of 1948/49 he embarked on a project to apply twin-stage supercharging to the six-cylinder ERA engine upping the power from 165 bhp to around 220 bhp, but the extra weight so far forward completely upset the delicate balance of the ERA and was to result in the accident in the 1949 British Grand Prix that changed – and almost terminated! – Bolster's career.

He understeered off at Stowe, hitting the haybales in those pre-Armco days. "The ERA rode up on the bales and over-turned while I was still at the wheel. Gaining momentum, it rolled over for a second time, flinging me into the road. Naturally the speed was still considerable, and I skated along the ground, losing most of my clothing and suffering a very large area of road burns. Meanwhile, the car somersaulted end-over-end, during which caper it caught up with me again and damaged the few parts of me that were in one piece up till then. It was as uncomfortable an accident as one could possibly have."

Among his injuries was a broken neck and there were fears that he would be crippled for life, but, Bolster being Bolster, he set about what he described as "an almost miraculous recovery."

In a quirk of fate, Murray Walker was making his first Grand Prix radio commentary from Stowe at this race. He was horrified at the enormous accident happening before his very eyes and he was convinced that Bolster had been killed. Murray went on to greater things in television commentary as we all know, but this accident also opened the door to a new career for Bolster in radio and television when he was offered the chance to be a course commentator at Goodwood. This led to TV commentating and he became famous all over again in his distinctive deerstalker and check jacket.

Raymond Baxter, ever the velvet voice of the BBC, had heard Bolster's track commentaries and invited John to broadcast with

him at Silverstone. They were initiating the art of live broad-
casting from the pits.

"The whole scheme, of course, was crazy" Bolster recalled in
Motoring Is My Business. "All I had was a microphone and a pair of
headphones on the end of 100 feet of cable. I was to rush from pit
to pit, whenever a car came in for repairs or to refuel, and describe
the action on the spot. It was a terrifying experience, because half
the time the noise was so great that I could not hear Raymond's
commentary. Somehow, I heard enough to start talking at the
right moments, but the task of dragging the heavy cable from pit
to pit was immense. It seemed impossible that anyone could hear
me over the roar of the engines – and I was worried all the time in
case a mechanic would use 'that word'"

Bolster was well versed with the f-word, seldom used in gentle-
manly conversation in those days, never mind in mixed
company. At a grand end-of-season dinner at the Dorchester, a
waitress passing John's table dropped a tray of plates with a huge
crash. The room was hushed and Bolster said in his distinctive
high voice "Shall I say f**k for you?" The room was double-
hushed until someone dared to laugh.

The secret of Bolster's success was his huge enthusiasm for
anything with which he involved himself and this included his
writing, his driving, his drinking, his sheer zest for living. That
Bolster spirit was certainly all about with the thrashing of chains
in the Prescott paddock in 2003.

Spollen's 1936 supercharged ERA was fastest up the hill at
42.14sec but times were not of the essence, more a means
of keeping personal score. Prescott is about having a good
time.

A change of pace and location now to the racing world of
the 'sixties and the Goodwood Circuit Revival the following
weekend where *Forza Amon!* my biography of Chris Amon, the
New Zealand driver who had led the Ferrari and Matra Formula
1 teams in his prime, was being launched. I now have a fresh
respect for the energies and abilities of Murray Walker, a man in

his 80th year, who went round the world recently promoting his autobiography and signing copies. So what's so special about getting a free trip round the globe and signing a few books, I hear your cry? It's like this. I spent the Goodwood weekend signing 500 copies of the Amon book and I ended up absolutely knackered by Sunday evening. This might have been in some measure the result of the efforts of my dealer friends, Ted Walker and Laurence Edscer in maintaining my fluid levels, but the absurd concentration required in signing your name so many times was mind-numbing. I'm not complaining, though. I'm just mentioning that the mental effort needed, amazed me and gave me fresh respect for Murray, him being a year or three older than me.

I also applauded Murray's Goodwood tribute to the late and great Barry Sheene, a sportsman like Martin Brundle, who turned to the microphone on retirement and was so effortlessly polished at the art of stand-up off-the-cuff commentating, that it made you wonder why they'd ever wasted all that time in the saddle. Or at the wheel, in Martin's case. Murray said the Sheene tribute was hard to do because he had been very fond of him and he felt very emotional.

Goodwood was glorious as always and it seemed the only person who stayed away was the weather. There had been dire forecasts but we saw only a few vague showers from time to time. Crowds were up again, a measure of this being that all the lavish programmes had sold out by noon on the Sunday. Last year I swept down from Bookham to Goodwood in a Jaguar XJ in exactly an hour, but this year in the stop-start queues we were nearly two and a half hours for the trip. But we did have the consolation of cosseting in a new 3-litre X-Type Jaguar, a performer with such style that I felt the only gilding to this lily would have been automatic transmission. I must be getting older than I thought. Jaguars are also getting smaller. Remember the Jaguar ads in the 1950s and '60s for 'Grace, Pace and Space'? The grace and the pace are still with the X-Type but Michael

Clark and Peter Renn were both over six foot and they almost had to have the car surgically removed from their shoulders when we arrived at Goodwood.

High point of the Amon book signing came when this bloke came up and stood there, looking at the book and then at me, and furrowed his brow for a few considered moments before he said "'ere... This Forza Amon bloke? Is 'e Chris's cousin, then?" Made the weekend worthwhile!

We were having a Pitpass.com sort of weekend, Pitpass being the popular website motor sport magazine edited by Chris Balfe. Michael Clark sent columns from New Zealand, I did occasional contributions and so did author Dr Mike Lawrence and F1 commentator Bob Constanduros. We all of us got together at Goodwood. Michael Clark and wife Sandy were over from New Zealand and the good doctor Lawrence was Michael's Goodwood mentor on the Saturday. He arranged for us to be chauffeured (if that's not too grand a word) in a 1960s Fiat Multipla (!) around the outside of the circuit and dropped off at the exact spot where Sir Stirling crashed his Lotus on Easter Monday, 1962. I'd never been there before. I've driven around the track heaps of times, but I'd never been on the outside and had a spectator's eye-view of the crash scene. Sent a cold shiver down my spine. And in modern terms, you were so *close* to the action. We watched the motorcycle race and then realised we were running out of day and the option was walking back around the circuit (Me? Walk any meagre distance if there wasn't a sustaining drink at the other end? You should know that my local, The Royal Oak in Bookham, is just 47sec from my front door!) or flagging down a ride. A WW2 Jeep came bumping around with a driver and two pretty ladies on board. Dr Lawrence stepped in front of the jeep and it stopped. Did they have room for three exhausted journos? The driver said they didn't. So we climbed on board anyway and crushed three of us large blokes into what might have been one spare seat. They turned out to be congenial company but then I suppose they'd have to have

57

been at such close quarters in the Pitpass capture of what was nominally a fighting vehicle.

Bob Constanduros turned up on the Sunday, fresh (well, sort of) from Brno that morning where he had been commentating at a West-McLaren promotion. He was endeavouring to hide the modern silver-grey West team shirt under his 'sixties Goodwood-style hacking jacket, trying not to be Tomorrow Man in the glory of yesterday's racing weekend. We decided that the 1962 stack-pipe BRM couldn't have been authentic because the exhausts on Irvine Laidlaw's car had stayed resolutely attached to the 1.5-litre V8 engine throughout the race. When the car made its debut at Zandvoort in '62 there were broken exhausts bouncing all over the place. Just kidding, Irvine. It sounded fantastic. Bring back stack-pipe exhausts...

Bob, who celebrates 20 years in the commentary box in 2004, can lay claim to be the only Grand Prix commentator in the world with not one but **three** Facel-Vegas in his motorhouse.

In the Sussex Trophy on Sunday afternoon, Bob was speculating on the size of the repair bill for Sporting & Historic Cars if their two cars, disputing the lead with some vigour, started swapping paint. Peter Hardman topped the weekend for me, watching him lead the early laps in a glorious power-slide through Woodcote in the 1957 Aston Martin DBR1. Tony Dron had been swallowed up from pole in the S&HC team's splendid Ferrari Dino 246S and it took him a few laps to get on to Hardman's tail. They may have been grandstanding as they swept into Woodcote side by side in the braking area, but they did it damned well! The Ferrari was three years younger than the Aston which was probably a year or two old when it was new in '57, but it was a race to remember. Just the sort of wheel to wheel excitement that Goodwood used to dish up when the races – and the racers – were for real.

Then there was Beaulieu. The autojumble at Beaulieu is the granddaddy of them all, a mammoth gathering of the rusty and the rare – sometimes both combined – but always a personal challenge to find a treasure. The great thing about Beaulieu is the sheer scale of the event and the fact that every one of the tens of thousands that come through the gate each day of the weekend has a different goal, a different item that they're out to find. Finding it is only the start. Then there is the ritual haggling endemic in autojumbling which really seems like a waste of time when you consider that the trader knows as well as you do that there will be a lot of calculated verbal before the price is settled...the fact that the trader has already added on the estimated amount of haggle, never seems to be taken into account. But I suppose there is a feel-good factor involved somewhere. The buyer inevitably goes away with a secret smile *knowing* that he's had a result and managed to get the price down as well. The trader – or at least the bloke on the other side of the counter – has got a secret smile as well because he's been trying to shift whatever it was, for *years*.

It reminds me of Mike Hallowes, Pink Floyd drummer, Nick Mason's right-hand-man at Ten Tenths, despairing of selling stuff he'd been taking to Beaulieu year after year and finally on the Sunday afternoon he laid out a dozen items with a notice that said ALL ITEMS ON THE TARPAULIN ARE FREE. No sooner had he set out his wares than a chap stepped in, picked out an old suitcase and gave Hallowes what had been on the original price-tag. Another prospective punter asked Hallowes why he was standing over his de-priced display. "To make sure that nobody nicks anything..."

You hear every language and accent at Beaulieu. It's a fully international happening. American collectors Bob Ames and Dale La Follette, veterans of their U.S. equivalent autojumble/swapmeet at Hershey, sprawling over an even greater area than Beaulieu, were making a professional approach, armed with walkie-talkies. Reminded me of American dealer, Charlie Schalebaum, a big, comfortable older chap who I was with at an earlier Beaulieu when he asked a dealer the price of an item that had taken his fancy. The guy said he was asking such-and-such a price. Charlie put his arm around the startled vendor's shoulders and said "Son, where ah come from, when you ask what something costs you want to know how much it costs..." The vendor blurted out a price somewhat south of what he was asking, and Charlie peeled off the required number of notes... Simple as that.

My favourite dealer at Beaulieu is a Frenchman who offers a wide range of early motor racing material gathered at Gallic fairs during the year. I won't tell you who he is or I'll find myself in a queue next year. Like Henry N. Manney III, writing for *Road & Track* in the 1960s and listing the hotels he preferred staying at during the season. The next year he couldn't get a booking because they were all *Complet* with Americans who had read his guide...

Suffice to say that this year I bought a beautiful illustrated Michelin successes book devoted to the 1903 Paris-Madrid. The cover art shows the French Bibendum riding a Spanish bull with a huge PARIS-MADRID 1903 flag. The race, as you will learn later in this book, was stopped at Bordeaux because of the carnage to man and motorcar. Motor racing was banned in France and it's a miracle that motorsport didn't stop right there. And you wouldn't be reading this. And Bernie would still be selling second hand cars.

I also found the British Intelligence illustrated report on the German Motor Industry during the war years. This included photographs and details of the Grand Prix cars that included the Italian Cisitalia because it was designed by Dr Porsche. It was also this learned publication that professionally suggested that the Volkswagen Beetle would probably never be a commercial success. Yeah, right. In fact this book is nearly as rare as the companion report on the German Grand Prix and Speed Record cars. So it was a good Beaulieu visit for me, one way and another.

A glass or two of toothsome *rose* with Laurence Edscer and Ted Walker on their joint stand in E Field. Ted Walker, who runs

Ferret Photographic, was Ted the Metal Man at Beaulieu with nary a photograph in sight and a table of rare hardware that included a pair of incredible aluminium manifolds for an 8C/35 8-cylinder Grand Prix Alfa Romeo as fielded by Scuderia Ferrari in 1935. The Ferret had priced these museum pieces at £800 for the pair and scoffed at my suggestion that there were probably more punters in E Field looking for Austin A35 bits than Alfa 8C/35 bits. He also had a beautiful polished metal sculpture in the form of twin-choke SU carburettors on a manifold and linkages for bolting on to an FPF 4-cylinder Coventry Climax racing engine. These were said to be a bargain, by folk who didn't show much sign of reaching for their wallets, at £700. Or you could have a long manifolding with three Dellorto carburettors that might have been from an XK or an E-Type Jaguar, at £450. There was a string of experts passing by and offering conflicting advice or information. You could have had a pair of uprights for a Lotus 41 at £100, rear uprights that might or might not have fitted a Chevron B24 at £400, a diff for a Lister-Bristol at £700, a Manx Norton gearbox at £100 and a complicated cushion-mounted rev counter for the same Manx was £275. I couldn't get my head around the gearbox being cheaper than the rev counter, but my mentor Peter Renn observed that the gearbox might have been full of neutrals... Then there was a pair of Lister Jaguar rear callipers at £250. Or how about a Ford GT40 illustrated glossy colour fold-out publicity brochure. Was it original? For twenty quid, Ferret figured it wasn't worth arguing about...

And how were his prices reflected in sales? On the Friday 'setting up' day he sold the Coventry Climax SUs, the Jaguar Dellortos and the Lister Bristol diff.

Meanwhile down at Monza my mate Nigel Roebuck always has his loyalties split between the Grand Prix cars wailing past the big windows of the media room above the pits and Mario Acquati's emporium of motor racing books and memorabilia. Roebuck phones for an opinion on a delectable and incredibly

61

rare packet of Achille Varzi documentation that includes a hand-written letter from the deep and stormy Varzi, a hand-written entry form and a receipt for the entry. Varzi raced a Bugatti that summer, scoring just a singleton victory at Tripoli. The price does not bear banter in a public place like this, but suffice to say that the Roebuck homestead may be mortgaged and Nige will come back on Monday with an incredibly valuable piece of kit. Varzi stuff is *extremely* thin on the ground, to the point where I can't remember ever seeing anything with his signature and The Buck has just scored a *pair* of signatures! Makes the Grand Prix seem almost irrelevant. And of course it *was* irrelevant to all the enthusiastic punters at Beaulieu...

We drove down to Lord Montagu's packed paddocks in a Peugeot 206 CC, a little whizzer with the initials standing for Convertible Coupe, I presume. I could *not* open the boot. I even scorned the habit of a lifetime and consulted the handbook. Peter Renn knows about things mechanical. He supercharged his Spridget which must mean something. It gave me a huge amount of satisfaction to see that he couldn't open the boot either. The Peugeot test car delivery driver had advised that the pull-out luggage cover in the boot had to be pulled across before the coupe lid would crank itself down and hide and he also warned not to interrupt the controlled-collapse of the hardtop or it would all end in tears. Peter said we'd give it a go anyway and all the whirring and lifting and cranking began...at which point the boot miraculously lifted itself in a mechanically orchestrated fashion...showing that it was actually hinged at the *rear* which explained our inability to open the boot in a normal fashion!

But there's more and it gets worse. The boot does not open from the front either, so I call Sunny Mondair, the Press Fleet co-ordinator at Peugeot. This is not going to be an easy conversation. "Er, I have this problem in that I am incapable of opening the boot on the 206 CC." There is a silence which I interpret as Sunny thinking 'Omigod, we've got another journalist who can't get into the car, never mind driving it.' But she didn't say that. She said 'Did you push the key in and then turn it?' Ah...no. So I pushed the key in and, amazingly I could open the boot lid. From the rear. Which means that the wizards at Peugeot have designed the boot-lid on their cheapest convertible to open either from the front if the top is coming down, or from the back if I'm trying to get in there with my luggage. Hinges both ends. Front or rear entry. Heavens...

Which puts me in mind of a story Les Leston told in a speech after a function at a stately home in the UK where, for reasons unclear, both of us had been co-opted as judges for a Concours d'Elegance. Les was clear who he did *not* want to win, and it sort of went on from there. The owner of the stately pile made an ingratiating speech about Les's racing career after the awards were over, and then Les indicated that he would also like to speak to the assembled company. He thanked his host and then said "In fact my first ambition was to go on the stage but I lost my place in the RADA study group because I miss-read the stage notes. They said "Enter Ophelia. From the rear..."" Nervous laughter.

Then came an international old-car weekend suggested by the genial Nick Brimblecombe who runs the splendid Grand Touring Club, hosting rallies and visits to events all over the world. Would I like to be the guest of GTC and the Austrian Tourist Board and cover the Alpenfahrt Austrian classic rally? A mille-second of consideration and I agreed. You can't rush into these things.

Driving the Mercedes 1955 190SLR, a museum replica of the car that won the Macau race in 1956, was the icing on the Alpenfahrt Rally cake. It was like sister-of-Stirling's Mille Miglia winner, a 190SL that had been stripped and modified for competition but was totally overshadowed by the 300SLR successes in 1955 so that I was never aware that a 190SLR existed until the museum car turned up in Austria.

I discovered that a British army sergeant, Doug Steane, had

finished second to an Austin Healey at Macau in 1955 and won the race in 1956. Celebrating the far-away success of the racy 190SL, Mercedes offered an SLR performance kit for DM400 and sold 2000 world-wide!

I drove it the day after the rally ended, my only instruction being that the tank was full and I should bring it back before it was empty. It was bloody cold that September Sunday morning in the centre of Austria's ski country but it was bracing to be able to wind up the baby Mercedes racer on the alpine mountain roads, ever mindful of the fact that the brakes were very 1955 with long pedal and not a whole lot at the end of it. Until you were right into it, and everything was warm, I suppose.

I was to 'crew' on the rally for the amiable Dr Josef Ernst, PR Manager for the Classic Department at DaimlerChrysler, in a big 1964 300SE Mercedes saloon. We had massive brake problems when a director of one of the rally sponsoring companies with local knowledge, conducted the mighty Mercedes in the early stages of a day that took us most of the way up the stupendous Grossglockner hillclimb. It was coming down that our man seemed to underestimate the two tons of motorcar he was driving as well as a misunderstanding about kinetic energy and we reached the bottom in clouds of smoke and NO brakes. Make that NO BRAKES. At all. The car just rolled away and only paused with the handbrake. We waited over an hour for the retarders to cool down and then Dr Ernst was back at the helm and decorum was more or less restored. Which was not to say that the good Doctor didn't hustle to the point where we never saw our 'VIP driver' on the third day.

Austria is all surprises. First surprise was the two gorgeous blondes to meet my Ryanair flight at Klagenfurt and then swept me away to the ski village of Bad Klein Kircheim in an amazing Volkswagen Phaeton – the 5-litre limo with the silky smooth W10 340hp engine. It was like no other Volkswagen I'd ever been in!

The crowds in the towns where the rally timing controls were set up were hugely enthusiastic. In Strassburg they mobbed each car as they came into the town square. The idea was that the rally stretched for 1000 kilometres spread over three days – a short run on the Friday afternoon as acclimatisation, then a long run through the mountains on Saturday and skirting into Italy and Slovenia, and on the Sunday it was lakes day.

The good Doctor Ernst pressed on with the big 300SE despite my suggestions from time to time that he might do more Cruise and less Race. He would slow for a while and then gradually get back up to full charge. This was all very well, providing we didn't meet an Austrian coming the other way using the same bit of white line that we were. Mention of white line reminds me of our sponsor PR man who had driven on the second day. His company produced markings for roads and airport runways, and he described his products as *horizontal signalisation*. I was so amazed at that description that I asked him to say it again. Dr Ernst was only just avoiding laughing out loud. Made losing the brakes almost worth having him along.

Rallying in the big old 300SE was like flinging an Austrian front room up mountain climbs, complete with overstuffed armchairs! It had only done 47,000km when the owner died. The son didn't want it, the daughter wanted to flog it, so the mother presented it to the Mercedes museum instead. There were the usual entrants determined to win, rather than enjoying themselves, the event and the sensational scenery. Dr Ernst was of the opinion that we should do our best to make up enough time to be able to stop for lunch at a suitable restaurant. Definitely my sort of rally driver! We were all but last on the first day, locked in competition with Piero Lercher's 1966 Fiat 500 and on final results our big Mercedes was 92nd and Piero's baby Fiat was 96th.

The Alpenhfahrt began in 1910 when the cars were lucky just to be able to get over the passes at all, never mind set performance times. The roads were unmade when Rolls-Royce won in 1912 and re-named their rally Ghosts, Alpine Eagles. The rally was part of the World Championship when the last event was run in 1973 and it was revived last year as a classic happening with all cars dating prior to '73. There were over 100 entries this year including Rauno Altonen, now 65, in a 1972 Porsche 911S. He was remembering his Alpenhfahrts in the 1960s when many of the mountain roads were still unmade!

I'm not good at scenery. I've always figured that if you've seen one scene you've seen them all – but the Austrian and Slovenian scenery was jaw dislocation material with mountain faces climbing sheer from a river to the sky. Round every corner was a view more gob-smacking than the one we'd just gawped at. I hope this doesn't mean I'm becoming a tourist...

At one of the time checks, we had to do a 'Le Mans' start before moving on. This involved Dr Ernst and my goodself 'sprinting' 30 yards to the Mercedes. This was all rather undignified for a chap of my advanced years. I don't think I've ever run in public before. Jacky Ickx was right. Walking is the way to do it. Remember when he refused to run across the track at the 'real' Le Mans, and they decided to scrap the traditional running after the little Belgian had made his point by walking at the start...and then went on to win the race!

Driving a Bugatti
Type 59 Grand Prix Car
— *Par Excellence!*

Even Bugatti experts seem uncertain as to whether there were eight or ten of the beautiful Type 59 Bugattis built by the Molsheim factory, distinctive with their 'piano wire' wheels, aimed to provide brave if ineffectual French opposition to Mercedes and Auto Union in the mid-1930s. In New Zealand this summer I was privileged to drive the only Type 59 still being raced (albeit, as I later discovered, it was a 'late-build' car based on original parts). The others sit quietly in museums or private collections. British ex-pat Peter Giddings was racing this Type 59 on the Southern Festival of Speed and he let me storm it around the paddock roads at the Levels circuit near Timaru. 'Storm' may be a slight exaggeration, but it seemed like storming from where I was sitting, sighting down the long louvered blue bonnet. It was the first time anyone else had driven the car and Giddings was amazed at the sensational noise it made, a combination of mechanical music, the high register of the supercharger shriek, an orchestra of meshing gears in the long 3.3-litre straight-eight engine, that looks as though it had been hewn from solid metal. Ken Purdy wrote in *The Kings of the Road,* "Most Bugattis are noisy in every way a car can be noisy, plus a few ways peculiar to themselves...the Bugatti water pump is something to make strong men weep, and some of the racing models fling oil about like a gusher gone berserk. It comes out of everything but the tyre valves and gets into everything including your hair..."

Giddings is a true enthusiast with the wealth to buy such a pedigree vintage racing car in the first place, and then to really *race* it with such a furious enthusiasm that other drivers would hurry to viewing areas to watch the Bugatti being pressed to its limits.

Bugattis inspire almost fanatical enthusiasm among owners and vintagents with a wish-list worldwide. Addiction might be a better word. I remember Ken Purdy writing about *"rasping down from Paris to Nice"* in a Bugatti and the word *rasp* has always come to mind when the marque is mentioned. My favourite Russell Brockbank cartoon shows a Bugatti driver having braked to a halt on a poplar-lined French road, having knocked down a cyclist. As he runs back to help the irate fallen Frenchman his wife is calling back "Ask him if knows a good restaurant..."

Getting into the cockpit was not without effort, even considering it was a token two-seater, the last Grand Prix car built to take a riding mechanic. There was considerable contortion involved in sliding my legs down either side of the big wide wood-rimmed four-spoke steering wheel. Once I was in and endeavouring to be nonchalant and comfortable, Giddings suggested that it might have been an idea to take my boots off and drive in stocking feet to clear the pedals. He suggested I climb out and remove them but I said that always supposing I could get myself out, I'd be too exhausted to get back in again, so he wormed his way down into the pedal bay to unlace and remove my left boot. Now I could slide across between clutch and brake and cover the accelerator with my right boot. Ahead of me was a Jaeger rev counter blue-lined at 5000rpm, a *huile* pressure gauge, a Bugatti *essence* gauge for fuel pressure and a water temperature gauge. Fuel pressure had been a problem that was eventually tracked down to a deranged plunger boot on the hand pump below the instrument panel. There was a simple on-off ignition switch, an advance/retard lever, a handbrake, the head of the magneto and an elegant brass reservoir for starting fuel supply and for cleaning the fuel system after switch-off. Fuel is a complicated chemist's mix of methanol, petrol, acetone and oil. Driven in anger, the Type 59 does just three miles per gallon on this witch's brew. The distinctive twin fuel fillers on the tail just behind the cockpit both fed the same tank and allowed the use of two churns to speed pit-stops. The raised, riveted body seam down the centre of the tail is a distinguishing feature of the Type 59.

The gearlever is gloriously vintage and outdoors, a wooden handled blade that links amazingly smoothly to the gearbox by a cross rod below the driver's legs. The H-shift pattern has been drawn on the aluminium instrument panel as an *aid memoir* with first gear towards the driver and down, second is straight up, third across and down, and fourth gear straight up.

The car starts with a crash of sound, shredding the paddock air and stopping all activities. I am wearing my 'Tazio Titfer' flat tweed cap backwards as pioneered by such as Philippe Entancelin and first gear slides in silently. I am much impressed as I had expected to graunch and satisfy the onlookers who do not believe I am being allowed to drive this incredibly expensive piece of automotive artistry. The engine spins easily and I am aiming down the long bonnet over an aero screen. I am instantly Rene Dreyfus, the Bugatti works driver I came to know well when he visited Monaco on occasions, celebrating his win there in 1930. He invited me to New York for the launch of his autobiography "My Two Lives" at the 21 Club in 1983.

In fact I am really driving carefully around the rectangular paddock roads, mindful that everyone has stopped to watch my progress and willing me to make a mistake, but I am revelling in this reminder of what *real* racing cars were like in the Golden Era. I was hugely impressed by Giddings generous gesture.

If getting in had been an epic performance, squeezing a gallon into a pint pot, getting out was an equal effort and I was heaving myself out, hands braced either side of the cockpit, when I became aware that my left hand was becoming uncomfortably warm. Hot, actually. Bloody burning! That's when I realised I was heaving down on the hot exhaust... Sir Henry Birkin died from burns he received from the exhaust pipe on his Maserati. I survived to write again.

There are reverse quarter elliptic springs at the rear but with the axle sliding in blocks and located by radius rods. The front axle is hollow, split in the centre and joined by a collar, brake torque being dealt with by radius arms connected to De Ram shock absorbers. The brakes are cable operated.

The amazing wheels are another Type 59 signature and I have always known them to be 'piano wire', but in fact when Giddings had Crossthwaite and Gardiner in Britain make two new wheels they had to mount an international search for the correct swaged specification of wire...and eventually it came from a bicycle manufacturer in China!

Jonathan Wood describes the unique wheel design in his book "Bugatti – The Man and the Marque": "It was distinguished by two rows of thin gauge spokes but, unlike conventional wire wheels, they did not transmit drive and braking reactions. That was the role of a large serrated aluminium flange, to which the brake drum was bolted, riveted to a standard Rudge Whitworth splined hub. The teeth meshed with their opposite numbers on the inner edge of the rim. Like their predecessors, when the wheel was removed, the aluminium shoes of the mechanically actuated brakes were exposed to view for, if necessary, instant replacement."

Giddings tells the story of Dreyfus and his Bugatti team-mates deciding that they didn't like the unpleasant noise created by the meshing of the wheel rims and the fact that "when the clutch was let out, a little bit of slack would create a knocking noise. It sounded like a loose rear end, but it wasn't. It was only the wheels..." Giddings says that Dreyfus told him they drew lots and he was appointed as the driver to go and tell Ettore Bugatti that they were unhappy with the unsettling noise from the wheels and wanted standard wheels fitted instead. "Ettore thanked Rene for explaining the problem with the wheels but was afraid he would be unable to accommodate the drivers' requests for new wheels. He pointed out that if this was to be a major problem, the drivers might be kind enough to tender their resignations as he had a long list of drivers anxious to race his cars..." They stayed on to race!

"We did love the look of it," Dreyfus wrote in his auto-biography. "The 59 was gorgeous...a breathtaking machine to behold. But it felt strange to drive..."

The Rootes type supercharged engine was giving around 240bhp at 5,500rpm and at the 1934 Coppa Acerbo a Type 59 was timed at nearly 290kph (180mph). In 1998 Sean Danaher tested this particular Type 59 engine on his dyno in the UK and registered 230bhp. The 750kg formula for 1934 presented Bugatti with something of a problem since this was a maximum. A *minimum* of 750kg would have suited Ettore. It was said that the Bugatti team went as far as removing the brake shoes as well as the tyres, when the cars were officially weighed and that sympathetic French officials turned the Gallic equivalent of a blind eye while Molshiem mechanics placed tyre levers under the weighbridge and stood on them... Dreyfus's works Type 59 was officially listed as 749.5kg!

The Type 59s looked glorious but they were a generation adrift, racing against the might of Mercedes, Auto Union, Maserati and Alfa Romeo with dated weaponry. Dreyfus picked up a win in the 1934 Belgian GP and Wimille later won in Algiers but it was too much to expect the Type 59 Bugattis to live up to their 'vintage' looks and dominate as they had done in the halcyon days of the Type 35 before the German teams arrived with massive financial backing from Adolf Hitler. The works cars were sold in 1935 and campaigned by private owners thereafter. Benoist and Earl Howe finished 1-2 at Picardy and at the Mannin Moar race on the Isle of Man, Brian Lewis and Charlie Martin scored another 1-2. In 1936 Wimille won at Deauville and at Comminges with an unblown Type 59. In 1937 Wimille had one of his best seasons with the unblown car winning at Pau, the Bona GP in North Africa, the Marne GP, Tunis and he lapped

Montlhery at over 91mph to win a 400,000 franc prize – in fact he lapped the 12-mile road circuit for 162 miles at an average of 91.3mph, just a fraction below Von Brauchitsch's Mercedes record for *one lap*! Wimille's lap record in the Type 59 was 92.44mph.

The noise of the Type 59 Bugatti with its supercharged straight eight engine remains in the mind long after the thrill of the drive has been forgotten or at least lodged in my memory bank. Ken Purdy captured the sound on paper: "The discerning ear can pick out three distinct themes – first the excruciating sharp *crack* of the exhaust, a high-level ripping sound; second, the characteristic growling, rattling, bucket-of-bolts noise of the roller and ball-bearing engine. A racing Bugatti engine in good shape always sounds as it were about to fly to pieces. Third, there is the siren-like rising and falling scream of the supercharger. Ah joy!"

Peter and I never actually explored the pedigree of his Type 59 in detail so I tended to accept that I was sitting in a piece of history without checking its credentials. Realising that I was a vintage Philistine after reading this feature that ran in "New Zealand Classic Car", Albert Ross put the Type 59 part of the Bugatti world to rights and filled in an important part of marque folklore when he wrote:

'Eoin Young's article failed to mention or give credit to this car's creator, world-renowned Bugatti restorer, Richard I'Anson, owner of Tula Engineering in the UK, and in particular, to Michael Whiting who virtually single-handedly built six Type 59s over 12 years.

In the mid '80s the late Bob Sutherland approached Tula Engineering with the proposition of building for him a Type 59 on an original and unused chassis, which had been obtained from Molshiem, and was at that time available in the USA. Tula purchased this chassis, which had never been drilled to take bodywork, along with an original Type 57S front axle and a set of springs, these items forming the basis of the car driven by Eoin Young, everything else having been made by Tula.

A further original chassis was obtained from the same source. To make the project viable, Richard decided to make another four cars on replica chassis. A friend and myself had the offer of one of these for £150,000 in order to finance the project and get it started. This figure was about a tenth of the value of an original Type 59 at the time. We did not in fact take up the offer.

Tula Engineering is only a small firm of under six people, based in an old cow house in rural Gloucestershire, but it then started the mammoth task of making patterns and machining castings to produce engines, superchargers, gearboxes, steering boxes, axles, wheels and brakes for six Type 59s. Even more remarkable is that the vast majority of this work was done by one man, Michael Whiting.

With one man building six cars, progress was slow, and due to this, Sutherland took delivery of only a complete kit of parts, plus a rolling chassis less bodywork, some five years after the project started. Sutherland then had Peter Shaw, the well-known Maserati restorer at Grantham in the UK, complete the car for him. The engine had been assembled by Sean Dannaher. In the end, Sutherland received his complete car no sooner than if he had let it be completed at Tula Engineering.

The magnitude of this project can only be appreciated by examination of a Type 59. The fact that six cars were built by virtually one man, Michael Whiting, is even more remarkable and I suggest is very worthy of recognition.'

So recognition is now made where it is due and my thanks to Albert Ross, who also noted that Bob Sutherland, who died in 2000, sold his car to Peter Giddings in the late 1990s.

Memories of those Racing Minis

John Cooper would have loved the new 135mph BMW-built Mini Cooper featured on the cover of this book. With a supercharged 1.6-litre engine, 'drive-by-wire' electronic throttle, a 6-speed gearbox and over 130bhp at 6000rpm, it would have been John's ultimate recipe with high performance and long legs all in a new century miniature package. It isn't a miniature marvel like the original Alec Issigonis's Mini concept but then the world has moved on since 1960 and now demands its minis to be bigger. I didn't like the first of the modern Mini Coopers, mainly because it wasn't really a mini and didn't really do much that something like a Renault Clio Sport couldn't do better. But the new supercharged Cooper S is very much in the original Cooper concept and takes me back to my early McLaren days in the early 1960s when Bruce had his beloved new E-Type Jaguar and I was driving his Mini Cooper to races on the Continent. It made continental touring hugely entertaining because it was so fast for such a tiny car and always took the traffic by surprise.

The new Cooper S has a full-length sunroof, electric windows operated from period-type toggle switches that seem to go with the image of the car. Slot into sixth and you see it smoothing along at 3000rpm on the rev counter directly in front of you, and 70mph on the dinner-plate sized speedometer in the centre of the dash...just like the original car.

Makes me want to do a Continental tour in a Mini Cooper all over again but perhaps if I lie in a darkened room long enough, the feeling of Mini Cooper motoring euphoria will subside.

John Cooper was so much larger than life and I always felt that it was a pity that he carried on beyond the win-by date of his Formula 1 cars because he was truly the father of the mid-engined post-war Grand Prix renaissance. Colin Chapman would refine the Cooper racing car recipe but it was Cooper cars that won back-to-back world titles in 1959 and 1960 before Team Lotus ever won a Grand Prix. (Stirling Moss won the first GPs for Lotus in Rob Walker's privately-entered car at Monaco and Riverside in 1960)

John was a splendid character. When I arrived in Britain early in 1961 Bruce McLaren had arranged for me to use the Cooper team address (243 Ewell Road, Surbiton, Surrey) for my mail and in those days it was like a direct link to where Formula 1 was at. It didn't get much better in the summer of '61. In a motor racing context, it was like collecting your mail at Buckingham Palace. Hadn't Jack Brabham just driven Coopers to win two World titles? But in retrospect, that was as good as it was going to be, even though the team soldiered on well into the sixties, taking on the formula change in 1966 with the huge and unreliable Maserati V12 engines.

I preferred to remember John as I first met him in the early sixties when I was travelling the circuits with Bruce, who was now leading the Cooper team, and we would all dine together in the evening. When the mechanics went back to work and the drivers went to bed, John would suggest we went for a stroll...and he always knew the best bar for a coffee and several cognacs where we put the racing world to rights.

In 1973, when John had been out of Formula 1 for a long time, but still visited the British Grand Prix, I met him in the paddock when I was wearing a newly fashionable pair of ear defenders, like headphones. John asked what they were for. He clapped them over his ears and a look of puzzlement came over his face. "Can't hear a bloody thing, boy!" I pointed out that that was the object of the exercise. "Bloody nonsense. Might as well stay at home. Next thing they'll be getting pegs for their noses so they can't smell the cars either. Wasn't like that in my day..."

'Steady' Barker once took me for lunch at the grand home of

Alec Moulton, the man who worked with Issigonis on the rubber suspension units for the first Minis. He also created his little lightweight bicycles that could fold-up for putting in the boot.

There was a broad balcony looking out over the view at the back of the house and in the equally broad room below the balcony was a long colour painting of that same balcony with Moulton's friends painted in. I asked him if Alec Issigonis was included. He said he wasn't sure and excused himself, returning almost immediately with a pair of binoculars to study the painted people until he found Issigonis and pointed him out...

At the turn of this new century, I wrote a series of features on the good old days of Mini racing, starting with the season of '64 when Ken Tyrrell turned his management expertise to running the works Minis while John Cooper was recovering from a huge end-over-end accident in an experimental twin-engined Mini.

It was a Tyrrell-managed championship title that went largely unnoticed long before Ken started his Grand Prix team and winning Formula 1 World Championships. It was the summer of 1964. Jackie Stewart had just been discovered by Tyrrell and Cooper after a test in a Formula 3 Cooper at Goodwood. Tyrrell signed him to drive one of his Cooper Formula 3 cars powered by a BMC engine. His other team driver was Warwick Banks. John Cooper was spending all his spare time experimenting with a new toy – a Mini with two engines. Those who drove it, talked of Ferrari power-to-weight, of doubled performance with another engine installed where the back seat used to be. It was this quirky high-performance 'toy' that led directly to Ken Tyrrell becoming manager of the Mini team when something broke and pitched John into a huge accident. He was lucky to escape with his life when the car somersaulted on the A3 Portsmouth Road near Surbiton. His father, Charles, was so appalled at the crash which nearly killed his son that he refused to let anyone see the wreckage. He smashed up what was left of the car with a sledgehammer and had it trucked away as scrap.

With John Cooper in hospital, Ken Tyrrell was asked to

manage the Mini entries in the European Touring Car Championship. "I thought I knew all about managing a single-seater team, but touring cars were a different ballgame," said Tyrrell, recalling that crazy summer. The way the championship was scored, class-winners could win the overall title if they kept on winning and winning by the greatest margin in the event of dead-heats and title count-backs. The Minis could win the title overall with careful planning.

There were circuit races and hill-climbs counting towards the championship and Tyrrell discovered early that there were more ways than one of winning. They scored a class win in the Mont Ventoux hillclimb but then discovered that there were not enough entries to make a class and missed points. Minimum entry was six. "From then on we took a full class everywhere we went with anyone who would come along with their Minis," recalled Tyrrell , who drove a Mini himself in one of the hill-climbs! South African mechanic Tony Jefferies, inevitably nick-named 'Yarpie', was also called up to race one of the Minis in three events that summer. He had raced in South Africa and came to Britain seeking a drive but was advised by Tyrrell that he stood no chance. "He offered me a job as a mechanic instead but I still imagined I'd get a drive. I tried Lotus and BRM and after a month of knock-backs I went to work for Ken. He gave me the works Mini van as my transport, British Racing Green with the two white stripes down the nose and COOPER CAR COMPANY on the sides. This was big stuff for me!"

Roger Bailey, one of the Tyrrell team mechanics that season, later Chris Amon's personal mechanic at Ferrari, and who later headed the Indy Lights series in North America, remembers Jefferies racing in Budapest. "We were one short to fill the class and 'Yarpie' had an international racing licence so we grabbed Banks' road Mini, whacked a set of racing wheels on it, and he was a race driver again!"

Ginger Devlin, long-time Cooper man, was running the Mini team in the British Championship and he compliments Tyrrell.

"Ken was on top of it all. A marvellous tactician. You'd have to get up very early to catch Ken." Devlin was there when everything happened at Cooper. "When we first started racing the Minis, some bright spark at BMC thought it would be a good idea to tow the racing Minis on trailers behind Mini vans in matching team livery. The fact that the car and trailer weighed more than the towing vehicle never seem to occur to anyone upstairs. And when you added spares and wheels and oil... Most of the vans spent the season with their grilles stove in, having run up the backside of the car in front, unable to get stopped..." In 1964 the Minis were taken around Europe on a transporter.

Bailey has vivid memories of the transporter. "It was an awful thing, a car carrier that BMC used for new car deliveries. I'd never driven anything that big before but in those days it didn't seem to matter. Licence? What licence? If you were a mechanic you could drive a transporter. It's different these days. In the States even the truck drivers want to fly to the races.

"I remember driving the rig south from Zandvoort and just entering a big tunnel in the evening rush hour when there was a huge **_BANG!!_** I didn't realise how high the rig was fully loaded and the front Mini on the top deck was jammed under the tunnel with its roof caved in. It was chaos! There were miles of cars in the lane I'd blocked and here I was trying to reverse the car carrier and get everyone behind me to back up..."

Team drivers were Warwick Banks and Belgian driver, Julian Vernaeve but John Fitzpatrick and John Rhodes were also on the strength. "We used the 970S," says Banks. "It had a little jewel as an engine and which closely resembled the one used in the Formula 3 cars with which Jackie and I won almost everything that season."

Bailey and Jefferies were mechanics. Those were the days when mechanics were expected to work all the hours God made to get the cars to grid. More to the point, they *expected* to do that. And drive the transporter. It was all part of the territory. There were problems during practice at Karlskoga in Sweden with wheel-nuts coming loose and Jefferies remembers spending hours drilling wheel-nuts and fitting locking wire.

Their most memorable drive was to Budapest and back. Jefferies had raced one of the Minis there, but the drive he remembered most was the trip home. "We drove the transporter back non-stop to get the motors to the BMC Competitions engine workshop in Coventry. The heater had packed up and we drove it back in the freezing cold. Roger reckoned that it was the closest he'd ever been to death – and for Rog, that was saying something!" Bailey had been involved in a motorway smash the year before. He suffered serious injuries and the driver of the car was killed.

"At that race in Hungary, in order to win by the maximum amount, we wanted all of the Minis we controlled to be as far behind as possible in second, third and fourth," said Tyrrell. "The marshals couldn't understand why, at all our stops to refuel, we were washing windscreens...windows...even the whole car, just to lose time. Saab were up to the same time-wasting game, but they didn't do it in the pits --they stopped out on the circuit and had *lunch*!"

Banks remembers racing against a two-stroke *Wartburg* in their class in this four-hour event. "I can smell its awful fuel even now!" says Banks, laughing. It was a super cobbled-street circuit and we were lapping the Wartburg every 15 laps. As he was our competition, our other team cars were pitted, washed and leathered off to kill time. Alas, Ken's calculations were slightly too enthusiastic and the Wartburg finished second in our class!

"Zolder was another memorable race. DKW were our main class opposition and I swapped the lead on every lap with Dieter Mantzl's DKW. Every lap we were side by side on the straight, grinning across at each other. He finally dropped back, but not until we had some 20 laps of monumental struggle. Great fun but that was what racing was all about in those days." The camaraderie between drivers and teams and mechanics was one of the main memories Jefferies has of that championship season.

Banks and John Whitmore spent a week learning the Mont Ventoux hillclimb. "At the top we watched the French Air Force practising aerobatics – *below* us!" Their practice produced results. The Mini took one and a half *minutes* off the 1-litre class record.

The Mini brigade worked together. At Zandvoort, Tyrrell asked Rob Slotemaker, the Dutch driver who ran a skid school at the circuit and knew it better than the back of his hand, if he would use his bigger 1275S to tow Banks round in the 970cc works car during practice. "That worked amazingly well," said Banks. "There were about 30 cars on the grid, mostly 1275cc Mini Coopers. Rob put his car on pole – and I was second!"

On the 14.2-mile Nurburgring *Nordschleife* mountain circuit with 89 left-hand corners and 85 right-handers, the Mini was a delight. "In the six-hour race there I was lapping in the Mini at around 10min 40sec which compared with Fangio's fantastic 9min 17sec lap record set in a 250F Maserati in the German Grand Prix only seven years before. I thought the Mini was just amazing around the 'Ring, especially when you remember it was only 970cc..."

Tyrrell got himself into trouble with BMC Competitions boss, Stuart Turner after one of the hillclimbs. "We were beaten by a DKW there, but it was pointed out to me that the DKW didn't have carpets and Group 2 regulations demanded carpets. I put in a protest which was upheld and we won our class. If we hadn't (although we didn't know it at the time) we wouldn't have won the championship. Stuart Turner gave me a right bollocking. He said 'BMC *never* protest!'"

Monza was the clincher and the Ford team played tactics that impressed Tyrrell by their sheer ingenuity. The final race was a 4-hour refuelling race but without driver changes and *all* the class-winners were equal on points, so it was wide open. "This was when Alan Mann, who was running the Ford team, pulled a fast one. He wanted to stop us winning our class so he brought an Anglia which wasn't normally competitive but it might be at Monza with its long straights and no chicanes in those days. His trump card was bringing an extra Lotus Cortina, whose job was to tow the Anglia in its slipstream. That was *good*. Very clever tactics. The Lotus Cortina would come in and refuel and then wait for the Anglia, to carry on towing it. The carburettors were icing on our cars and Banks was running second to the Anglia but with a slight misfire. Over at Ford they were having fuel problems."

Other teams were towing. Fiat did the same with Abarth with a 1000 to tow the 850s and Alfa Romeo had a 1600 Giulietta to tow the 1300s which were too heavy on most tracks, but worked well at Monza with a little outside assistance.

Banks recalls that John Young was the driver of the Alan Mann works Anglia. "There was no way that we could compete but there was an element of luck and mismanagement when they forgot to take into account the extra fuel consumption and ground to a halt very near the end. Another thing about that Monza race was that it was a single-handed four-hour race and they wouldn't let me out of the car – for *anything*!" Tyrrell takes up the story. "At one of his refuelling stops late in the race, Warwick started unbuckling his harness and climbing out of the car. I asked him what he was doing and he said he was going for a pee. I pushed him back in and said 'Do it in the car – we're trying to win a championship here!' And we did."

The final at Monza was a blessed relief and the championship win was a major achievement in Mini terms yet it only earns half a paragraph in Peter Browning's book "The Works Minis".

Tony Jefferies remembers a light note about that Monza race which paints a picture of team life and Tyrrell's paternal management style. "We had driven the works cars back from the circuit to the Hotel de la Ville and parked them. I was out of my car and making sure it was locked. Ken Tyrrell was going up the steps into the hotel when John Rhodes roared into the car park with tyres screaming, did a three-sixty spin turn almost at Ken's feet, and slipped into a parking space. Rhodesy climbed out all nonchalant-like. Ken's jaw had dropped as he watched his driver's antics, his eyes went big – and he just shook his head and walked inside. Rhodesy said 'Jesus – I've upset the gaffer, haven't I!' But Ken took it all in his stride. We were all part of his team. It was really more like a family than a team."

When Mini people talk about racing back in the 'sixties, someone always remembers the story about the stuffed-up 'dead heat' at Spa. Ken Tyrrell and Sir John Whitmore have vivid memories of a staged three-car dead-heat finish to the 1963 touring car race at Spa that didn't quite work out as planned. Tyrrell would team manage the works Minis when they won the European Touring Car title the following season, but at Spa the year before they were so far in the lead that it was decided to stage-manage a dead-heat finish. "Because of the continuous high speed at Spa we were having a problem with the oil getting to the gearbox bearings, but in the race we were running 1-2-3 so comfortably that we arranged for them to cross the finishing line together, side-by-side. As luck would have it, one of our cars had trouble with its gearbox and the other two waited for him, but as they came down from the last corner to the finish, a DKW caught and passed them on the grass. We were beaten by half a car's length!

Sir John Whitmore was one of the Mini trio with Jimmy Blumer and Bill Blydenstein. "We were more than two minutes clear at the start of the last lap when Bill began to have gearbox trouble so we slowed to stay with him and thought we had loads of time. Round the final hairpin he was going really slowly but I thought he could coast down the hill from there and still complete our three-abreast winning finish. But half way down the hill from La Source I looked in my mirror and saw the DKW! I had a real dilemma now. I couldn't signal the others because they wouldn't know what I was on about. I had to make a quick decision about whether to put my foot down and make sure we won the race...but if I'd done that and my team-mates finished second and third, I'd have been a shit...so we didn't make it and the DKW won!" So much for being a gentleman.

Murray Walker in vintage mood
at Donington.

Eoin Young at the wheel of the 1903
Jarrott Napier with John Bentley.

Daughter Selina, with grandson Alfie,
age 3, learning to draw.

Eoin Young with cap, showing Tazio Nuvolari wearing a similar titfer.

David Young (left) remembering his C-Type Jaguar, with Gavin Bain and Eoin Young.

Phil Hill lunching with Ford at the Italian GP.

Eoin Young singing
IT BEATS WORKING.

Eoin Young snug-fitted in works
908 Porsche at Hockenheim.

Lou Meyer, 3-time Indianapolis 500
winner, and Eoin Young at Indy in 1991.

Rick Mears Mum and Dad
celebrating his Indy win in 1991.

Sir Stirling Moss, Howden and
Judy Ganley, and Gail Barwood
at Silverstone.

Euan Sarginson and Eoin Young.

Vintage McLaren lineup:
Tyler Alexander, Teddy Mayer
and Eoin Young.

Nigel Roebuck (left) and Keke Rosberg.

Eoin Young with serious cigar at Pebble Beach in California.

Rob Walker, Sir Stirling Moss and Sir Jackie Stewart.

John Cooper, Ken Tyrrell and Stirling Moss lunching at the Barley Mow.

Jack Brabham and Roy Salvadori
at Goodwood.

Brian Redman – Jenks rated him as a
'nice lad' in his 1968 Belgian GP report.

Photograph of Delahayes at Ards in
1936, hanging in the famous butcher's
shop on the TT course at Comber.

Jenks at the Nurburgring 1000km
in 1969 with Harry Calton
(Ford PR) left, Eoin Young and
Michael Bowler of 'Motor'.

Eoin Young with 1930s Mercedes
works driver, Manfred von Brauchitsch
in the south of France.

Eoin Young in the big front-engined
Indianapolis roadster.

John Cooper and Ron Dennis with Mini Cooper and the F1 McLaren road car at the Barley Mow.

Motorcycle champion Geoff Duke having his first car race in a Gemini Formula Junior at Silverstone in 1960. It was also Jim Clark's first single-seater.

John Bolster's 4-engined Bloody Mary Special at Prescott in 1938. (*Ferret Fotographics*).

Pop singer Chris Rea, Eoin Young and Nigel Roebuck over lunch at the Ford F1 motorhome.

Eoin Young in his 1928 supercharged Stutz.

John Cooper and Eoin Young with photo of the 500cc Cooper streamliner.

Eoin Young making notes during test drive with 1922 TT Sunbeam in New Zealand.

Denny Hulme and Jack Brabham – World Champions in 1966 and 1967 in Brabham's cars.

Carroll Shelby and Roy Salvadori, Le Mans winners in 1959.

If a tweaked Mini could be so fast with one engine across the front, surely there was a case for fitting a second sideways engine in the back and double the power and performance? The amazing thing about the twin-engined Minis was that there were so many of them built by various companies. Mini creator Alec Issignois was naturally one of the first when he dropped a second engine across the back seat of an open Mini-Moke, presumably for military use as Citroen had done with their twin-engined 2CV *Sahara* for the French Foreign Legion. Having proved that it could be done and the problem of linking transmissions and throttles could be coped with on the Moke, it was obvious to make a twin-engined car. Issigonis had two versions built at BMC, one with 110bhp and a racer with 170bhp which would be entered in the Targa Florio in 1963. Paul Emery and Daniel Richmond at Downton Engineering built twin-motor Minis of their own, but it was assumed that John Cooper would obviously build the best twin-engined 4-wheel-drive road car.

The unlikely Targa Florio entry was driven by John Whitmore who was vastly impressed at being paired with Belgian Paul Frere who had won Le Mans in 1959 and 1960. "In practice I did a lap at about 47-minutes which was quite fast," says Whitmore. "But we used up a complete set of tyres in one lap, so we decided to run at 50min laps and save rubber. In a sense it was a bit silly because you could easily have done 50min laps with an ordinary Mini! On the second lap of the race the rear radiator sprung a leak so we had to shut the rear engine down and run on the front engine alone – the result was that we were racing an ordinary Mini and carrying a spare engine in the boot!"

It is clear that Whitmore was no fan of the Twin-Mini. "It was bloody fast but we always had a problem getting the gear linkages to work. There were rods and links all over the place and to change gear on both engines at the same time was more luck than judgement. It didn't handle particularly well. The weight at the rear of the car gave it a momentum of its own, a pendulum effect. You couldn't hurl it into the corners like a normal Mini because the back would just go wandering out..."

It was reported at the time that Whitmore had a problem with the front engine during Goodwood tests, shut the engine down and lapped faster than the Mini lap record with only the rear engine. "Complete nonsense," says Whitmore, now Sir John.

Each engineer had their own ideas of how the controls should be coupled and the placement of the fuel tank but the amazing feature was how innocuous the car looked from the outside. There was an air-intake scoop on the right hand side and an air exhaust grille on the left. The Cooper car had vents in the boot lid which was permanently propped open *a la* Abarth. John Cooper drove me down to Goodwood for an F1 test session in the twin Mini and it was an understated roadrocket, crammed full of machinery with the rear engine boxed to insulate occupants from heat and noise.

The instrument panel was crowded with a pair of rev counters to the right of the single speedometer with oil pressure gauges for the front and rear engines on the far right in the river's sightline. There were ignition keys for both engines. The gear linkage was complicated with a pair of levers coupled so that both gearboxes could be worked at once. If there was a problem in either engine, it could be switched off and the gearshift link unhooked.

The Cooper Twin-Mini was actually built in a shed in Ken Tyrrell's logging yard at Ockham in Surrey, a small building that would later see the creation of his own Formula 1 car – and be considered for preservation as a building where engineering history had been made. Neil Davis was in charge with Roger Bailey. "It was John Cooper's idea and we did the initial work," says Davis. "We cut the rear floorpan out and fitted in a complete sub-frame unit in the hole and reinforced it under John's instruction. It then went back to Cooper where Roger fitted it out with the fuel tank and wiring and general installation. Jack Knight did the gear linkages, coupling them together." Davis said they also built a twin-engined version of the hydrolastic 1100. "I suppose we fitted that with a couple of Cooper S 1275cc engines. Ginger Devlin drove it up to BMC and we never heard of it again."

Bailey says the Twin-Mini was a winter project and remembers a test with John Whitmore when the front engine failed. "We pulled the pin out of the linkage, disconnected the gearlevers and set off for Surbiton on the back engine. Then that failed as well and we had to phone for a trailer to get home!"

Ginger Devlin, in charge of engineering at the Cooper Car Company, recalls that the main problem with installation of the second engine was that it went into the back of the car facing the same way as the front engine so the gear linkage had to go through every sort of twist and turn and right-angle tweak to join up with the other linkage. The exhaust system from the second engine went through similar tubular gymnastics to join the front exhaust and emerge as a single pipe with a strange 8-cylinder growl.

Interest in the Twin-Mini project evaporated when John Cooper crashed heavily on the Kingston Bypass on his way to dinner with Roy Salvadori. It is generally assumed that one of the locked rear steering links snapped and a wheel flicked sideways triggering the somersaulting accident which left Cooper hospitalised and out of action for months. Devlin's opinion is that the 'iffy' rear linkage selected second while the front was in top and the rear engine locked up.

Of Men and Motors

Piers Courage was a talent waiting to blossom and it was one of the tragedies in Sir Frank Williams' life that Piers met his end in a fiery crash at Zandvoort in 1970 driving the De Tomaso that Frank was fielding in the 1970 season. In 1969 he had sent a Brabham-Cosworth to the Tasman series for Piers and I had obviously written something about his performance that gathered his total attention. I recently found the handwritten letter he had sent in February:

'Dear Eoin,

I never normally like putting pen to paper about anything written against me in the papers. However on reading your recent article, I feel that I must make some comment as I obviously have no defence against anything you like to say in the press.

I have only done this since one or two of your colleagues, whom I saw the other night, remarked that there must be some feud between us for you to write what you had.

Regarding your article, firstly you know very well that at Lakeside I had a good chance of staying with Chris during the race and that with Graham holding me up to the tune of over a second a lap, I had to get past him early in order to stay in the picture. As it was, Graham meted out to me the same treatment he gave Jackie at Levin although I noticed no criticism of him at the time.

About Warwick Farm, I have no excuses except that for you to say that the Brabham on Dunlops should have been a 'good wet weather machine' was a bit presumptuous, considering your experience of competitive driving in these conditions, whilst in actual fact the car had done exactly one lap in the wet since it

86

was built and was consistently out of balance at the time.

I had no wish to be in front of Amon and it was only due to the fact that he had himself 'lost it' on the corner before that put me in this position. Your comment will probably be that I can't stand criticism but I have suffered under your pen for about three years now, with, I think you will admit, fairly good humour and I am sorry that I have been driven to writing to you, which is something that, I assure you, I would not have done if I thought your comments were fair.'

I replied, apologising for 'riling him' and offered a platform in my *Autocar* column the following week to put his views. I told him that what I had in mind was a piece leading with 'There are always two sides to every racing incident and since I have come down rather hard on Piers Courage after his early exits at Lakeside and Warwick Farm, it's only fair to hear his side of the story since he was sitting a lot closer to the action than I was. Take it away Piers...' I also added 'Oh, talking about poison pens, don't forget I used the same typewriter as I did on the 1968 series 'Down Under' and I felt there was stacks of credit where it was due then. I was even ticked off at *Autocar* for being to pro you!'

Piers replied a few days later 'I appreciated what you offered to do in *Autocar* but as you know I am not one to bear a grudge and I would much rather forget the whole thing and say nothing. I think that as the Tasman Series is now 'history' it would be stupid to stir it up again and I would never go into print about it myself. There is nothing as dead as yesterday's news so I am sure that it will soon be forgotten, even if it hasn't been already.

Anyway, I shall enjoy proving you wrong this coming season!

Seriously though, I have always had a lot of respect for you as a journalist and having got what I had to say off my chest, I should like to let bygones be bygones. See you at Brands.

Yours, Piers.'

* * *

This is 1966 when I am renting an apartment from Mike Hailwood in a point block at Heston, five floors above his. 'Signs of the financial times: Outside my flat the other morning were a brace of identical white Ferraris, one left hand driver and the other right hand drive. Rich racing drivers? Wrong. Rich motorcycle racers. They belonged to Mike Hailwood and Jim Redman. Just goes to show that there must be plenty of gold around for the quicker sprocket men.'

* * *

Robert Ramsay Campbell Walker was a true gentleman. In fact an American journalist described Rob as 'A gentleman in terms of one word as well as two.' He had raced a Delahaye at Le Mans in 1939 finishing a worthy 8th starting in a dark suit with collar and tie, and stopping at dawn to change into a sports jacket. As a gentleman did in those days. That same Delahaye won a special challenge race at Brooklands immediately pre-war to decide the fastest road car in Britain and in 1978 Rob loaned the car to me to take to the 50th anniversary of the Tourist Trophy races at Ards. When I asked him why he didn't take the car over himself, he said that his wife worried about him going over to Northern Ireland when 'the troubles' were still present, if not exactly manifest. I drove over in convoy with Denis Jenkinson in one of the 'GO' Talbot team cars and we had a great weekend despite the weather. I asked Rob when he wanted the Delahaye returned and he said 'Oh, when you're bored with it.' I gave it back two years later.

The Delahaye was such a delight to drive with its Cotal electromagnetic gearbox operated by a little switch on the dashboard, so simple to operate that even I could manage it. The car felt almost 'modern' to drive and I was fascinated to find a splendid article written in 1936 by John Dugdale, one of my predecessors on *The Autocar*, who was covering the Ards TT and the day after the race he was offered a drive around the course with Rene Lebegue in the Delahaye (a twin to Rob's car) that had set the lap record:

'It was with considerable though suppressed excitement that I donned one of his white crocheted helmets, borrowed a pair of Brunet's goggles that he was just about to pack, and climbed into the Delahaye. Helmet and goggles were *"absolument neces-saire"* according to them, so it looked as if we were going to have some speed work.

We drove fairly gently down to the beginning of the straight, waited for the oil to warm and the road to clear, and then *Un, deux, trois, quatre, CINQ!"* and with spinning wheels and a deep throaty roar from the engine, Rene let her have it. Up to four-five in second, four thou. in third, and then it was three thou. in top immediately. I clicked the watch. 84mph in nineteen seconds. Good going!

'Now we try 4,000 rpm?" Lebegue queried – that meant over 110mph. He turned the car round. The road was clear...away! Like the wind, we roared towards the aerodrome. Three-five in top in a flash, but she was naturally slower accelerating between 100 and 110. A car appeared in the distance at the bottom of the road. We only reached 103mph. Lebegue immediately slowed so no acceleration time is available. He is far too good a driver to take needless risks. (In the race he had reached 115mph, equivalent to 4,000rpm).

'We continued the reverse way of the course to Belfast. I asked what he thought of the circuit. "Difficult," was his immediate answer, and of the twists down Bradshaw's Brae he volunteered, "Very difficult." In Belfast the car was absolutely controllable in traffic. The brakes were first class, as was demonstrated at a rather hasty stop for traffic lights.

'What a road car this Delahaye makes with a maximum of 120mph on ordinary petrol and without the help of a super-charger! Road-holding is splendid. There is independent sus-pension for the front wheels. The car feels absolutely right, and

89

Charlie Martin, who drove one in the race, described it as like a 2.3 Bugatti to drive, I cannot say more…"

* * *

Rob Walker gained fame as Stirling Moss's entrant in Formula 1 providing him with the luxury of choice between a Cooper and a Lotus taking both cars to Grand Prix courses. After Rob's death, I met up with one of his early mechanics who said that Rob had asked him if he could devise a way of being able to identify his car when he was holding out the pit signals board during a race. The Walker colours until then had been a plain dark Scottish blue. Overnight the mechanic painted a broad white stripe around the nose incorporating the white circle for the number and this became the Walker racing colours for the rest of his racing career. At the Goodwood Circuit Revival meeting in 2003, the top seller in the Goodwood shop was a rugby shirt in Walker blue and white with Moss's favourite racing number 7.

I once asked Stirling whether he had ever longed to be World Champion and carry the number one on his car. The only reason he would have wanted the number one, he said, was that it would have been easier to paint on. Which takes you back to the early Moss racing days in the late '40s and '50s when you painted your own number on the car. Then came the Les Leston stick-on race numbers and the inside of the boot-lid on every racing driver's road car was festooned with random numbers peeled off the car at the next meeting when your race number would be different in the programme. And you saved the old number in case you needed it again, but you never did and Les Leston made more money. Contrast that with the modern fashion of having no discernible number at all because the timing is done electronically as the car crosses the line and numbers take up valuable advertising space on the flanks.

Rob Walker was a legend in his early racing days for consumption of the family product – Johnny Walker whisky – but by the time I arrived in the early 'sixties he was the soul of sobriety. Aston Martin team manager John Wyer observed in his splendid book *The Certain Sound* that Rob was timekeeping for the Aston team at the Dundrod TT in Northern Ireland and they were staying in the same hotel. "At about midnight Rob noticed that his glass was empty and as the staff had gone to bed, he did the natural thing and broke into the bar. He was presented the next day with a considerable bill for damages.'

I loved Rob's remark when he arrived down at the pits for the first day of practice at the first Grand Prix in Las Vegas. He was staying at the MGM Grand and he said "You know, these Americans must be very lazy...they shave in bed." I asked him how he could possibly know that and he said "There are mirrors on the ceiling of my bedroom!"

Grand Prix course commentator Bob Constanduros has a thing about the Franco-American Facel Vega and has three in his garage, one of which had been owned by Rob. Bob had tracked down the garage that originally serviced the car for Rob and the foreman asked if he was aware that Rob had had the speedometer 'clocked'. "Do you mean he had the mileage cranked back?" Bob asked. "No, we re-calibrated the speed-ometer by twenty miles an hour so that when Rob was doing 100mph it was only registering 80mph on the speedo because Betty, Mrs Walker, didn't like Rob speeding."

Bob was intrigued with the story but confided that he didn't know how to broach the subject with Rob. I offered to handle the task on his behalf and we were walking across the dusty paddock at a Spanish Grand with Rob and Betty when I asked Rob if there was any truth in this matter. He turned and said quietly that it wasn't really a question he could answer just at the moment. But in fact he had answered the question...by not answering it!

* * *

There was a time when I measured all road cars against the original S1 Bentley Continental and in January 1982 I wrote in *Autocar*: When the conversation veers around to what sort of car you would buy if you had the funds to indulge, my contribution always raises eyebrows. I suppose I should say I've always wanted a Ferrari but the fact is that I have *never* wanted a Ferrari. The Bentley has been a fading dream of mine for years now, ever since I drove one briefly in the early 'sixties. The dream has been fading in direct ratio to the increase in prices. I came within half a day of buying a doctor's Continental, low mileage, one careful owner, St George's Hill, Weybridge, heated motor-house. That was £2,400 in the early 'seventies. I don't know what happened to the other half of the day but I failed to become a Bentley owner.

The Bentley was my dream. At a lunchtime drinks party in the New Year the conversation was deep into cars we would have owned 'if only...' and I wheeled out my desire, so far comprehensively thwarted, for an S1 Continental. "Oh really?" said Robert Cowen. "That's interesting. I've got two. Would you like to borrow one?" It seemed as though Santa was a little late this year. Instant acceptance.

Memory tended to fine down the size and shape of the Continental. I had driven XJ-S Jaguars on occasion and always placed them as the logical successor to the mantle of the Continental, so perhaps I was expecting more of the modern Jaguar and less of the gothic Bentley. My problem is that I am continually raising my sights when it comes to motorcars and what was yesterday's maximum comes close to being today's minimum. Although I can enthuse over vintage cars, I think it would drive me potty to own one.

The Bentley looked a million dollars when I picked it up from Robert Cowen's home at mid-Holmwood near Dorking. It was the H.J. Mulliner two-door with the long down-sweeping ramp of a tail recalling the first and most famous of Continentals – the R-Type. It was the most beautiful motorcar. I was mentally tucking my napkin into my collar, preparing to enjoy everything about it. The enormously wide door opened into opulence. It was like being shown into the morning room of a stately home. Two huge leather armchairs. New carpets and trim. It could have been Earls Court 1956. Immaculate wasn't too strong a word.

Robert had left instructions on cold starting. Horrifyingly apt, as it turned out. I eased the seat closer to the enormous black steering wheel and gazed with awe and not a little apprehension over the long bonnet. It was six feet from the laid-back 'B' of the mascot to the windscreen. Under that long black bonnet was the last of the 4.9-litre big-six Rolls-Royce/Bentley engines. The next models would have the V8. Horsepower is always said to be 'sufficient' in these sort of cars. Figures are never quoted. Suffice to say that it needed all its power because it was a *large* car to push around. I couldn't believe how big it was. Quiet, comfortable, quick – but *big*.

Snow was forecast but the roads were dry and the sun was shining. Such a magnificent motor needed a good run so we headed down the A24 to Worthing. A heady pace was easily achievable but somehow it was a little slower than I remembered. But then I was thinking 1982, not 1956. It took some miles down the Worthing road before I could get myself cranked back to 1956 when Moss was in a Maserati, Fangio in a Ferrari and Coopers were trying to get into Formula 1. In 1956 I was driving my mother's Austin A30 in New Zealand. I had never actually *seen* a Bentley at that point. Bentleys were rather thin on the ground in the Colonies then.

This was more like it. Seventy miles an hour came sharply into focus. The long sweeping dual carriageway sections of the Worthing road converted to the N7 and we were motoring fast down to the South of France. Road tests of the time talked of 120mph and Robert had talked of 110 but it didn't seem to be the time or the place (Honestly, officer) to tempt fate. I didn't want to scatter (a) the engine or (b) myself on the A24. It was

93

motoring in the Grand Manner. You sat behind the wheel in a sort of upper-class sprawl with arms stretched long and wide to grip the wheel.

If you apply yourself to the marque you can wallow in vintage Bentley Le Mans victories. The Bentley was sweeping along, now. The brakes which had seemed alarmingly meagre at first were now working in splendid fashion. I had to remember it was 1956 and you had to get on the pedal *hard* to produce results. Worthing was achieved and I struck out across the smaller lines on the map to get home. That was a mistake. The big Black Continental wasn't cut out for minor roads with dusk approaching and the sky leaden and heavy with snow. We made it to Horsley and home with some relief. That night it snowed. The Continental sat cocooned in its own classic-shaped igloo for the rest of the week. Walking was dangerous enough. My Golf GTI could cope and so could most cars with engines over the driving wheels. I couldn't imagine what the Bentley would be like so I refrained from putting it to the test. I thought I would prefer to remember the nicer parts of the re-acquaintance, the sweeping curves on the Worthing road and not the tight squeezes in the half light on the road to Shere. The open-mouthed looks of frank admiration for a truly superb style of motorcar. I gather Bentley people tend to dismiss the S-Type Continentals while only grudgingly accepting the R-Type before it. If pressed, they probably dismiss any Bentley built after W.O. left the company. But I still rate the S1 Continental as a gentleman's classic GT. A Grand Tourer in the best possible meaning of both words. And not quite at the King's ransom asked in the balmy days of a mere year ago.

If I'm being honest, perhaps I don't pine to own a Continental *quite* as much as I did. Is it just that there is more of me age-wise and otherwise? It was like riding the Concorde down from Paris to Rio for the Grand Prix. I thoroughly enjoyed the trip as an experience but I probably enjoyed the cuisine and the service as much as the speed. I thought it was a splendid advertisement for first class air travel because Concorde fares made first class seem cheap!

That's the way I feel about the Bentley. It was built by craftsmen, it looks like an automotive work of art and it will still be admired when the last of the XJ-S Jaguars have rusted away. It must be the Philistine in me. That and not having the money to buy one now. It's a buyer's market. *Adieu*, Continental, if I can ever get you out from under the snow...

* * *

Denny Hulme's father died in September 1982 and I wrote "If you thought Denny Hulme was one of the toughest nuts to win the World Championship until Alan Jones came along, you should have known Denny's dad. If you imagine Denny as the traditional 'Chip off the old Block' you start to form a picture. Clive Hulme was a hero and son Denis had a hard act to follow. Denny must have been delighted that he was able to deliver a World Championship title to his father in 1967 to prove that he was a true son of his father. Clive Hulme died in New Zealand at the age of 71. In World War 2 he was awarded the Victoria Cross for bravery under fire during the evacuation of Crete in 1942 and he was serving as a sergeant in the New Zealand Canterbury Regiment. In a series of rearguard actions over eight long days and nights, Clive Hulme continually fought back until he was seriously wounded.

I can remember Denny reminiscing about a visit to Crete that he made with his father and his father insisting on following the path of the retreat through the hills, and how the villagers remembered him. At one stage during the retreat Clive was positioning rifles along a ditch facing down a stretch of road and running back and forth along the ditch, firing each weapon in turn to give the impression of a force of men to the approaching enemy.

In later years Clive discovered that he had the ability to heal by faith and also to divine for water and for minerals. It's easy to doubt these abilities in others but not so easy when you hear tell of the results. I remember being most anxious that Clive should go out to the car when he was visiting us, and bring his divining rod in for a demonstration. I was still sceptical until he offered to hold one side of the handle and I would hold the other – when the end of the rod dipped suddenly it almost tore it out of my hand, and I could see that he was putting no pressure on his side at all! It served to demolish my scepticism and to bolster belief in the stories that Denny had told of his father's amazing career.

* * *

Motor racing ran in Patrick Head's family. His father, Michael, raced a C-Type Jaguar in Finland in 1954 when Keke Rosberg, the man his son made world champion, was just five years old. 'Michael Head's C-Type was the famous Tommy Wisdom car that had been raced by Stirling Moss and Tony Rolt and it was rebuilt by Head at home. "I can still hear the female yell occasioned by the discovery of the cylinder head in the airing cupboard." This C-Type was one of the original 50 series production cars with drum brakes so it could be used for production sports car races, or easily modified to more potent form for out-and-out racing events. Michael Head decided to campaign the 'C' in a series of international races in Finland and Sweden in May 1954 and would drive the car between races with his wife as passenger.

This particular car was chassis 005 and I can sympathise with Mrs Head travelling as passenger together with luggage and tools in a space that was cramped enough just sitting there, without other encumbrances. My baptism to motor racing travel was in a similar seat (C-Type chassis 039 to be exact) with David Young, driving between 1959 events in New Zealand. It took most of the weekend before you could hear properly again because the exhausts jutted out beneath the passenger's side...and then you had to face a drive of several hundred miles home again. It seemed like fun in those days!

The track in the centre of Helsinki was likened by Michael Head to Hyde Park and there were 85,000 paying spectators to watch Patrick's dad win on the narrow tree-lined 1.5-mile course against a selection of Ferraris, Allards, XK120s, a Lago Talbot and another C-Type. This was the Djurgardsloppet and the next event was Lapeenranta which was a different prospect with the majority of the track hard-surfaced but the sharp bends were loose gravel. Hardly the ideal course for a car that had been designed to win at Le Mans with its smooth surfaces. Mr Head (or Brigadier to give him correct honours) quite enjoyed the rough and tumble and won again in the Jaguar, noting 'The Finn is a tough chap with lots of spirit at all times.' Son Patrick would have echoed those comments with Keke in mind...

* * *

From my *Autocar* Diary in July 1985:

I always seem to have these moments when positive thought deserts me. This time it is the cold sober light of 10 o'clock on Saturday morning in Detroit. The Formula 1 cars and the rain have just started. There is only one other chap waiting for the hotel lift. He would have called it an elevator. He has the morning papers and a coffee-to-go, obviously going back to his room too. For 30 floors up the Weston Hotel I'm in this two-in-a-lift situation: do you make conversation or stare up at the changing floor numbers. It's embarrassing enough under normal circumstances but, when the only other person in the lift is Paul Newman, *the* Paul Newman, the situation reaches an immediate flash point.

There are people out there who would kill for the chance to travel 30 floors upward with Paul Newman and here I am casting about for something to say more positive than does he think the rain will clear. He thinks it might. He hopes it does. His race is this afternoon. Silence. Further altitude. Now for the classic gaffe.

Since what I know about TransAm racing could be comfortably engraved on the pointed end of a pin, I ask The Man what car he is racing. This immediately ranks me with the masses who queue just to touch him and to be told that he doesn't sign autographs. I've proved beyond reasonable doubt that I am not worthy of this trip to the top with a star. I've proved that I know who he is but not what he drives, and he goes racing purely to be accepted as a sportsman, a real live hero – more than a celluloid celebrity. He probably went racing so that he could get away from morons like me.

Sorry Paul.

Oh, he races a Datsun. I have the next floors to reflect on what I might have asked him.

* * *

I gather that I have something of a reputation for being less than enthusiastic during motor races (witness my nodding off sitting beside Nigel Roebuck six feet from the speeding cars during a Canadian Grand Prix) but if the subject is raised, Roebuck always draws the attention of the company to my behaviour during then 1991 Indianapolis 500. In my 5 June Diary column I wrote: 'Never mind sitting on the edge of your seat with excitement: in the last 10 laps of the Indianapolis 500 this year I was jumping up and down on mine and roaring support for Rick Mears who had snatched the lead in his Penske-Chevy and was hightailing it for home.

Most unseemly behaviour you may think, for a seasoned reporter of the grand prix scene these past 30 years, but when you have half a million people around you doing the same thing you tend to get carried away.

We had seats in what you would call 'the gods' if you were at the theatre: high above the 'short chute' between turns one and two, with the Mears family in front of us.

Dan Luginbuhl at Penske Racing had organised our seats, and if it had seemed remote when we first scaled the heights that morning to await the rain-delayed start, we found we were in the thick of the lead action when Pa Mears switched his radio scanner to Rick's frequency and we could keep track of what it was like from the inside. Ma Mears kept her fingers on both hands tightly crossed throughout the race, and it worked. Her son won his fourth Indy 500 from his seventh pole position and 11th start from the front row in his 14 races at Indianapolis. Mears joins A.J. Foyt and Al Unser as the only drivers to win Indy four times.

Mears owes his success to the patronage of Roger Penske. Robin Miller, in the *Indianapolis Star,* reminded me the morning after the race that it was Penske who poached designer Nigel Bennett from Lola, and Penske who put together the Chevrolet engine deal with Mario Illien and Paul Morgan at Ilmor Engineering. It was the eighth Indy win for Penske's team, proving that the more he practises, the luckier he gets.

* * *

There was a pause in the conversation at Indianapolis after lunch two days before the 1991 '500' and Louis Meyer suddenly said: "Thirty-three, I think I was then. By the end of May we'd lost five guys. Those old tanks we drove then...you hit the wall and you snapped your neck. We didn't have hard helmets, we didn't have safety harnesses, things like that. We just raced." And then he wandered off into the muggy heat of the afternoon, an Indy veteran wearing his red baseball cap with a Speedway Oldtimers badge on it, 87 years old and a living part of Indianapolis tradition.

Louis was the first three-time winner of the '500', with victories in 1928, 1933 and 1936. He was the first Indy winner to drink the now traditional bottle of milk ("they paid me $100 to do it when I won in 1928"), the first Indy winner to keep the pace car (a Packard) when he won in 1936 and the first driver to turn a lap of the 2.5-mile speedway at over 130mph in 1939.

It amazes me to be able to talk with a racing driver who was winning at Indianapolis when Bentleys were winning at Le Mans, a man who confused Nuvolari with Ascari when I asked him about the Ferrari challenge in 1952. But it was a slip of the tongue that was readily excusable because he'd known both men during his career. Tazio had turned up for the '500' in 1938, presumably in some sort of VIP capacity, and he was pictured at the wheel of a big front-engined Bowes Seal Fast Special but he did not feature in the race coverage.

Rudi Caracciola was another grand prix driver that Lou met up with at the Speedway: "He and Alice came out to our house in California and I took them to the midget races at Gilmore Speedway. He was really amazed at the midgets and he must have taken half a roll of film before he realised he still had the lens cap on. You should have heard Alice chew him out!"

* * *

Chris Amon celebrated his 60th birthday during 2003 and Michael Clark and Chris's wife, Tish, conspired to put together a surprise dinner to celebrate Christopher's amazing achievement of six decades. When he arrived in formula 1 aged 19 there would not have been many who would have wagered on him making *two* decades. Michael and I contacted motor racing folk around the world to acquaint them with Chris's great age and to solicit what we used to call 'telegrams'. I thought Mario Andretti's message was wonderful. Mario had won the Indianapolis 500 in 1969 and the F1 World title in 1978 having driven for Ferrari and for Lotus. He wrote: 'Chris, as you celebrate this milestone birthday, I welcome the opportunity to wish you a very happy 60th and reflect back on an event in which we co-drove decades ago.

'It was 1969, the 1000km of Monza. I can still picture the banking on the old track and taking the Ferrari through its paces. Do you remember that I drove the first half of the race because I had to be in Atlanta the following day for a USAC race? I distinctly recall being in the lead when I turned over the car to you and telling you to call me collect after the race. But I never heard from you whether or not we won. Did you ever finish? If you can recollect any of this, do let me know what happened.

'I wish I had some 'dirt' on you, Chris, to share with your dinner guests but you were always such a straight arrow that I think your proper behaviour might even have rubbed off on me – for a little while, anyway...'

* * *

Michael Clark and Gail Barwood have a lot to answer for. I had written a book on Chris's life and racing career at a time when he was totally committed in the sale of his farm and without the time or the will to get involved with anything that would divert his attention. The book was finished and the manuscript delivered when Howden Ganley arranged a far-away lunch in Auckland for members of the British Racing Drivers' Club in New Zealand. Howden was the 'forgotten fourth' New Zealand Grand Prix driver. The world knew that Bruce McLaren, Denny Hulme and Chris had all achieved in Formula 1, but Howden's two seasons in BRM and two seasons in March tend to be overlooked, mainly because both teams were bouncing along the bottom in the early 1970s and Howden's talents were effectively stifled by his machinery. As a director of the BRDC, his lunch in the colonies, which also included top New Zealand drivers, was a major success. The night before, we had all gone out to dinner but I had faded early. I woke around 4am, realised I was alone and pounded down the motel stairs to find out where everyone was. I need not have wondered. The lights of the Amon unit were still blazing across the courtyard and all of the night-before's dinner people seemed to be still there! Of course there had been a fair amount of liquid intake to stave off dehydration and promote enthusiasm for anything mentioned and during this session it had been decided by Michael, with enthusiastic support from Gail, that Chris should tell me some of the stories he had been regaling *them* with during that long and hazy evening. I failed to see that 4am was the ideal hour to be advised that my carefully-crafted, completed manuscript was now to be re-opened and announced this loudly (and probably, on reflection, churlishly) to the assembled company before returning to my motel and my bed. To their credit, Michael and Gail took it upon themselves to gather in the extra stories and both of them visited the Amon home in the next few weeks. The extra gems were added in and "Forza Amon!" was launched with a flourish at the Goodwood Circuit Revival in September as recounted elsewhere in this tome.

* * *

You're going to hate me for this tale:

I was with *AutoWeek* editor, Leon Mandel, in Peter Revson's McLaren pit at Watkins Glen in the early 1970s. Leon was writing a book with Peter (it would be printed after Peter's death in 1974 as *Speed With Style*). Peter's latest girlfriend was in the pit too and as it was nearing the start of practice, Revvy wanted to concentrate his mind on other things, so he suggested we get out of his hair and go down to the Glen Motor Inn for lunch.

She was a very attractive girl, as Revson's women tended to be, and the three of us embarked on random conversation over lunch. She knew that I lived in England and said she would be going to London soon. I suggested that she give me a call if she was at a loose end. She said she didn't think they were allowed to make phone calls out. I asked if she was perhaps going to prison? How come she couldn't make phone calls? She said she was involved in the Miss World contest. I asked if she was maybe a fashion writer. No. She was Miss America. Oh. Right. Marjie Wallace was an intelligent stunner and the judges thought so too because she became Miss World! And she had managed to find a phone to call me before the contest began. She was the feisty lady who kicked the Miss World title into touch because she didn't want to do the contracted year in promotional service. She wanted to travel with Peter.

A year or so later and Sandra, Selina and I are flying out to New Zealand. The flight stops briefly at Honolulu and we are filing back into the Boeing 707, passing through First Class to our seats at the front of economy. No Club Class in those days. Selina and Sandra had gone ahead when this vision of loveliness rose from a First Class seat and said "It's Eoin isn't it?" Stupefied, I gabbled that it was indeed me...and then I realised it was Marjie. I hadn't seen here since that Watkins Glen lunch, apart from a time or two on TV news. Could she come back and sit with us? Ummm. Help! How do I explain this to the family? So we went back, there was a spare seat, and heaven knows what we talked about but I can remember Selina being old enough to be saucer-eyed. How could her father possibly know Miss World? There have been times when I wondered about that myself... I asked her why she had chosen to ride in economy for a while when she had a perfectly good First Class seat. She said the guy in the window seat was 'hitting on her'. Can't say I blamed him.

* * *

The Spooky Thrills of Spa-Francorchamps

The first lap of the 1966 Belgian Grand Prix produced a series of crashes that beggared belief and set all-time records for Formula 1 mechanical mayhem. There has never been such an opening lap. If you had made a movie featuring that opening lap in the deluge, it would have been deemed as simply too contrived for belief. And yet Phil Hill was following the field from the start in a special space-frame McLaren fitted with a 4.7-litre Cobra V8 and festooned with cameras shooting footage for John Frankenheimer's *Grand Prix* movie.

I was covering the race for *Auto News* and reading that report now makes me want to pinch myself to make sure I'm not making it up. Spa is a victim of the Ardennes weather. If you can see down to the swoop of *Eau Rouge* (then the first turn after the downhill start; the grid is now further back on the run up to *La Source*) it's about to start raining – if you can't see *Eau Rouge* it is raining already. The Spa weather is still like that, but there has never been a race like the 1966 Grand Prix.

My report reads like a thriller, starting with the rather unusual situation (considering the modern political tyre scene between Michelin and Bridgestone) where Ferrari, John Surtees, Dunlop and Firestone were waiting for the weather to make up its mind. John's V12 was sitting in the pits shod with dry-weather Indy Firestones but the front wheel nuts were loosened, and when the sky finally darkened over, the Firestones were whipped off and Dunlops screwed on. Bandini's 2.4-ltre V6 switched from Firestone to Dunlop on the dummy grid.

'Clark and Spence (in their Lotuses) were on wet-weather Firestones, but Bonnier was sitting rather uncomfortably on dry-

104

weather Indy Firestones. The rain spattered with the flag, but it was bucketing down on the far side of the circuit and the first signs most of the drivers had of the inclement weather was either a view of the way they had just come, or a frantic lock-to-lock dodging match as cars spun everywhere.

'Surtees had almost set his tyres alight at the start, but Stewart's BRM was slewing sideways as he took off. Clark's mechanics had slipped a rag under Jimmy's wheel so that the car wouldn't roll down the hill at the start, but at the last minute an official whipped the rag away and with the car rolling Jimmy couldn't find first gear and had to settle for second. The Lotus just made the top of the hill before stopping with what the mechanics thought was a dropped valve as Jimmy over-revved at the start.

'There was so much high-speed action on that first lap that it is hard to know where to start. Bonnier's Cooper-Maserati on its low-profile dry-weather tyres was first to go as the bunched field headed into the right-hand sweep after *Burnenville* and he spun in clouds of spray bouncing off fences and walls as others collided trying to dodge Bonnier and each other.

'Mike Spence in the Parnell Lotus-BRM skidded down a steepish bank on the right-hand side of the road without flipping or hitting anything too hard and could have got back into the race if he could have gotten the Lotus back on to the road without a crane. Denny Hulme in the Brabham and Jo Siffert in the Walker Cooper-Maserati touched with Hulme's Brabham getting a bent steering arm which kinked the wheels out, and Siffert's rear wheel was hauled off true.

Meanwhile Bonnier's red Cooper had knocked all its wheels off, climbed the bales and was see-sawing on top of a stone wall like a cigar with Bonnier easing himself out ever so gently so as not to tip it over into the farmyard 20 feet below.

Hulme drove down from the scene of the spins, stopped to kick the front wheel into line and was driving on when he saw the spray from the approaching leaders in his mirrors. Considering damp discretion to be the better part of drowned

105

valour, Hulme stopped, left the Brabham ticking over on the side of the road and scooted back to the fence while Surtees and the rest of the bedraggled 7-car field splashed through!

Now read on. Surtees and Rindt had been battling through the first half lap, nose to tail with the Ferrari just in front when Rindt lost the Cooper at the kink between the farm buildings in the Masta Straight (he must have been doing 120 – Graham Hill said it felt like 300!) and said he spun it four times and on his final revolution in slow motion he saw Bondurant's white BRM going off backwards.

Bondurant had hit what must have been a small river across the road in the middle of the flat-out-in-the-dry kink, spun backwards, then sideways and rolled with the car coming to rest upside down on his left shoulder. Petrified peasants hauled the car off him, and he got back to the road to see Graham Hill's BRM backwards in the bales just up the road. Graham had hit the same patch of water, ground-looped the BRM into the bales and was out of the car trying to get back on the road when he saw Stewart's BRM wrecked in the ditch below him. The monocoque was stove in on the little Scot and there wasn't much Graham and Bondurant could do until a toolkit appeared from somewhere...'

A week later, I had found out more about the consequences of that amazing opening lap at Spa and wrote in my column: 'Graham *could* have made sure that Jackie was still with us, and then battled back into the race as his BRM was still race-worthy and he could have been placed high enough to get some more championship points. Right at that moment with Jackie being quicker than his team boss on most circuits the opportunity to steal a march had certainly presented itself on a plate. But to his everlasting credit Graham stayed with Jackie and, helped by Bob Bondurant, he removed the steering wheel and lifted the little Scot out.

The fuel tank had ruptured in the crash – sideways into the end of a stone wall at around 120mph – and Jackie was soaked in fuel which was causing him considerable discomfort, in addition to his cracked collarbone. The two drivers carried their patient to a barn and waited there until the ambulance arrived to take Jackie back to the field hospital behind the pits. Only then did Graham think about getting on with the race, but as he had lost nearly five laps on the leaders he knew his chances of qualifying as a finisher were pretty remote and he jacked it in.

'The story didn't end there. Jimmy Clark's Lotus had expired before it even got to the scene of the first accident and the good Jamie had trudged back to the pits in the rain. When he heard that his fellow Scot (I'd actually written, cringe-makingly, 'Doon-Hamer') was in the field hospital he went in and sat with Jackie until he had recovered enough to talk to his wife, Helen. When the race finished Jackie was taken by hospital to Verviers and Jimmy and Helen went with him.

Jimmy arrived back at the Val d'Ambleve Hotel at Stavelot, still in his overalls when everyone else was just finishing their dinner. Now all this might not sound like much, but it certainly is a far cry from the people who condemn today's racers as money-hungry bigheads only out to increase their bank balance.'

And that was written nearly 40 years ago! Reminds me of Charles Jarrott writing about motor racing being ruined by commercialism – in 1906!

In 1968, as related elsewhere in this tome, Denis Jenkinson wrote a different version of his normal straight factual report in *Motor Sport* and I used this as my special memory of the man in the tribute book *Jenks – A Passion for Motor Sport*. He wrote a brief formal précis of the race and then produced what he called his Francorchamps Monologue as though you were sitting beside him and he was chatting during the long laps of that spookily fast road course.

As I wrote in 'my' chapter in the book, I will cherry-pick for you and bring you the typically Jenks observations that always reflected his enthusiasms and his prejudices, those little written digs that so appealed to his reader and so infuriated the person to whom the dig referred.

"There's the 1min board; what a magnificent noise all those racing engines make; no wonder I'm going deaf after 20 years of Grand Prix racing. They are all rolling down the hill nicely; must be tricky on this downhill start to keep everything on the boil with only two feet to operate clutch, brake and accelerator. I suppose they are all doing a heel-and-toe act on the brake and accelerator. . .

"Here we go; stop creeping, Ickx, even if this is Belgium; wow!, the revs the Ferrari are using, how fascinating to see the throttle slides jiggling in and out like that. . .

"To see those two Ferraris going up the hill in first and second place is quite like old times. That was the Honda in third place. Talk about red rags to a Honda. This should make Surtees cast off a lot of worries and inhibitions and show us the great racing driver that he really is. He will not settle for following *two* Ferraris for long. Bonnier was going slowly, wasn't he; wonder if he will make it back to the pits to collect his starting money?. . .

"It must be wonderful to be leading the pack round the long Stavelot bend, knowing that you have a completely clear run ahead of you up the long incline to *La Source* and through those super-fast corners; 170mph, 175, 180mph, who knows? Revs, tyres, gear ratios are all very well, but only an accurate beam would ever record the truth. . .

"This is Grand Prix racing, and it's not for the faint of heart. Imagine taking that long downhill sweep of *Burnenville*, the car all twitchy and all four tyres sliding; they must be doing 130mph past the little café. Wish I was there, but I can't be everywhere. There's only one place from which you can really see a motor race, that's alongside the driver. Pity we can't have two-seater Grand Prix cars. . .

"Oh ho! The Honda has nipped by Amon. How about that? Surtees really leading a Grand Prix in the opening phase, that's more like it. Pity he's only got Amon and Ickx to race against. He should have Gurney, Hill, Brabham and Stewart all around him. That would make a Grand Prix, and I suppose poor Clark would have been in front of them all. Hill is not really getting into his stride, he ought to be past McLaren by now, and Redman is holding off Brabham. I suppose 'Black Jack' cannot see any prize money in view, so he's not going to strain himself. There's Rindt coming into the pits; the Repco 4-cammer still needs a lot of development. Rindt is not exactly being the Ace of Aces he thinks he is. . .

"Here they come again, Surtees still leading Amon; Amon is making it very obvious that he'd like to get by, but he'll never do it. Nobody goes past Surtees when 'Big John' is really having a go, not even Brabham. . .

"That's the end of Rindt's 4-cam Repco engine. Wonder if he's ever seen the mess that a loose valve seat makes inside an engine when the bits fall into the cylinder at 9,000rpm?... (As an aside, Jenks never took to Rindt, to the point where he announced that if Jochen ever won a Grand Prix, he would shave his beard off. Rindt did, at Watkins Glen in in1969, and Jenks was as good as his word and shaved off his trademark whiskers!)

"Oh dear, the ambulance is going off, wonder who has pranged? Redman, Oliver and Bianchi have yet to appear on this lap. The loudspeakers say it is Redman. Hope it's not serious. Nice lad, Redman. Been having a good season, too. Unlike him to crash. Wonder if something broke?...

"Looks like oil coming out of the Ferrari nose. Poor Amon, last year Brabham threw stones at him at Silverstone and Nur-burgring, now Surtees has done it, right through the oil radiator, and there is a wire mesh guard in front of it, too. I wonder sometimes whether drivers like Surtees and Brabham carry a pocket-full of stones, just in case!...

"Hulme is now first. Doubt whether he and Stewart will really race and get nasty; too docile and friendly these chaps, and anyway, Stewart said after practice he could not take any chances with his right forearm in that plastic corset device...

"Stewart leading! Surprising that Hulme let him by, he must have forgotten all the old Brabham elbows-out training...

"PUMP OIL is written on Tyler Alexander's signal board and it's for Hulme. That will be the Bendix pump that returns the oil from the catch-tank to the main tank. I thought it was switched on all the time. Those Cosworth engines aren't right, they shouldn't breathe that much oil. Bet that surprised Alexander, Hulme leading again; surprised me...

"McLaren leading his bunch again, that's the orange cars second and third. Where's Hulme? I spoke too soon. He's missing. McLaren and his bunch are now racing for second place...

"Twenty-five laps gone. Stewart's dropped 10sec. He's all right. I expect he's looked across the fields at Stavelot to keep an eye on them, and McLaren's orange car must be easy to pick out. With the keen eyesight these chaps have got he can probably see the McLaren at the hairpin in the mirror from the top of *Eau Rouge*...

"After this lap, one more lap for Stewart. Matra will be so pleased with their victory, it's been on the cards since South Africa. On Dunlop tyres too. Long time since Dunlop have won a Grand Prix, and at one time they had a monopoly. Always felt they got over-confident and complacent in those days! Too easy to do. We'll hear Stewart coming out of *Blanchimont* soon and through Virage Seaman. Wonder how many people pause to pay respects to that small stone by the Clubhouse that marks where Dick Seaman crashed. Was it 1938 or 1939? Remember actually weeping when I heard he was dead. Have got hardened to racing drivers being killed nowadays. Perhaps I haven't. Wept genuine tears at Brands Hatch when I heard Clark was dead. Only two months ago. Seems like a different age altogether...

Here comes Stewart, one more lap to go. Good grief! He's in trouble. Coasting down into the pits. Oh my goodness, what a panic. There go McLaren and Rodriguez, racing to win now. Like

Monza last year. They are putting petrol into the Matra. It won't
re-start. Another battery. The starter motor must be cooked. And
here's Oliver, the Lotus is out of fuel. This is ridiculous, they've
all miscalculated. Oh Tyrrell, you've thrown the race away. That
really is too bad. It's re-started. He'll finish, but in fourth place...

"Here's a jubilant McLaren, the lucky devil, to win like that.
It's justice really, for Hulme should have won...

"There's McLaren. Good for him to win, and with his own
car; must feel marvellous. Well done, congratulations. You really
didn't know you'd won? Not until Phil Kerr greeted you in the
paddock? But you waved your arm in jubilation as you crossed
the line? Pleased to finish second! It was some race. Always is at
Spa..."

He had literally been thinking out loud, painting word pic-
tures with his pen, for he wrote everything long-hand. I thought
it was a marvellously evocative piece of writing, nearly as good
as being out there and doing it. But because *one* reader wrote to
say he didn't like the change in Jenks' style, he never wrote like
that again...

Champagne Pace at Reims

Spell it Reims or Rheims but say it *Rraarns* if you fancy it in French. Whichever way you spell it or say it, Reims was a special race in the Grand Prix season, certainly a circuit with style, not a country track like Magny Cours, masquerading as a venue for the French Grand Prix, miles from anywhere and unloved by drivers or teams. No class. And yet the French Grand Prix was where it all started. They didn't call the first one the *French* Grand Prix, it was just *the* Grand Prix because it was the only one when it was first staged over twelve laps of a 64-mile circuit around Le Mans in 1906, the race being run over two days with the Hungarian driver, Ferenc Szisz winning in the works Renault.

The Reims circuit in the centre of the champagne country in northern France was in the form of a large triangle of public roads, the fastest leg being down the Route Nationale N31, the Soisson to Reims road. The first races were run in 1925 as the Grand Prix of the Marne. In 1932 the race assumed full Grand Prix status, staged by the Automobile Club de France and it was won by Tazio Nuvolari in a factory Alfa Romeo, averaging a cracking 92.297mph.

Motor Sport took a languid approach to that Grand Prix in 1932. The first page of the report was taken up in scene-setting which sounded thoroughly enjoyable. You could have been sitting alongside the scribe as he penned his notes in the early evening.

'Brilliantly lit cafes down the length of the street, crowded tables and the bustle of waiters; an endless procession of dusty travel-stained cars, Bugattis and Delages from distant parts of France, Lancias and Alfa Romeos from Italy, cut-outs open and engines revving – and swarms of Citroens, Renaults and Peugeots; fireworks and crackers thrown into the road; the continuous peal of musical horns, the church chimes to theme-songs; noise, laughter, excitement and gaiety!

'We were sitting at a café in the Avenue Drouet d'Erlon, Rheims, on the eve of the French Grand Prix. We drank champagne, the finest in Europe – for was not the festival celebrating the discovery of Champagne held in this very city only a few weeks ago? It was midnight, and so warm was the perfect July night, so beguiling the sparkling wine, and so gay the spectacle before us, that we had little inclination to walk back to our hotel and sleep!

'A sports saloon drove slowly down the street. Suddenly the back wheels locked and the car came to a standstill. Something had seized in the transmission, but the driver and his girl companions only laughed. Twenty people pushed, but the car would not move from the crown of the road. Still laughing, the occupants got out and ordered drinks at a café on the pavement, leaving the car in the middle of the road, with all four doors wide open. What did they care – they had arrived at Rheims! The car was still here when at last we strolled back to our hotel.'

And all this as the lead-in to a Grand Prix report in the august monthly, "Motor Sport". I asked veteran editor, William Boddy, who might have penned the report and he told me that he did not start with the magazine until 1934. He thought it might have been written by artist Roy Nockolds who drew the illustrative art of Nuvolari's Alfa Romeo passing Chiron's Bugatti that appeared in *Motor Sport* with the race report.

It was noted that for this race the grandstand had been completely rebuilt in permanent reinforced concrete as had the pits and the control tower and the press room on the opposite side of the track. I assume these were still being used when I first went there in 1961 with Denny Hulme who was competing in the Formula Junior race. They still stand now, gaunt and lonely structures, lost in the countryside as a mute reminder of some amazing motor races in the past.

113

In those days before transporters and motor-homes, the cars were fettled at garages in the town and driven to the track by lucky mechanics. You could buy champagne by the bottle or the glass in the paddock. Denny and I had arrived late at Rheims because he had miss-read his diary and we went to Monza instead, having to make an overnight dash from Italy. We probably got the last hotel room in town at a seedy establishment but we counted ourselves fortunate that we didn't have to sleep in the car. On race morning as we left the room, a driver in the ubiquitous blue Dunlop overalls was coming out of the room next to ours. I asked Denny who he was. "Dunno," he replied. "Never seen him before." This was not surprising because it was the first proper Grand Prix he had been in. His name was Giancarlo Baghetti and that afternoon he would win his debut title race for Ferrari. And he never won again. We were living next door to history...

Bridgette's Bar was the most popular nightspot in the town and there were lurid tales from the times of Mike Hawthorn and Peter Collins. Later mayhem included the wheelnuts being removed from a police paddy-wagon while the *gendarmes* were inside endeavouring to quell the racket. Loud applause when the police van lurched into the pavement as the wheel came off as they tried to drive away. I have vivid memories of my first visit to Bridgette's and watching in amazement late one evening when John Cooper arrived in style, clambering through the window, followed moments later by the even more spectacular style of movie star Jill St John – also through the window. That was when John startled the imbibers by announcing that he was painting his cars – traditionally British Racing Green with dual white stripes up the nose – red for the race. When asked why, he replied that only the red cars seemed to be going fast in that summer of '61 when Phil Hill would win the world championship. There were four Ferraris across the front row in the Grand Prix the following day and Bill Gavin took a dramatic photograph of the front row

114

hunkered down under power with smoke pouring from spinning rear wheels.

* * *

It might have been Jimmy Clark's ambition to miss a Grand Prix because of a 'bird' as in beautiful girl, but it was the feathered variety that dropped him from the 1966 French Grand Prix at Reims. 'Jimmy was put out of action by a sparrow, of all things! Earlier in the day he had clobbered a partridge which whistled out of the corn, but at 170mph the sparrow must have hit him right between the eyes like a bullet and Jimmy had been lucky to hold the car on the road, let alone drive it back to the pits.

'He was badly shaken and covered in feathers and blood and he was taken straight to hospital where the doctor advised no more racing that weekend. The blow had cut his nose and bruised his eye seriously.'

* * *

Brigitte's Bar was closed by the police on the night after the Grand Prix in 1966 and I noted the lack of social action in my column in July 1966:

'Reims was quiet this year compared to some of the hectic sessions that have been known to occur at earlier GPs in this French town. The rozzers weren't running the risk of giving the wheel nuts whipped from the paddy wagon on race night this year – they went as far as to postpone the prize-giving until the Monday morning and spread the word that Brigitte's Bar was shut. Sacrilege.

But I gather that a few persistent hell-raisers did manage to persuade Brigitte to open the bar for a while. There have been some fair old scenes at Reims when the racing was finished. Like the time the law opened fire over the heads of a fine, although slightly inebriated body of Englishmen, who were in full flight, running down a darkened street. And when one of them slipped and fell, the others thought he'd been shot...

Or when the shoulder-to-shoulder crowd at Brigitte's was getting a little unruly and the good lady summoned the law who arrived in force to hear a strident chorus suggesting that all coppers might have been born a while before their parents were married...and Innes Ireland was on the phone at the end of the bar having dialled the Reims equivalent of 999 to ask for some further support for the *gendarmerie*.

Living Upstairs from the Monaco Grand Prix

They were seven floors above the grid in Roy Salvadori's Monaco apartment and forty-odd years away as Roy and his old Cooper team-mate Sir Jack Brabham reminisced about the good old days, looking out over the modern multi-million dollar Formula 1 scene. The summer of 1959 had its share of important memories for both men. Roy won the Le Mans 24-hours race for Aston Martin with Carroll Shelby and Jack won the Monaco Grand Prix for Cooper and went on to win his first world championship. He would win three. Brabham won Monaco in 1959 – and lost it dramatically in 1970 when he misjudged the very last corner lapping a slower car and slammed into the barriers, letting a hard-charging Jochen Rindt through to win. Jack limped home second.

Roy and Jack were Formula 1 team-mates at Cooper when the little company first went into Grand Prix racing in 1957. "We got on well together. Never any arguments," Roy remembers. "In those days we used to have one good 2.2-litre Coventry-Climax 4-cylinder engine and Jack would use it one weekend and I would have it the next. In those days it was an achievement to get *one* good engine." Their second-string motor was a 2-litre racing against 2.5-litre foreign opposition.

Roy was contracted to Aston Martin for sports car racing and when they built a front-engined formula 1 car they wanted Roy to bring Brabham with him from Coopers to use his testing talents on development. Brabham knew that Coventry Climax were building a special new 2.5-litre engine for 1959 and reckoned that the Cooper mid-engined design, then unique in Formula 1, would be a better bet than the big Aston Martin. He urged Salvadori to stay with him at Cooper for 1959 but Roy was committed to Aston Martin. Brabham won the world championship that summer and Roy regretted his decision because the Aston Martin was beautifully made but sadly uncompetitive.

"I had rather committed myself to the Formula 1 Aston, and Jack to a lesser extent," says Salvadori. "I had discussed it and I was going to go over to Aston. We were also being paid a reasonable retainer, which one would never have got from Cooper. . . I have to say that I did try hard to get out of my verbal agreement with Aston's F1 team manager, Reg Parnell. He said 'Look, Roy, you've done so well with Astons. . .it's made you. . .you owe us a little loyalty. . .' In the end I was talked into keeping my agreement with them."

The way Brabham remembers it, he was asked to switch from Cooper to Aston Martin. "But I never really had any intention of going. We just *talked* about going. And then Reg Tanner, the Esso racing manager, made sure that I didn't leave Cooper by signing me up to a £10,000 contract!"

Roy agonises over the fate of the Aston Martin GP project. "The project was stillborn, really. . . The prototype was built and tested in 1957 but nothing really happened until the 1959 season, so it was dormant for two years, which was a shame." The Aston GP car was put on hold while John Wyer's team put their full works support into sports car racing. Grand Prix was for prestige; sports car racing was for selling David Brown's Aston Martin sports cars.

Looking back, Salvadori rates himself honestly as a racing driver and thinks that the development of the Aston suffered by not having Brabham's input. "I wasn't that good as a tester. I could establish a lap time and if it was a good car I could do a decent time. That was my contribution. What I couldn't do was tell them what to do with the car, what to change or modify, how to improve it. I just drove. Basically the Aston was extremely good. The road-holding was great – even the rear-engined cars weren't any quicker at that stage. It was a heavy car and it didn't have much torque while we were testing in 1958 and getting ready for the 1959 season. We were doing most of the testing at Goodwood but we really couldn't get a comparison on times because although everyone tested there, unless you had a spy – which we couldn't afford – you didn't know what the opposition was *really* doing. But on paper, we looked good. Our times were quite sound.

"What we didn't realise was that Goodwood was a very good circuit for the Aston, it flattered the car, so it was shining there and when we got to our first race – the 150-mile Daily Express International Trophy – the car went extremely well. I was on the front row with Jack and the Ferrari and the BRM. I finished second and made fastest lap. But I couldn't stay with Jack, who won in the Cooper. He just showed immediately that the rear-engined Cooper was going to be a winner.

"My second place was a very good performance for the new car, but that was as good as it ever went. It was deceiving us. At Aintree the car suited the circuit and we had another good race. I made fastest time in practice but Jack had done the same time a moment before, so that although we were tied on lap-times, he had pole and I was next to him.

Roy's race was ruined when he realised that fuel was swilling into the cockpit and he had to make a pit-stop. "They had over-filled the tank and I was being saturated with fuel. I eventually finished sixth – still a good result but from then on we just didn't perform."

There was also a problem with restricted revs on the 2.5-litre 250bhp six-cylinder engine. They couldn't take it over 7500rpm otherwise they suffered bearing problems. "Torque was very poor and reducing the revs just crippled it. Really, that was the crux of the matter...

"We continued into 1960 but then withdrew. It was a damn good car but it was just too late. It should have been racing in 1957. Compared to the 250F Maserati it was much quicker. It was quicker than the Ferrari – or as quick, certainly."

119

In an odd twist of fate, Salvadori's decision to leave the Cooper team meant that the young New Zealander, Bruce McLaren, Brabham's antipodean protégé, was given the drive – and the cars that carry his name are still winning GPs and world titles. If Salvadori had stayed at Cooper, McLaren might have missed his vital opportunity and drifted into obscurity.

The Aston project had been abandoned but Roy stayed loyal to Reg Parnell's team and drove Formula 1 Coopers sponsored by Yeoman Credit in 1961 and Lolas sponsored by Bowmaker in 1962. Perhaps Salvadori's best race in Formula 1 was the U.S. Grand Prix at Watkins Glen at the end of the 1961 season. The sleek shark-nose Ferraris had dominated the season but when Wolfgang von Trips was killed in the Italian Grand Prix at Monza and Phil Hill clinched the world title, Ferrari decided to withdraw and America's first world champion was denied a drive in his home race. The British teams heaved a sigh of relief. Innes Ireland made Lotus history by winning the first GP for Team Lotus at Watkins Glen but that race was Salvadori's finest. In the final stages he was overhauling Ireland's leading Lotus and was five seconds behind and closing fast but with three laps left the engine failed in the Cooper.

Roy switched then to sports cars and saloon racing with Tommy Atkins' private team with a Cooper-Monaco, a Shelby Cobra and the new E-Type Jaguar. When the Formula One Cooper team was sold in 1965, Salvadori became team manager.

Brabham is 75, Salvadori nearly 80. There is a lot of racing history in the Monaco apartment that Roy and his wife Sue have had since Roy quit racing and the motor business in Britain. A rare original oil painting by Frederick Gordon Crosby on the wall features Sue Salvadori's father, Johnny Hindmarsh on his way to winning at Le Mans in 1935 with a Lagonda. Roy has a Dion Pears painting of his Le Mans winning Aston Martin in 1959 but it has been consigned to storage.

Unusual that husband and wife have such family racing links? It gets better. Ask for further details of Johnny Hindmarsh's racing career and Sue says, almost embarrassed, that her *mother* was probably more famous in the world of motoring. As Violet Cordery, sister-in-law of Noel Macklin who built Invicta cars at Cobham in Surrey, in 1927 she became the first person to drive around the world – in an Invicta tourer, naturally – and drove these cars on endurance records at Brooklands, Monza and Montlhery.

Her pioneering world trip covered 10,000 miles and took five months motoring through Europe, Africa, India, Australia, the USA and Canada. The Invicta open tourer was grossly overloaded (the onboard crew included the RAC observer, a mechanic and a trained nurse as well as young Violet who did *all* the driving) and yet she still managed an overall average speed of 24.6mph.

When she married John Hindmarsh she retired from motoring competition. Hindmarsh was a journeyman racer in Talbots and Lagondas with his Le Mans win the high point in his career. A test pilot for Hawker, he was killed when his prototype Hurricane fighter plunged into St George's Hill, not far from Brooklands, in 1938.

Roy Salvadori raced through the Stirling Moss era before the big money when the idea was to race as many different cars as you could in one day and then party with the pretty girls that night. They were getting paid but they weren't getting rich. But they didn't know that then. The millions came along a few decades later. Danger was a necessary part of racing in those days. Added a touch of excitement, doncherknow. Earl Howe, then President of the British Racing Drivers' Club once famously said in the 'fifties at a driver's briefing "Motor racing is dangerous – let's make sure we keep it that way!"

Moss and Salvadori chased 'crumpet' after the races and both were adept. The suave Roy was nicknamed 'Smoothadori'. When Moss wrote a book called "All But My Life" the lads in the pit-lane reckoned it should have been "All But My Wife." Different days.

Even Salvadori's name suggested a continental air of racing

intrigue. Some suggested that he had made it up for more starting money. In fact his mother Zelinda's maiden name was Ferrari before she married Gino Salvadori and they left their home at Lucca in Tuscany to buy a home at Dovercourt near Harwich in 1920 and set up in business making ice-cream. Roy was born there in 1922.

Like his father-in-law before him, Roy's Le Mans victory was perhaps the high point in a long career and his decision to stay with Aston Martin, while honourable was unwise in hindsight and the Salvadori star was on the wane.

When John Cooper's father, Charles, died it became apparent that while John was a jovial genius in the workshop, fettling with new racing cars, he was unable to handle the administration side of the business which his father had always handled on an extremely conservative basis. John Cooper had survived a huge accident on the Kingston Bypass when a suspension part failed on an experimental twin-engined Mini Cooper and John let Salvadori know that he wanted to sell the racing team.

"I knew Jonathan Sieff of the Chipstead Group then BMW importers for the United Kingdom (also a member of the Marks & Spencer founding family) and I arranged the sale. Chipstead were also involved with Maserati and when the formula doubled from 1.5 to 3-litres it was a family deal that the Cooper Formula 1 cars would use Maserati V12 power. The problem was that there was not as much available horsepower as the factory claimed. "It soon became apparent that the 360bhp that Maserati were claiming for their engine was not as powerful as Brabham's 320bhp Repco V8 and to prove it we arranged to run the Maserati engine on the Coventry Climax dynamometer and invited Maserati engineer, Alfieri over to observe the test."

The most exciting part of the Cooper Maserati was Jochen Rindt sitting in the middle of it, soldiering through a three-year contract that must have seemed like a good move when he signed the contract.

"Jochen was very good but very disgruntled when I arrived as team manager. He had a deal that he thought was wicked. It was for three years and his retainer was something stupid – in the hundreds of pounds and these were the days when it was just starting to happen and the drivers were being paid good money. Or what they thought was good money then. His contract was a good deal when he signed it. It always is when you sign it but it loses its appeal after three years if you strike form.

"Also, he didn't like his mechanic. Jochen *was* a little difficult to get on with. He wasn't the easiest guy. He was a bloody fine driver but quite temperamental and there were a few explosions.

"He was rather upset when he failed to qualify at Monaco in 1965. He was driving the bloody tyres off the car but he couldn't get up to pace. He was *adamant* that it was the car and his mechanic insisted it was the driver. And when we examined the car he was only getting three-quarter throttle. The mechanic had re-routed the throttle cable and the way he had hitched it up, restricted the throttle. The poor bastard had been trying to qualify at Monaco with only three-quarter throttle travel!

"He had a *flaming* row with John Cooper but John wouldn't accept the blame. Then the mechanic admitted what he had done and apologised but from that point on, Jochen didn't want to know. He said the mechanic he wanted was a very young Ron Dennis. I said 'But the guy's a youngster! He's only 18-19.' He was an apprentice then but he was shaping up very well. Even so, I couldn't just put him in charge of Jochen's car. But he stuck to his guns. 'He's the guy I want,' he insisted and I thought 'Christ, it's getting worse and worse', so I eventually put Ron in charge of Jochen's car and we never heard a squeak out of Jochen from then on.

"Ron followed Jochen when he eventually switched to the Brabham team. That was the secret of Ron Dennis's success. He had the ability to instil confidence in Jochen and that was half the battle..."

Salvadori signed the Mexican driver, Pedro Rodriguez to join

Rindt in the Cooper team for the opening Grand Prix of the 1967 season in South Africa.

"Jochen didn't take to Pedro at all. There was no real problem until we got to the race and Pedro made a very good time in practice with the Cooper-Maserati. We had worried about tyre-wear and we noticed that Jochen's wear was terribly heavy while Pedro's was very, very light and our race was obviously going to be decided on rubber.

"There was a slight hesitant period when Jochen's engine was flat out and he wanted to take Pedro's car. I refused because it would have knocked Pedro's confidence and he was doing very well. I told Jochen that we'd never snatched *his* car and given it to another driver. (Not that there was anyone better to give it too...) I said that wasn't the way we worked. Then he got Denny Hulme to try and make me change my mind but that only made me more determined that Pedro would keep his car.

"Bernie Ecclestone had come down to South Africa with us and we spent a day at a makeshift circuit around old gold mine tailings with Jochen charging around in the blazing sunshine trying to get rid of the misfire. I remember this well, because Bernie and I put out a table and chairs and we were playing gin rummy. In the race Jochen went well until the gearbox broke but when we looked at the tyres, he'd never have made it without a stop. It wasn't the tyres so much as the way Jochen drove the car. Pedro had been close behind Jochen early in the race until he lost second and third gears and he was plugging around – but amazingly he finished...and he *won*!

"Jochen had lost the race but Pedro had won it and that was where the hate campaign started. Jochen had always wanted to join in with Bernie and myself playing gin rummy but we didn't think he was the right material. We eventually relented and taught him to play but even when he *did* get a good hand or two, he was always losing. He never seemed to do the right thing and he wanted to play for *money*. On the plane back from Johannesburg I was playing cards again with Bernie when Pedro decided he wanted to play too. He was a loser with me and he was a loser with Bernie...and Jochen just couldn't wait to play with him. We reckoned that they weren't mates now so what would happen if anything went wrong with the card game?

"They started playing and I've never *seen* such hands as Pedro was being dealt. It sounded as though he was being sarcastic because he really didn't know and he was showing us four aces and saying 'Is this good? Is this good?' We didn't know what to say so we'd sort of mumble that it was not too bad. Jochen didn't know how to bet and he was starting to wonder whether Bernie and I were in it together with Pedro. He'd call on Pedro's hand and then see these four bloody aces or a run that he couldn't tackle! Pedro just *slaughtered* Jochen and Jochen was furious. He went back to reading a book. When the plane made a fuel stop at Nairobi, Jochen got off. Took his bags with him. He'd decided he'd had enough of us!"

Roy started racing in 1947 with the P3 Alfa Romeo that Tazio Nuvolari had driven to win the 1935 German Grand Prix on the Nurburgring, defeating the might of Mercedes-Benz and Auto-Union. The 25-year-old had a hectic debut. "To say that the car was unstable, doesn't make a start on it. Coming up behind another car I was offered three choices – hitting the car I was passing, hitting the fence...or getting by unscathed. Frightening.

"I first met Bernie around 1953 at Crystal Palace. Actually I saw him having a big shunt in his Cooper 500 – he used to have a few of them – but he was a real enthusiast and his cars were always beautifully prepared. I got to know him better when he backed Stuart Lewis-Evans. Bernie had bought a couple of Connaughts at the team's closing-down auction and sent them to New Zealand in 1958 for Stuart and me to race. He told Stuart to sell the cars out there. When Stuart announced that he had sold one, I asked how much he'd got for it. He said it could be worth a lot of money and that it all depended on how much the stamp collection was worth. He said he'd taken a stamp collection from a Hungarian guy. I suggested that perhaps he'd better check with Bernie on the phone before he did anything else. When he came back he was *ashen*! He didn't say anything so I don't know to this day what Bernie said. It was surprising, really, because Bernie was a wheeler-dealer and if he'd been there, he might well have taken a chance on the stamps.

"Then there was the time at Monaco in 1966 when Jochen, Bernie and I decided to charter a yacht in the harbour over the Monaco weekend. Bernie arrived first and bagged the best suite but by the time we had arrived he had had enough of the rocking and booked a suite at the Metropole Hotel. He had asked the skipper to put a table and chairs on the quay and he was sitting there having a cup of tea and was quite happy to pay his third share as long as we had our meals and played gin rummy anywhere but on the boat!"

The Salvadoris moved to their Monaco apartment in the late 1960s and enjoyed hosting their old racing friends over the Grand Prix weekends. This year Maurice Trintignant, winner at Monaco in 1955 in a works Ferrari and in 1958 with Rob Walker's Cooper, was swapping notes with Maria Teresa de Filippis, the Italian lady who raced in Formula 1 in 1958 and 1959 with a 250F Maserati, a Behra-Porsche and a Lotus. Cliff Allison, an original Team Lotus driver in 1958 and with Ferrari in 1959 and 1960, was remembering his huge accident during practice at Monaco when he was flung out of the Ferrari cockpit and suffered a badly broken arm. A dramatic wire-service photograph made front pages around the world with Allison spread-eagled down the nose of the Ferrari.

The *Ancien Pilotes* celebrated their annual luncheon beside the pool at Mike Sparken's Cap Ferrat home a couple of bays from Monaco on the free Friday. Their main problem these days is a dearth of younger members and they worry that the name of the club may be a deterrent. This year the turn-out included Tony Brooks, Clay Regazzoni, Cliff Allison, Roy Salvadori, Sir Jack Brabham, Maria Teresa di Filipis, Robert Manzon, Tim Schenken, Les Leston, Henry Taylor, Maurice Trintignant, Jochen Mass, da Silva Ramos, Gino Munaron, Paul Frere, Tim Parnell, Nanni Galli and Jean-Pierre Beltoise who won the 1972 Monaco for BRM in the rain.

Sir Jack Brabham lost a bet at the luncheon. Jean Sage, the French *Ferraristi* who was Renault Formula 1 team manager in the turbo years, had taken a wager with Brabham who said that he had never raced a Ferrari. He was *certain* that he had never raced a Ferrari and was perplexed when Sage produced a photograph from a report of the Spa sports car race in "The Autocar" of August 25th, 1957, clearly showing Jack at the wheel of a 2-litre 500TRC Ferrari which had been entered by the American millionaire, Temple Buell. Brabham offered to buy Sage dinner in the best restaurant...in Australia. Jabby Crombac observed that there wasn't one. Best restaurant in Australia, that is.

On the Thursday afternoon I strolled through the paddock with Sir Jack as he met up with old racing friends, bemoaning the fact that his son Gary, who raced for the Panoz team, had a new car that is slower than last year's car. Bernie Ecclestone shook hands warmly, laughing at memories of his days as owner of the Brabham team after Jack's retirement. There were chats with Niki Lauda and Bobby Rahal at Jaguar and with Ferrari driver turned team owner, Stefan Johannsen. Modern fans recognised the historic driver and pressed autograph books through the high paddock fence. Jack met up with his fellow-countryman, Paul Stoddart, for the first time at the Minardi motorhome on the quayside. Stoddart was proud to make Jack's acquaintance and Jack was interested in the modern economics of Formula 1.

A French journalist requested an interview for a one-to-one series he was writing on drivers talking about other drivers. Would Jack talk about his old team-mate Bruce McLaren? We sat for half an hour under the Minardi awning while Jack recalled his young Kiwi protégé who would follow his example and leave Cooper to build his own cars. He told one story that I had never heard before. "The day after the Indianapolis 500 in 1970 I flew back to Heathrow on the same plane as Bruce and he was telling me that he was definitely planning retirement at the end of the season so that he could concentrate on engineering and testing. I told him that if he was retiring he should stop driving altogether because in those days there were no rescue or medical facilities during test sessions. The next day he was killed testing his new CanAm sports car at Goodwood..."

Three Decades of Diary Stories

My columns that started in the 'sixties acted as my personal diary that everyone could read, a recollection of all the anecdotes, the funny and the intriguing stories that had happened during the week. They were comment on the news, *not* the news itself so I didn't have to get bogged down with the minutiae of gear ratios and lap times or asking slow drivers what their problems were. Or recording the comments of the winning drivers when you knew exactly what they were going to say before they took their helmet off. I used to tell people that I was only writing down the stories that my mates wanted to hear in the pub when I got back from a race. They all *knew* who won but they wanted the gossip, and that's what I wrote each week. The chapters that follow on thirty years of racing are not meant as day-to-day records but more a collection of anecdotes and quotes that form a reflection of racing in what now seems like the far-off past. Remember that in over 30 years of *Autocar* columns we are talking a total of over a million and a half words...maybe there's yet another book in that stack of 1600 magazines!

The John Surtees at Le Mans for the test weekend in April 1967 seemed to have undergone an uproar transplant. Calm was the order of the day in the Lola-Aston Martin pit after the mayhem endemic at Ferrari in earlier days. I wrote: 'Big John's fire-breathing seems to be a thing of the past. At one stage Eric Broadley and the Lola team were out on the track in front of the pits waving frantically at Surtees to slow down. A mechanic had discovered one of the pins securing the tail, still in his pocket while the Lola roared out of the pits; and scrutinizing the cars as Surtees went by wondering what on earth was happening,

129

they realised that one of the other body-fastening pins was starting to come loose as well. Someone, it seemed, was due for a verbal beheading but Surtees said nary a word.

'He ran out of fuel on the Sunday and sat on the side of the road while Scarfiotti acted as messenger boy and loaded a can of fuel and a filler into his P4 Ferrari and went out to rescue his ex-team mate. Again, no sharp words about who hadn't put in enough fuel. The *grand finale* of Surtees' calmness came when the Lola arrived late at the pits with John hanging on to the tattered remains of the passenger's door which had come un-latched near *Tertre Rouge* and blown off. Surtees climbed out of the Lola and said "The door blew off." A masterpiece of quiet understatement. . .'

And then there were road test cars that I *didn't* like. In May I had driven a new Ford Mercury Cougar to the VSCC Silverstone and was a tad embarrassed. "I drove up in the 2+1-sideways and felt I was doing a rather unseemly thing by nosing this rather large piece of American ironware in among the countless examples of antique European engineering expertise. I didn't much like the Cougar. It handled like a row of books falling off a shelf, had an even greater thirst than me, and generally acted very much like the boulevard cruiser that it is. The Mustang is a vastly better motorcar."

The new Ford-Cosworth DFV V8 missed Monaco and would debut a fortnight later at Zandvoort, but the Ford brass were on hand in the Principality. 'I gather that Stirling Moss asked Ford Director, Harley Copp whether he would sell him one of the 3-litre V8 Formula 1 engines if he (Moss) had still been racing, to which Copp replied "We wouldn't have to – you'd be driving in our team!" But Moss says that if he was still in the steering business today, he would be driving a Brabham for Rob Walker using – and he reckons he could have got one – the Ford engine.'

In 2003 it was said that owners of red Ferraris should memorise their number plate because there were so many parked around Monaco. It has always been the ultimate to get a parking place in Casino Square when the cars aren't racing through. In 1967 "Getting back to the free show at the Casino Square, a low little English-registered Lotus Europa had a sign on the dash that read: 'Together we chose a Lamborghini but instead we bought seven Europas and £1000 stayed in the bank.'"

There used to be a serious sudden hill on the straight behind the pits at Zolder and for some reason at dinner in June 1967 it prompted discussion about concentration and the way it is affected when one eye is closed. "Static tests were conducted at the table by shutting one eye and plugging a finger in the top of a bottle. Ken Tyrrell apparently doubted the validity of the argument when transferred to the race track. Jim Clark asked him how he would like to go over the brow of the hill at Zolder with one eye closed. Robin Widdows chimed in with the classic reply from the aspiring racer to the already-great: 'You mean you go over there with one eye *open*?'"

After the one and only French Grand Prix on the short Bugatti circuit at Le Mans, I suggested that Ing. Forghieri was signalling Chris Amon to go faster. At the next race he took me aside to explain what he had actually been doing: '"Chris wasn't driving *hard* enough. I would never tell a driver he wasn't driving *fast* enough, but Chris drives the Formula 1 car as though it is a Prototype in a long-distance race. He brings it to the pits and the brake pads are un-marked – the gearbox is like new. He doesn't drive to the limit of the car. The Ferrari will take more than Chris gives it." He went on to say that he had the greatest respect for the ability of Amon as a driver and also a personal friend, but he felt that Chris was being too gentle with the car. Forghieri gave me the impression that he wouldn't mind if Chris broke the Ferrari, just as long as he know that Chris had been fully using the car. He wouldn't dream, of forcing a driver over his personal limit, or even suggesting that he should do so. "I love my drivers," he said, after a partly successful battle for words with his interpreter.'

A.P.R. 'Tony' Rolt started racing in the late 1930s, gained fame winning Le Mans with Duncan Hamilton for Jaguar in 1953 and in July 1967 we were talking about speeds on the Mulsanne Straight. "When I was racing a Nash Healey in the early 1950s, 145mph was really motoring down Mulsanne. When you reached *Tertre Rouge* you had time to stretch out, ease cramped private parts and even unwrap a barley sugar and pop it in your mouth without getting tangled up with the paper!" I doubt whether (that year's winners) Foyt or Gurney would have had time to worry about barley sugar at 220mph in this year's race – or if they did, they'd have eaten the paper as well.

More Rob Walker: In October 1969 he told me that he never gave Stirling Moss pit signals saying PLUS or MINUS. If it was a plus time, the figures were in black, or on the odd occasions when it was a minus, the figures were in red 'So that he could remember as though they were figures in his bank balance,' Rob explained.

Keith Duckworth was at Riverside for the CanAm race in November 1969, still talking about his visit to Detroit to see the Ford race engine department: 'Repeatable comments were his description of the valve gear on the huge 8-litre Ford V8: "It's like lying on your back underneath a giant piano and playing it with an 8ft stick." Or his suggestion for the huge inlet manifolds: "They should cast arrows in them to show the air which way to go..."'

In December 1969 I was writing about the RAC Rally and Paddy Hopkirk on television. 'He was asked through the window of his works entered 2.5 Pi Triumph what he thought the hardest thing about the rally would be. "Winning it in this car!" was the boyo's reply which must have done wonders for the cardiac condition of any British Leyland brass watching the box. Then there was Paddy's comment during the London-Sydney rally as the competitors streamed ark-like off the P&O liner *Chusan* at Fremantle after their crossing from Bombay. What did Mr Hopkirk think of the sea voyage, asked the TV commentator? "Best advertisement I've ever seen for air travel..." They couldn't win.

I arrived at the BRDC clubhouse at Silverstone one year and was talking about the hot air balloons we had seen in the sky on the way in. I wondered where they were going to. Paddy pointed out that hot air balloons don't actually *go* anywhere. You go where they take you. Then he told about a flight he had taken in a balloon with friends and they had lost their bearings so they whooshed down low over a Sunday afternoon garden barbecue to shout for details of where they might be as some guide to where they might be going to. "A guy with a very Australian accent shouted up 'Aren't you Paddy Hopkirk?' I said that I was and he shouted back 'I bought some wing mirrors off you a couple of years ago and they fell off after a fortnight...'"

As the decade turned from the sixties to the seventies, I was in philosophical mood, noting that: 'One of the most significant points about motor racing in the 'sixties was that Bruce McLaren won the opening Grand Prix in the Argentina with the works 2.5-litre Cooper-Climax and one of his own Grand Prix McLaren-Fords won the final race of the decade – the Mexican Grand Prix – driven by Denny Hulme. Before 1960 racing drivers drove the racing cars and the car-builders built them but in the 'sixties a new generation of drivers with engineering backgrounds started coming to the fore and set about building their own cars. Jack Brabham left the Cooper team and was running a Grand Prix Brabham in 1963. Bruce McLaren started building his own sports cars while still a works Formula 1 driver with the Cooper team, and then left to campaign his own Formula 1 McLaren in 1966. Dan Gurney also assumed the role of driver-constructor in 1966 when the first Eagle appeared on the Grand Prix grids. The latest driver to turn constructor is John Surtees. His F5000 TS5s have been winning races in 1969 and 1970 will see the first Surtees car in Formula 1 with John at the wheel.

Fortunately the racing drivers were more successful at their go-it-alone ventures than the established constructors had predicted. Brabham was the first driver to win a Grand Prix in a car with his name on the nose and he continued the winning streak in 1966 to take the World Championship – another first. McLaren won a Grand Prix in a McLaren at Spa in 1968. Gurney won at Spa in 1967 in his Eagle.

'Ten years ago Jim Clark and John Surtees were preparing for their first season in Formula 1 racing. Clark had signed with Aston Martin but was to switch to Lotus, joining Surtees and Innes Ireland. By the end of the decade Jim Clark had won 25 GPs and two world championships before he was killed in 1968. John Surtees had won six GPs and one world championship. Clark had hitched his wagon to the Lotus star and stayed with Colin Chapman, but Surtees had a restless 10 years switching from team to team.

'If there was a car of the decade it has to be a Lotus – the Type 25 and its derivatives. When the first rear-engined Lotus appeared in the Argentine at the beginning of the 1960 season it caused a stir and Ireland qualified second fastest to lead in the opening laps. Stirling Moss was so impressed he persuaded Rob Walker to persuade Colin Chapman to sell him one of the new cars. Rob describes the scene well: "In those days Colin was virtually unheard of and for Stirling to want one of his cars must have been like God coming to you and asking..."

'They won first time out at Monaco to give Lotus its first Grand Prix victory. By the end of 1969 Lotus cars had won 36 GPs as compared with 13 Ferrari wins, 12 BRM wins and 12 Brabham wins in the same period. For students of statistics, the decade also saw nine wins each from Matra and Cooper, four wins from McLaren, two from Honda and one each from Eagle and Porsche. The last two are interesting from the point of view that long, tall Dan Gurney was driving on both occasions.

'Driving victories in the sixties show Jim Clark well out in front with 25; Graham Hill is next with 14; Jack Brabham and Jackie Stewart are level on 11 each, John Surtees scored six, Denny Hulme five, Dan Gurney four and Stirling Moss four before his retirement after his Goodwood crash in 1962. Bruce McLaren, Phil Hill and Jacky Ickx won three GPs each, Taffy von Trips won two, and Baghetti, Bandini, Ginther, Ireland, Rodriguez, Scarfiotti, Siffert and Rindt all won one GP.

'Looking at the number of wins which gave each world champion his title during the 'sixties, we see that Clark again heads the list with seven wins in 10 races counting towards the 1963 title, and six wins in 10 races in 1965. Jackie Stewart took the championship this season (1969) winning six races out of 11 in the Matra. Phil Hill (1961), John Surtees (1964) and Denny Hulme (1967) won the championship with only two GP wins each. Graham Hill won the title in 1968 with three wins out of 12.

'In 1960 the British entrants refused to race in the Italian Grand Prix at Monza because part of the race was to be run on the banking. Phil Hill won the race in a front-engined Ferrari – the last GP win for a car with the engine in the front, and the first American driver to win a Grand Prix since Jimmy Murphy did the trick in a Duesenberg and won the French GP at Le Mans in 1921. The following year Phil won the world championship.'

The Seventies

There were several American drivers on the 1970 Tasman Series, now open to 5-litre single-seaters raced as Formula A in the USA and Formula 5000 in Britain. Bill Simpson, the man behind the Nomex driver suits in the States, turned up for the Levin race: 'He discovered that it wasn't much fun using an actual race as practice for heeling-and-toeing – a new and wonderful art for him – because he was arriving at too many corners in neutral. He had been used to driving USAC cars in America without using the clutch except for starting, and placing his left foot on the brake for the rest of the race. After the Levin race, he spent an hour in the cockpit of his Eagle parked safely in the garage, making loud revving engine noises by mouth and trying to teach his right foot the correct sequence for swivelling between the brake and the throttle. It's easy when you know how, but learning to do it must be like trying to write left-handed.' Always assuming you're not left-handed to start with, of course.

Chris Amon was officially on holiday during the 1970 Tasman Series and doing different things: 'In addition to his commitments with March in GP and CanAm, McLaren for Indianapolis and Ferrari for the occasional sports car drive, Chris has involved himself in another horsepower problem. The power of one horse, to be exact. At the Trentham yearling sales in New Zealand recently, Chris splashed starting money from a couple of Grand Prix races on buying a filly which will be looked after on his father's stud farm at Bulls. As the newest horse-trader in motor racing Chris says he and his father will breed from the filly and also race it. What will they call it? "We'll have to sit down and think of a name for it, but it will probably have a motor racing association to it." Other horses in the Amon stud have been named after race tracks – two of them being Spa and Daytona.'

We like to think that motor sport does not suffer the violence of football crowds, but at Warwick Farm, the crowd at Creek Corner was a law unto itself: 'Ice, pies and beer cans flew across the crowd at Creek Corner in sporadic battles between races. A trumpeter on the heights of the embankment stirred the drinkers and occasional spectators to arms at the start of each race, and when a luckless Formula Ford car sagged to a stop with broken rear suspension going into Creek Corner, the trumpeter played a solemn Last Post. The police patrolled the crowd from the comparative safety of the space between the safety bank and the spectator fence, only occasionally venturing into the packed tipsy embankment crowd to speak with the thrower of a too-accurate missile – if he could be identified.'

At the end of the Tasman Series, Sandra and I flew across to South Africa to go on Safari with Bruce and Pattie McLaren and baby Amanda:

'I'm tapping this column out in a little air conditioned hut in Lower Sabie up in the Kruger Park game reserve. Last night there was wild excitement when the natives spotted a wild elephant coming up from the river not 50 yards from the hefty wire-rope fence. Cars on the road upset it and it broke into a lumbering run up the road, stopping to munch up half a tree a leisurely stone's throw from our front door. Even the natives were impressed.'

Bruce had arranged to borrow a huge air-conditioned Ford Fairlane for the trip and met us at Johannesburg airport. He packed our luggage in the huge boot and because the sun was up and the day was warming quickly, he took off his jacket, folded it on top of the luggage, and slammed the boot-lid. That was the instant when he remembered that the car keys were in his jacket pocket and we were locked out! He phoned the Automobile Association and the serviceman arrived to be acquainted with the situation. He took it all on board and, obviously not being a Formula 1 enthusiast, said to Bruce McLaren in his broad Afrikaans accent "How do I know it's *your* car, eh?"

Ken Tyrrell was fielding a pair of over-the-counter March 701s in 1970: 'Speculation was rife in Kyalami as to whether the March cars performed better with or without their distinctive side 'pod' tanks. I asked Ken Tyrrell whether the side-tanks really did provide additional down-force and were an improvement. "Funny you should say that," grinned the burly Tyrrell. "Brabham's just been along and asked me the same question and I told him it cost me £9000 to find the answer and I wasn't about to tell him!"

I went to Sebring for the 12-hour race where movie star, Steve McQueen, made headlines finishing second to Mario Andretti, but it wasn't a performance that found favour with Mario. I wrote: 'Mario Andretti was driving the wheels off his Ferrari 512 sports car in the closing stages of the race, battling not only to win for himself and the Scuderia but to beat *Bullitt*-star Steve

McQueen and Peter Revson who was sharing the actor's 3-litre 908 Porsche Spyder! The 5-litre Ferrari Andretti had been sharing with Merzario, broke its gearbox when it was 10 laps in front with an hour and a half to go so the little American took over the third-placed Giunti-Vaccarella 512. The Gulf-Porsche driven by Siffert-Rodriguez was leading with the McQueen-Revson 908 in a fantastic second place. The Ferrari was down on power with what Mario thought might have been a dud valve, but he was flying through the night, lapping only 3sec slower than he had been when he was leading during the day. He was straightening the esses and scattering rubber marker-cones everywhere. Concern for the concours appearance of the car was definitely in second place to Mario's determination to win the race. "I was driving my butt off in that thing. No way was I going to let an *actor* win the race!" Andretti closed on McQueen just after the Gulf-Porsche had suffered its second front suspension breakage (and the team's fourth!) so for a few Hollywood-style miles a film star was out in front of an international race!

'At breakfast the next morning Andretti was praising Revson's performance in the race and saying it would be a shame if McQueen got all the credit in the newspapers. But we observed that Mario's three co-drivers didn't exactly come in for the lion's share of the publicity in the morning papers... Certainly Revson drove a very good race because he is a very good driver, but McQueen's drive, in my opinion, was exceptional because he had smashed a bone in his left foot in a motorcycle race the weekend before and he was driving with a hefty plaster cast on his clutch foot.'

I sat on the back of a pick-up truck with McQueen before the race and he told me about his plans for a movie on Le Mans and his personal problems with insurance companies: 'They pulled me out of the car when we were making *Bullitt* and they pulled me off the motorcycle in *The Great Escape*."

'McQueen is no powder puff and grease-paint film star. He's tough. The week before Sebring he was riding his Husqvarna

400 when he came off on the fourth lap of the 100-mile off-road race at Lake Elsinor. He broke a bone in his left foot in six places, but he got back on the bike and finished sixth out of a field of 500 starters! No wonder his insurance company is jittery...'

'McQueen plans to share a 917 Porsche with Jackie Stewart at Le Mans (EY: They didn't) and he will be entering his 908 as a specially-equipped camera car to be driven by Jonathan Williams. Although they are making a film around the race, McQueen says he will drive in the race as a racing driver, not as a film star. Stewart says he thinks they have a chance of winning the race, and after seeing McQueen perform at Sebring, I'm inclined to agree. As we saw at Le Mans last year, it isn't always the fastest car that wins the race. The filming will start with the first day of scrutineering and will finish when the chequered flag falls. And that's when the film-making *really* starts and McQueen takes over to shoot the driver's off-duty scenes which will make up the story behind the race. McQueen wants to bring racing as it really is, into the popcorn crunchers in the front stalls. "For example, a lot of people are very naïve about what is involved in night racing. – driving as far as you can see in the beams of your lights...the flash of lights in your mirrors..." In fact, before Sebring, Steve was one of the naïve ones too although he didn't realise it. He did after the first night practice though! It should be a great film'

In fact I didn't think it was a great film, even though I spent some time at Le Mans while the fiction bits were being shot around the pits and on the course. To my mind there were too many long Hollywood-style smouldering glances. I initially thought that John Frankenheimer's *Grand Prix* movie was a travesty of the real thing, but after seeing *Le Mans* in the cinema in London I began to warm to the Frankenheimer flick...

Those were the days. Before Monaco, I was waxing lyrical about the Principality: 'I like to walk around the circuit during the Grand Prix watching the maestros at work from close quarters, but I prefer to watch the Formula 3 race from the Metropole Hotel balcony overlooking the Mirabeau Hairpin. It's reasonably safe there and the chocolate éclairs go down a treat with a nice cup of tea (EY: Well it *was* a long time ago!) In the past I have always driven down to Monaco, but this year I've got to rush back to jet across to Indianapolis for the first qualifying runs of the following weekend, so I'm travelling on a Page & Moy package tour which has to be good value at 83 guineas (EY: I told you it was a long time ago...) for five days demi-pension at the Metropole – and that includes the air fare!'

Jackie Stewart – World Champion the first book on JYS written with fellow-Scot Eric Dymock, came out at the start of the European season, and I mentioned in my *Straight from the Grid* Diary column in *Autocar*: 'Stewart tends to be outspoken about things he believes in and like many personalities who back their opinions, he has his detractors. But the Stewart I get along with best is the non-serious relaxing Stewart who is very entertaining company. Shoulder-length hair isn't everybody's cup of Brook Bond, but Stewart probably feels he can now afford to do what he pleases. He wasn't about to buy Rolex watches and suits from Blades when he was banging away at plastic pigeons...'

The hardest column I ever wrote came out in *Autocar* on June 11th, nine days after Bruce McLaren's death: 'This is the most difficult column I've ever had to write. It's difficult because I thought I would never have to write it. Not about Bruce McLaren. I never imagined that he was immortal, but I just didn't consider that he could get killed in a racing car. If you are any sort of motor racing journalist you have to know the drivers on a friendly basis, but I knew Bruce McLaren better than I knew anyone else in the sport. I met him in New Zealand in 1959, and in Australia at the beginning of the 1962 season he asked me if I would be his secretary in England. He said he wasn't sure that he needed a secretary and he didn't know quite what I would do, but he said he'd think of something. I suppose we did quite a lot. He introduced me to Formula 1 motor racing in

Europe and to everybody in it. In 1963 he started his own racing team with a staff of three – himself, me and Wally Willmott. When he started sports car racing, Teddy Mayer and Tyler Alexander joined the team. Bruce's cars worked because he was a sound engineer and he knew what should be built into them. Teddy Mayer brought his American business talents in behind Bruce's track ability, and the business mushroomed. What had started as almost a hobby for Bruce, running his own racing team was suddenly the foundation for a million dollar motor racing facility. In 1966 I left the team to become a writer, but I was very much aware that I owed whatever success I achieved solely to Bruce. That's why this column is so difficult to write.

'It's hard to take an objective look at a man like McLaren because he never seemed to have any bad points. It didn't seem possible that anyone is his line of business could be cheerful *all* the time. When things weren't going right, he just smiled a little less often. The success of his racing team probably stemmed from the fact that he was the same age or younger, than most of the mechanics, engineers and designers, and he worked with them. A visitor to the factory would have been hard pressed to pick out the worker who had his name on the wall outside.

'The team operated more as a family. He was proud of being a New Zealander and if a prospective mechanic turned out to be a fellow countryman he usually stood a better chance of getting a job. Denny Hulme 'clicked' in the McLaren set-up and when he and Bruce travelled together they were like two brothers out for a treat. They joked together, but when the situation demanded it they could be serious with each other. At breakfast on the morning of the 1969 Mexican Grand Prix which Denny was to win in his McLaren, I remember Bruce saying something that made Denny laugh. He rocked back on is chair and tittered as only Denny could "You know, the reason this team is so successful is because we have a better time than anybody else." And he was right.

'When Denny burned his hands at Indianapolis, Bruce was

terribly concerned for his friend and fellow driver. When Denny heard of Bruce's accident, he was desolated.

'The death of a driver is hard to accept. You can say that those who live by the sword should be prepared to die by it, but deep down you don't really mean it. If drivers like Bruce went racing only for the money, perhaps such an attitude would be apt, but Bruce went racing because he really and truly enjoyed doing it. The fact that he was also successful and made money at it, was something of a bonus. He didn't have to be at the factory with his sleeves rolled up every day. He could afford not to, but the hours that he worked in his own factory would have outraged any union official. He did it because he sincerely enjoyed racing and enjoyed building something that worked well.

'Someone gave him a plastic model kit of the M8B CanAm car that he won the series in last year and he was looking forward to building it up. That's another of the things he won't be doing.

'But racing is like show business, and the show must go on. The McLaren entries for the Belgian GP were withdrawn but the remaining two CanAm McLaren M8Ds were air-freighted out to Canada for the first race of the 1970 series at Mosport. Bruce would have wanted it that way, I know...'

Phil Kerr, joint managing director at McLaren with Teddy Mayer, put it well when he said that motor racing would not only miss what Bruce McLaren had done during his career, but it would also miss what his death prevented him from doing. "Bruce knew as much at 32 as Jack Brabham and Colin Chapman do in their early forties. Just think of the tremendous promise and potential...

'Safety in racing is a little bit like a leaking roof when the sun is shining. Nobody ever complains until it starts raining. Likewise, the people who burst into print in publications usually only mildly concerned with racing on clear days will offer advice on how we can make racing cars safer.

'Piers Courage's fatal crash (at Zandvort) drew attention again to the lack of fire equipment at Grand Prix tracks, and started some people wondering whether there should be new safety regulations. Using methanol fuel instead of pump petrol was suggested because methanol is less volatile, but as Denny Hulme pointed out, the problem with methanol is that you can't see it burning. It has a clear flame. Denny's burns on his hands when his gloves were soaked with methanol-based fuel leaking from a breather during Indianapolis testing, were made more serious because the fire crew went on past him to chase the car. They couldn't see that his gloves were alight. Likewise when Roger McCluskey hit the wall late in the '500'. Fuel was running down the track to form a wall of fire but the drivers couldn't see it. Brabham spun right through it!

'Another suggestion that perhaps merits more consideration is to ban the extensive use of magnesium in the construction of the cars. The De Tomaso had magnesium bulkheads and mag sheet forming most of the monocoque, and in the fire this was extremely difficult to stop burning. A solution might be mandatory use of steel bulkheads and aluminium sheet for monocoques. But I don't really think that these sort of restrictions are the real answer. I just wish I knew what it was.'

The Dutch fire rescue crews came in for criticism and the following year they put on a demonstration of how their training had improved their fire-fighting. An old BMW saloon was set alight on the infield as the media watched. They couldn't quell the blaze...

'Helen Stewart, Jackie's wife, was sitting above the Tyrrell pit armed with her stopwatch and a big pad, but she wasn't in a flap trying to time every car in practice. "Ken told me that instead of getting nine cars wrong, I should try and get three right..." But Helen could certainly pick the form. The three drivers she was timing were Jochen Rindt, her world champion husband and Jacky Ickx. And that's the way they finished in the race: first, second and third.'

Four-wheel-drive in Formula 1 came and hastily went in 1969 and was something of an embarrassing blind-alley subject that the sport was not at all keen to discuss. At a barbecue before the Watkins Glen CanAm race, I noted that technical writer Karl Ludvigsen had announced that he had worked out the solution for the McLaren 4-wheel-drive F1 car: '"First of all you will have to tell us how we can get the rust off it..." replied Jo Marquart, a Swiss who started his design career with an omnibus company in Edinburgh before shifting to Lotus and then to McLaren.'

'Full marks to the Brabham mechanics for their quick work during

the Austrian Grand Prix when Jack stopped with water pouring from a fist-sized hole in the radiator. A rock had gone through the stone guard and ruined the radiator, but in just six minutes they had drained the radiator, removed it, fitted anther and sent Jack back into the race. "Six minutes!" said an incredulous Denny Hulme. "We couldn't even *find* a radiator in six minutes!"'

'Peter Gethin had language problems in Austria and a puzzled waiter went off to bring back three Martinis on a tray. Peter was equally puzzled because he had only asked for a dry Martini. *Ein, zwei, drei.* Got it? Peter got it. Three times!'

I drove a 914/6 Porsche press car from Stuttgart through to Austria for the race and I didn't much like it: 'It may be uncouth and untidy of me to want to take my coat off and sling it in the back seat, but at least I'd like some sort of back seat to sling it into! The seat-backs in the 914 seem to be bolted to one side of the firewall and the engine is bolted to the other, which means that (a) you have to endeavour to get comfortable sitting bolt upright because you can't adjust the seat back, and (b) you have to learn to live with the noise of the engine. It was great to start with as we barked down the Autobahn and I was sure I could come to terms with the noise and the need to think exactly where I wanted to put the lever before you changed gear, but I soon got tired of it. To the point where I asked the Porsche team manager if he could arrange to have the car driven back to Germany and I would fly home to Heathrow. He said it would not be a problem. A few days later and the phone rings in Horsley. "Herr Young? Ve haf your Porsche at our service station near the track. Vill you be collecting it? You left it in the paddock with the key in the ignition..." Bugger. A phone call to Porsche to find that they had forgotten to bring it back and they had to fly someone back to Austria to drive the 914/6 home.

August 1972 and we were at the Nurburgring: Jackie Stewart drew upon the dummy grid after a warm-up lap round the (old 14.2-mile) Nurburgring with a worried frown. He pulled down his face mask and said to Ken Tyrrell who was leaning into the cockpit "It's really going to be bad out there in the race. The track is starting to break up at the edges..." He probably wasn't ready for the Tyrrell reply "You think you've got troubles – England are 179 for 9!"

In my Diary in September '72 I was in self-congratulatory mood:

'Talking travel, it's a source of constant amazement to me that I can be back in England at 9 o'clock on a Monday morning after a Sunday CanAm race in the States and yet I rarely manage to get back in England before Monday afternoon after a Grand Prix much closer to home in Europe. Last year I flew over 100,000 miles going back and forth to races in America. Well, it impressed me, anyway.'

Russell Brockbank, motor racing's cartoonist laureate, told me over lunch just before Christmas (1972) that he didn't always draw his themes for racing rib-ticklers from the Surrey remoteness of his country cottage in Thursley. In 1953 Brock was perched in the pits at Le Mans doing the night lap-scoring for the Cunningham team. "I was picked for the job because I could memorise groups of headlights. I could remember the pattern of the headlights and spotlights and it meant I could pick out each individual car in a group of Jaguars coming up out of the night from White House corner..."

Tom Wheatcroft's Donington Collection had just opened in March 1973 and it included the Ferguson P99 which Stirling

145

had driven to win the 1961 Gold Cup at Oulton Park to score the first Formula 1 win by a 4-wheel-drive car and the last win by a front-engined car in Formula 1. My favourite Ferguson memory is from a decade ago in 1963 when Innes Ireland drove the P99 until it literally dropped in the Lady Wigram Trophy. They both gasped into the pits (Graham Hill had said it was like racing a stove when he had almost won the New Zealand Grand Prix a couple of weeks earlier) with the 4-cylinder FPF Coventry Climax engine so cooked that even the spark leads were charred! Innes reported, as only Innes could, that all the gauges read zero except the water temperature, the needle of which was almost wound around its stop!

The 'Eighties

October 1981 and Clive James is writing about Murray Walker's Monza commentary in *The Observer*: 'Under James Hunt's exemplary tutelage, Murray has quietened down considerably lately, so that you can almost hear the cars...The running gag of the Grand Prix series is that whereas Murray, safe in the commentary box, sounds like a blindfolded man riding a unicycle on the rim of the pit of doom, the men actually facing the danger are all so taciturn that you might as well try interviewing the cars themselves.'

November 1981 at the McLaren TAG-Porsche announcement: 'I couldn't help remarking on the fact that Porsche engineer, Mezger was wearing two wrist watches on one arm. Was he perhaps in a small way smuggling to help cover the cost of his trip from Stuttgart, or was there some incredibly technical reason why engineers at the top of their trade *need* two wrist watches? Herr Mezger was a shade embarrassed about it all. No, he wasn't smuggling, it was just that he had this complicated new digital watch with two faces so that you could set one to suit a second time zone, but so far he hadn't been able to work out how to set

146

it, and at the last minute it seemed easier to grab his old reliable analogue off the dresser and leave it on Stuttgart time. It's a relief to know that I'm not the only person baffled by the inner workings of my digital watch,'

In February 1982, before the season started I wrote that it was great to see Keke Rosberg in a competitive car at last – a Williams – and it would be great to see if he could take full advantage of the opportunity: 'As I understand it, Rosberg was born in Stockholm, brought up in Finland as a Finn, and now lives out of Monaco, Ibiza, England and a suitcase. His style, while making his way to the top, offended many of the pundits on the sidelines who reckoned that his kerb-jumping and tail-sliding was not the mark of a champion-in-the-making. But the pundits have said that about men who became champions before now. Jochen Rindt for instance. Rosberg has a lot of the Jones aggression and has always impressed me as a driver who takes charge of his car rather than letting the car take charge of him. He is a personable young man out of the cockpit. In my book we need more drivers like him and if he follows Alan Jones to an eventual World Championship title, I for one won't be a bit surprised..." And he did.

As a Rosberg postscript, I took a photo of Keke introducing his young son Nico to Jackie Stewart at a Grand Prix, and a few races later I gave Keke the prints. He was delighted. "Nico will be so pleased, because he was meeting a *World Champion*." I pointed out that he, Keke, was a World Champion. "Oh no – that's not the same at all. Your Daddy is just your Daddy..." And now young Nico is carrying the Rosberg name on in European racing.

Niki Lauda had returned from retirement to drive for McLaren again and on the eve of the season in February 1982, I wrote: 'John Watson must be wondering why he ever volunteered the quote that Niki Lauda would have to be prepared to accept Grand Prix racing today as it was and not as he'd like it to be. That was when it was first suggested that the battle-scarred

Austrian was considering a comeback. Early on the morning of the first day of practice for his first 'comeback race' at Kyalami, the aforementioned Niki Lauda herded all the Grand Prix drivers into a bus and locked them all together in a hotel for 24 hours. If that isn't changing racing to the way you want it to be, I don't know what it is!' The drivers were rebelling against restrictive clauses in their FIA superlicences, and Niki was heading group action.

Monaco for the Historic Grand Prix in June 1982: "They don't make them like that any more," I said to Brabham designer, Gordon Murray, as he was studying the rear suspension of a 1960 front-engined Dino Ferrari. "Thank goodness for that," retorted Gordon. He is a designer with a soft spot for racing machinery of the past, but his new habits die hard as I discovered when I suggested perhaps we should abandon the present Formula 1 with its endless bickerings and bad feelings (EY: So what was new there then?) and switch the World Championship to historic events instead. The effect was electric but the reply wasn't exactly what I'd expected. 'That'd be great,' said Gordon with a gleam in his eye. 'We could design a car that looks just like a 250F Maserati but with a carbon-fibre body and all the weight tucked low down. We could have double leaf springs with independent suspension units tucked away inside. Wonderful!'

July 1982: 'I was watching the historic race at Brands Hatch with Innes Ireland and wondering how much faster some of the cars would have been with drivers of slightly more calibre at the wheel – or perhaps less investment in the machinery. "If you or I were out there, it'd be different, laddie!" It most certainly would have been. Innes would have been quicker and I would have been slower, but I pointed out to the man who won Team Lotus their first Grand Prix that (a) I didn't want to drive, and (b) I couldn't imagine anyone letting him, so the suggestion was really a rather nebulous one.'

Rob Walker's wife Betty was victim of a freak accident in the Brands Hatch paddock when tyres fell from the Pirelli truck

148

and knocked her out momentarily. Afterwards, when Betty had recovered, Rob was able to say, remembering his days as a team owner, "To think of it...all those years when I used to dream about tyres falling off the back of a lorry and when it does happen, they have to hit Betty..."

December 1982 at the announcement of the Nimrod Aston Martin Le Mans project at Goodwood House: "Victor Gauntlett, Joint MD at Aston Martin, very much a Bulldog Drummond sort of chap, British and proud of it, told the luncheon gathering that he felt getting involved in motor racing on this level was a lot like making love to an elephant. "If you get it right, you hear nothing for two years. But if you get it wrong, you get kicked to death." If Gauntlett has a fault it is making pale shadows of those about him.'

Long Beach in 1984 and Frank Williams is trying to tempt Alan Jones out of retirement: "I offered him many hundreds of thousand of pounds and we discussed his various contractural obligations in Australia. He said he would phone me back within six days, but he didn't. So I suppose that's my answer..." Charlie Crichton Stuart, the man who makes sure the sponsors are sweet in the Williams team, is also lifetime president of the Alan Jones fan club. "If we could get Alan back and put him in the new FW08 for Imola, we'd brain them," he said, referring to the rest of the field...'

Then there was the time I pre-empted the news by accident: 'The Long Beach paddock was buzzing with speculation as to which driver Williams might hire. I had been chatting to Frank Williams, but he was giving no hints, and then I went back to the motel room I shared with Irish writer colleague, Maurice Hamilton. I walked into our room to find it full of Irish people which can be a little disturbing when you imagine it's going to be empty. Derek Daly is perched on my bed talking to Maurice and Mrs Daly is perched on the carpet reading the newspaper. Groping for a comment to broach the situation, I say 'Hi – how's the new Williams driver?" D. Daly looks as though I have

149

caressed his temple with a ball-peen hammer. "What?" he says. "What are you talking about? Who told you that?" This reaction is much better than I had imagined, considering he was the last person I had expected to find in my motel room anyway. "Oh, I was just chatting with Frank Williams before I left the garage..." True statement. By now I have well and truly gathered D. Daly's attention. "What? What did he say? I said noncommittally that we had just been discussing who he might sign as a driver. "Did he mention my name? Are you serious about this?" By now the situation is getting out of hand. Any minute now this agitated Dubliner is going to be on the phone to the Williams garage, or worse, leaping into his hire car and presenting himself to sign the contract. Francis will not be amused with me. So I have to confess that while my story is mostly true, it does lack credence in some areas. D. Daly thought it probably wasn't the funniest thing he had heard all weekend. No doubt he cheered up a little when it all came true a few days later.'

Phil Hill – Much more than just a World Champion

One of the best things about the Italian Grand Prix at Monza was lunch with Phil Hill in the paddock during the summers that I hosted press guests at the Elf and later Ford motorhomes. Phil led a tour group of Californian enthusiasts to Monza each year but he would always contrive to slip away for a relaxed lunch. He may have been a top racing driver but he is so much more than just a World Champion. Phil has a way with words in print and over lunch that always made a table of journalists envy his ability to capture scenes and people from the past and describe them with such uncontrived eloquence.

Unfortunately for Phil, the first American world champion Grand Prix driver, motor racing history captures him in the haunted portrait photograph having just been told that his team-mate Wolfgang von Trips had been killed in the race that Phil had won to clinch the 1961 World Championship for Ferrari at Monza. The race had sapped him, the win had buoyed him and now the news of Trips' death had knocked him sideways. Phil Hill was and is a total perfectionist, a driver who demanded the best from himself and therefore it was a minimum requirement from those he worked with and drove for. An intense but hugely entertaining character, much more than a retired driver because he was always much more than a racing driver. In recent seasons we would look forward to Phil strolling round the corner of the motorhome at Monza for an hour immersed in Formula 1 gossip. He was eager for the inside news while we wanted Phil to scroll through his amazingly graphic recall with stories from what we looked at as the Good Old Days and just maybe he regarded as the Awful Old Days.

As a top Californian sports car racer, Hill's target was a drive with the Ferrari factory team with a place in the Grand Prix squad as his total ambition. Philip Toll Hill, Jr. was born in Miami on April 20th 1927, and his family later moved to California where his father became postmaster at the Santa Monica depot. Phil was a car person from his school days and he would have revelled in the knowledge that their home was not far from the original Santa Monica road course where the first American races ran early in the century. At three, he thought he *was* a car. At age seven he knew all the specifics of the current cars. He paid ten dollars for a Model T Ford when he was 12 and drove it round a nearby dirt track in Santa Monica Canyon getting the feel for the skills that would make him famous. He tried racing a midget car. "They told me I looked like a cow walking across an icy pond so I gave that up."

Phil was avid for the history of racing and read all the books he could find in the 'forties, remembering Barre Lyndon's "Combat" and "Grand Prix". He still regards passages from Charles Jarrott's "Twenty Years of Motors and Motor Racing" published in 1906 as some of the best writing about the sport. Hill has become a noted writer on the subject himself, applying his extensive appreciation of the best of all aspects of cars and racing, with a polished pen. After Phil had left a Monza lunch one afternoon, we agreed that we wished we could be like him and write the way he spoke.

Written words can't cope with Phil's conversation as Christopher Hilton noted in his book "Grand Prix Showdown!". He had been quoting Phil on team-mate Von Trips: "I got along fine with von Trips. He was happy-go-lucky, and maybe I didn't find him sort of serious enough. Perhaps he was, but not in my way of being serious. I've never had much empathy for drivers who didn't have a key interest in the mechanical side of it and von Trips didn't have that. He knew what spark plugs were and that was about the end of it."

Hilton felt he had to paint in the colour of Hill's conversation, the extra layer of emphasis. *I must, I feel, soften this impression of Phil Hill because the printed word faithfully recording a man's word cannot capture the timbre of his voice, the sounds of the sentiments being expressed and thus how they are being expressed. That is important. Hill, long matured in the ways of the world, is recapturing something honestly and without a trace of rancour. He's not criticising von Trips, just telling it the way it was.*

Phil is a great raconteur but is not always quite as patient as a listener if his attention is lost. He has this wonderful way of nodding and saying "I'll be darned...I'll be darned..." and you know that it's all over.

He bought and modified an MG TC when he was 19 then worked for International Motors, a major west coast importer of foreign cars, and was sent to England where he worked in training programmes with Jaguar, MG and SU carburettors. He came home with a new XK120 Jaguar and raced it on the Pebble Beach road course, now the high-dollar park that hosts the annual concours events. His early races with the XK120 bring grimaces in retrospect. "I just sort of drove *over* everybody, if you want to know the truth – and they all knew I'd run into them so they got out of the way. God! The lack of rationality connected with that sort of driving scares me to death today!" And this was written in 1959.

Richie Ginther worked with Hill at International Motors and both would wind up driving in the Ferrari works team but in those days, Richie was Phil's sidekick. "Phil was nervous, quick to get excited – he was always a perfectionist and he was certainly annoyed with himself a lot more than he was with other people. He had more real education in a broad sense, more than anyone I knew. By himself he had studied literature, architecture, medicine, music...he played piano, alto sax, guitar and drums at various times. He quit them all because he didn't think he was good enough."

The XK120 had its limitations and Phil traded it on a true competition classic – a 1937 2.9-litre supercharged Mille Miglia

Alfa Romeo that he raced during the 1951 season and then sold it. Today the car is priceless. Phil sold it because "I couldn't get parts and the engine swallowed 30 quarts of oil in the engine and another 30 in the crankcase."

In its place he bought a 2.6-litre Touring bodied Ferrari from former racer and Le Mans winner, Ferrari's U.S. distributor, Luigi Chinetti who would be instrumental in Phil getting into the works team.

In 1952 Hill took Ginther as his navigator on the Carrera PanAmericana, a 2000-mile road race though mountains and plains from Mexico's southern border to the Texas border. "That first time it was all 'Uncle Phil's taking me racing' and it was all wonderful, but the next year we went over a cliff and after that, all he could do was shout *'Slow down!'* Phil laughs now as he remembers Richie in those early drives. In the mid-fifties Phil was suffering from a stomach ulcer and it added to the stress he put upon himself anyway. This was probably where his reputation arrived as a driver who raced on his nerves, who existed on baby food and Complan. When he was interviewed by Alan Henry in 1974, his parting shot was "I'd like you to nail once and for all this nonsense about me having a 'nervous wreck' mentality. I've never been nervous, it's just that I used to get completely absorbed with what I was doing and didn't like people bothering me with stupid questions just before a race."

Hill was so determined to shift his career to Europe that he shipped his own Ferrari and it was during the voyage from Houston to Catania that he had a telegram asking him to visit Enzo Ferrari when he arrived. The result was an invitation to drive at Le Mans in 1955, the year of the huge accident when Levegh's factory Mercedes hurdled the safety barriers opposite the pits and plunged into the crowd, killing more than 80 spectators. Phil was standing on the pit counter, helmet on, waiting to take over from Maglioli and saw the crash happen but didn't appreciate the enormity of it. He was told not to look at the mayhem when getting into the car for his stint. Hardly an encouraging debut for a driver sensitive to a good deal more than sheer speed.

He would win the Le Mans 24-hour race in 1958, 1961 and 1962 but the perfectionist in Phil wanted to be in Formula 1. Enzo wasn't sure, so Phil forced the issue and borrowed Bonnier's ageing 250F Maserati for the French Grand Prix at Rheims in 1958. He finished seventh, a lap down but it had the desired effect and he was given a works Ferrari in the Italian Grand Prix at Monza. He finished third behind Tony Brooks' Vanwall and Mike Hawthorn's Ferrari, having been signalled to stay behind Hawthorn to help his title points. Phil reckons he could have won his debut GP but for the teamorders.

For 1959 Hill was a Ferrari works driver with Englishman Tony Brooks and fellow-Californian Dan Gurney but the new rear-engined cars from Cooper were scoring wins. In 1960 it was again Cooper and now Lotus as the British cars demonstrated that front-engined cars were doomed. Phil scotched that at Monza scoring the last Grand Prix victory for a front-engined car but it was a hollow victory because the British teams had boycotted the race, which combined the dangerously bumpy bankings with the road course.

Brooks remembers Phil's arrival to the Scuderia. "It was a perfect year for Phil to get into Ferrari in 1959. It was a good solid reliable car with a beautiful gearbox and it gave a lot of satisfaction. As he had been driving front-engined sports cars in the endurance races it would have been easier for him to move into a front-engined Formula 1 car than a rear-engined one."

By 1961 Phil was the only 'English' driver in the team. This season was the first for the down-sized 1.5-litre formula and Ferrari had planned ahead with a rear-engined prototype running in Formula 2 in previous seasons. The shark-nosed V6 dominators swept all before them, sometime starting five cars with Hill, Ginther, Trips, Baghetti and Riccardo Rodriguez. Moss confounded Ferrari power at Monaco and the Nurburgring where the sweet-handling of the Rob Walker Lotus paid winning dividends. "Many, many times I'd have willingly traded my Ferrari's power for Moss's handling. The Ferrari was absolutely *awful* round circuits like Monaco."

Hill won at Spa and at Monza with seconds to Trips at Aintree and Zandvoort and after Monza, with Trips dead in the accident that also killed 14 spectators, Hill was the haunted world champion. It didn't help that Ferrari abandoned the rest of the season and Phil missed appearing in front of his home crowd in the season finale at Watkins Glen.

It got worse. In 1962 the British opposition had caught up in the power race with the Coventry Climax and BRM V8s coming on song. The once all-conquering Ferraris were simply blitzed and the political situation at the factory where defeat was blamed to all quarters, resulted in a revolt and many of the team's key characters left under Carlo Chiti to set up a new A.T.S. team. Phil went with them. He had been between a rock and a hard place. It made no sense to stay at Ferrari but how much sense did it make to switch to the brand new A.T.S. organisation? The new car appeared for the first time at Spa in 1962 and I remember studying the spidery car, lonely on its own at the end of the pitlane, without a pit box as a newcomer. Dan Gurney had ambled down to inspect Phil's A.T.S. and someone cracked a joke about the home-made look of the car. "Don't worry," said Gurney. "If it wins the race tomorrow it'll be the best-looking car here..." It didn't.

For 1964 Phil inadvertently jumped from the frying pan into the fire following his BP fuel contract to Cooper as team-mate to Bruce McLaren. Hill hated it. He and John Cooper clashed on a season-long basis, the angry situation culminating when Phil crashed and burned during the Austrian Grand Prix on the Zeltweg airfield circuit. Cooper stood him down for the next race at Monza, grudgingly reinstating him for the US and Mexican GPs as his home events, and the Grand Prix career of a champion simply ebbed away.

Paradoxically, Phil enjoyed his best single-seater races in a Cooper as team-mate to Bruce McLaren on the 1965 Tasman Series in New Zealand and Australia. For Hill it was the relaxed re-creation of everything he had enjoyed about the early races in his career. The series gave him everything he wanted, including the amazing opportunity to buy a huge and rare collection of player-piano rolls from a convent in Christchurch. This cathedral city also saw Phil in jail. We were waiting for him to join us at lunch but he was late, so we started. An hour later the doors burst open and Phil arrived. The other diners sat stunned as Phil announced 'Where have I been? I've been in *jail*, goddamit!" An American tourist had been robbed of a wallet that included several $20 bills and Phil had visited a bank to change a few...$20 bills... The police had been called while Phil was losing patience with waiting and he grabbed the notes from the startled teller and stormed out. He was walking down the footpath when he was aware that two men were following him, and asking him to stop. Figuring they were race fans who had recognised him and wanted an autograph, he turned, only to find a pair of constables with a cruising squad car behind them. He was invited into the back of the car and the driver turned to ask who they had apprehended. Phil recounted the situation with superb irony: "He *says* he's Phil Hill the racing driver." One of the police remarked on Phil's chronograph wristwatch. 'Nice watch, sir -- where did you get it?' 'Where did I get it? I got it for winning the Le Mans 24-hour sports car race.' And the policeman said if that was the case he presumed it would be engraved. I said 'Of *course* it's engraved, and I took it off...and there wasn't a mark on the back...' Eventually the situation was smoothed out and it became an after-dinner story for all concerned.

Phil's final single-seater race in his hectic career was in the McLaren Cooper-Climax on the long country-road circuit at Longford in Tasmania and it gave him huge personal satisfaction to have finished third. Bruce had won the race but Phil had battled wheel to wheel with Jim Clark's Lotus and both had thoroughly enjoyed the cut-and-thrust, each in total trust of the other on the high-speed track road circuit. "It reminded me of the original Elkhart Lake circuit in the early 1950s. Longford had bridges, crossroads, ditches, hedges and trees and everything else. I loved that kind of track, where you could see where you were going. Jim Clark and I got into a fantastic battle. He was going well enough and that Lotus was a wonderful car. We just went back and forth, back and forth, for ages. I finally found out where Jimmy's weak spots were. There was one place round the back, over a bridge I think, where my Cooper seemed to be better than the Lotus. Or I was taking it better than he was. I slipped past and can remember him looking annoyed that he couldn't do anything about me there. Bruce won from Brabham and I was third."

That last single-seater race had a sad note after a young Australian driver had crashed off the track, killing himself and a photographer. It had a profound effect on Hill. He told journalist Adam Cooper: "I didn't used to think that way in my earlier days. A blank slate would cover it up and it was all about getting on with the next race. But that was years earlier. I had been at it for too long, to tell you the truth and been to too many funerals. After a long period you run out of reasons as to why it's them and not you. When you're driving Grand Prix cars, you can't have any doubt at all about whether it's a reasonable and practical thing to be doing. And I think I sort of got to that point, but it was a joy to be able to go out of single-seaters on a high note."

There were long-distance races with the Ford endurance juggernaut and with Jim Hall's almost family team with the high-winged Chevrolet-powered Chaparral GTs with automatic transmission on European circuits. He shared the winning Chaparral with Mike Spence in the 1967 BOAC 1000-kilometre race at Brands Hatch and that was the end of a distinguished racing career. A culmination more than an end, really because it was a matter of Phil moving on to other things that interested him in the world of motoring. He had married Alma and they had two children, Vanessa and Derek who is now racing in Europe, and Phil could immerse himself in his first love, a senior figure in the rarefied Pebble Beach concours world of historic cars.

Phil is restless in his seventies and uncertain about finding himself the centre of a minor media scrum at a recent Goodwood Festival of Speed as journalists realised it was the 40th anniversary of his world championship. He gives the impression that his world title is past history and there are more important things to talk about.

Remembering Le Mans

Le Mans lasts too long. There, I've said it. I know that the famous round-the-clock race is known as the famous long-distance racing happening staged by the French for the British and that there are motorised legions of enthusiasts who regard being uncomfortable for 24 hours as something to look forward to from one June to the next. Racer Gordon Spice made Le Mans a specialty but even he said he had his reservations. "It always meant I couldn't have a drink for 24 hours," said the feisty Gordy.

Chris Amon was adjudged too young to compete at Le Mans in 1964 and yet the previous weekend he had driven in the Belgian Grand Prix on the superfast Spa circuit. Two years later the babyface Kiwi would win the 24-hour race for Ford teamed with fellow-countryman, Bruce McLaren. In 1967 he signed with Ferrari and would lead the Italian team for three seasons. He remembered one Le Mans race where he lost out all round. Christopher enjoyed a good dinner with the best of them and the Ferrari team had rented an elegant French chateau near the track, but he felt that he should be responsible on the night before the long race, and go to bed early. He went back to his room and was climbing into the big bed when he realised he wasn't alone. A pretty French girl that followed the Ferrari team and was known as French Susie, had found her way into Christopher's bed and was reclining *sans chemise*. Now Christopher faced a major decision. Does he abandon his sense of team responsibility or does he ask the naked French girl if she could make other arrangements. He decided that he would abrogate his responsibilities, shrugged into a dressing gown and knocked on the door of the Ferrari team manager, the lanky

Englishman Michael Parkes. Chris explained his problem, which at any other time and place would have been a problem he would have enjoyed handling himself, but Parkes understood and took over. "He scooped French Susie out my bed and set off down the corridor, banging on a door that was opened by a startled bespectacled Italian aerodynamicist. Mike said 'Here's a present for you,' and swept into the room, dumping the bare Susie on the bed. The problem was that I was out of the race early when I got tangled up with someone else's accident in the opening laps..."

I went to Le Mans with Bruce McLaren when he drove for John Wyer's Aston Martin team in 1963 and it was my first experience of the team's base at the Hotel de France in La Chartre sur le Loir. Wyer used it as his team base from the Aston days through his time with Ford, Gulf-Porsche and Mirage. It was a tidy drive from the circuit but it guaranteed peace and quiet away from the hustle and bustle of Le Mans. The drive back to La Chartre after the night practice was as good as being in the race. I remember Roy Lunn, the Ford engineer, riding back with McLaren as a passenger in the Ford GT to try and identify a misfire at speed. "Could I hear the misfire? Man, I was hearing angels singing!"

Roy Salvadori, who won Le Mans for Aston and Wyer with Carroll Shelby in 1959, had fond memories of the Hotel de France. "We stayed there in 1953 – my first year at Le Mans. It was a small family hotel with exceptional cuisine and a large garage in which the team could work on the cars. It was on the Loir, some 25 kms south of Le Mans. We used the hotel year after year and it gradually expanded, adding bedrooms, bathrooms and enlarging the dining room. The motor racing world patronised it during race week but they also visited during the year. After night practice when we used to return late to the hotel there was always an excellent meal ready."

A few years ago I went to Le Mans with John Coombs in his yellow D-Type Jaguar originally raced by Paul Frere for Ecurie

National Belge. We were in a cavalcade of D-Types which had dominated the long race in the 1950s and Frere would drive the car in the demonstration laps on the morning of the race which traditionally started at 4pm. On the way to the track on race morning we stopped for fuel at a big service station and John came back to the car chuckling. "The lady at the till asked me if I was in the race and I said I was. She asked how I thought I would go, and I said 'Oh perhaps fifth or sixth...'"

Frere, was a famous Belgian motoring writer and a racer who had won at Le Mans with fellow-countryman Gendebien in a works Ferrari in 1960. He was in his late 70s but it was as though he had never been out of the cockpit. The old smooth skill was still here but we swept past the pits at such speed on the opening lap that was I was sincerely hoping that he remembered that the track went right at the end. He did.

It was late morning when the demo laps were completed and I suggested to Coombs that we motor out to La Chartre for lunch at the Hotel de France. "Do you know how to get there?" I couldn't remember, but it seemed like being lost for a while would be better than kicking our heels at the circuit for the next five hours. I said I did. John left the D-Type, borrowed an XJ6 from Jaguar and six of us crammed in for the mystery trip to lunch. When we eventually arrived after a few wrong turns in the French countryside I was hoping that the lunch would be as good as I had promised it would be. I shouldn't have worried. I saw Madame Pasteau, wife of the owner, standing in the foyer and wondered if she would remember me. To my delight and amazement she came over, gave me a voluminous hug and said "Ah, M'sieu Yooong!" We soon had a table set out for us and Madame fussed around us making sure that we were satisfied. John Coombs is famous as a worrier and there were times late in the lunch when he was ostentatiously looking at his watch but it was one of those wonderful French lunches that expand to empty the afternoon and Madame whispered that she had 'made arrangements for your friends.' I went back to her private lounge and she had arranged armchairs in front of the television which was showing the cars setting off on their warm-up laps. Coombs was slightly mollified by the fact that it was now too late to get back for the start anyway and we might as well be comfortable. Half an hour after the start, the room was full of sleeping mature motor racing enthusiasts...

I never went to Le Mans in 1966, the year McLaren and Amon won for Ford but Chris said he remembered driving me back from the 1965 Le Mans race in a Ford Mustang. "I remember it because you kept shouting at me to slow down! I was only doing 120mph and it seemed slow after doing 200mph in the race..."

In later years I worked for the American Gulf Oil Corporation sponsors of the Wyer team and I went back year after year with John's GT40s, Porsche 917s and Mirages. Too late for the Wyer Aston Martin years but I felt I'd been there after all the stories that John told in those magic after-dinner hours over a cognac or two. Or three. In those days I suppose I regarded it as work but when I look back at it now, it is becoming part of history.

Then there was the year I drove over to Le Mans with Eric Thompson in an historic Aston Martin DB2 – VMF65 – specially prepared for Le Mans in 1950 but crashed by works driver Jack Fairman on the way over and the wreckage was returned to the factory. Eric had raced for Aston Martin and Lagonda and he had bought the famous old car for the trip that turned out to be the first time it had actually made it to Le Mans!

I was going to say that sliding in behind the wheel gave me a great sense of history, considering the great names that had sat there in the past after it had been repaired, but in fact I had great difficulty in gaining access to the cabin at all. It had a lot to do with an excessive amount of me, a high seat edge and a low wheel rim. Eventually I perfected a sort of foot-first contortion that seemed to work with a measure of decorum.

"It *sounds* fast, doesn't it?" shouted Eric as we stormed across France. The crackle from the twin tail pipes sounded most impressive. Putting your foot down made the noise move up a key in aggressiveness but that was about as far as aggressiveness went. The noise changed, but the speed didn't.

Eric said they used to see over 125mph on the Mulsanne Straight and they were lapping around 100mph. In 1951, when he shared the third-placed works DB2, they averaged 90mph for 24-hours. Forty years on and we didn't need to check the rev counter, Too hard in third and the cockpit filled with smoke; up around 80mph in top and the gearlever launched into a flailing rattle. Seventy was a comfortable lope to which you reconciled yourself and sat back to revel in the history of the old charger, maximising what you had rather than missing what you wanted.

At Le Mans we were promised a parade of old cars at noon on the Saturday of the start and the cars were lined up in the traditional angled positions across the road from the grandstands which were sparsely filled with four hours to go before the start. The electricity was definitely already in the air. We were promised five laps and Eric and I had agreed that he would start and hand over in a lightning driver-change somewhere on the back of the circuit. Then Eric changed his mind, said he had driven at Le Mans seven times before, after all, and I should drive. Which gave me a slice of Aston history, because these were the first laps the gallant old works DB2 had ever covered on the track for which it had been built four decades before.

We were sitting in the Aston waiting for the 'off', me feeling suitably nervous, and Eric ran his fingers over the complex row of switches and knobs on the instrument panel. I assumed he was going to give me a pre-flight guide, but instead he said "You know, I can't remember what *any* of these are for. . ."

Eric had great Le Mans memories to recount over meals that weekend. David Brown's dream had been to beat Ferrari at Le Mans in 1954 and to that end he commissioned a special Lagonda based on a bloated DB3S works Aston Martin fitted with a 4.5-litre V12 Lagonda engine. "It was an absolute pig to drive," said Eric, still shuddering at the memory today. "It understeered horribly. I've got a photograph of me going into a right-hand corner at Le Mans on full right lock yards before the apex. But it was very fast down the straights, I'll give it that. I was slow away from the start because the engine wouldn't fire and I was behind both Parnell and Collins. I passed Peter Collins on lap 6 and the Parnell/Salvadori supercharged DB3S on lap 15. I was on the tail of a Talbot going into the Esses and thinking about how and where I'd pass him rather than what I was actually doing and I got on the white line and spun into the bank.

Thompson eventually managed to extricate the big car after an hour, having hacked through a body outrigger with the hacksaw and hammered the bent bodywork clear of the tyre. "I turned it round and motored very slowly back to the pits where I received the old Death Ray treatment from John Wyer and they decided to withdraw the car."

John Wyer's bleak glare and cold treatment of drivers who had spun, crashed, or otherwise fallen short of his rigid command, was legend to generations of drivers, more than one of whom had been reduced to tears. His Race Reports were often brutal. In 1954, he condemned Bira for being too slow and Jimmy Stewart for being recklessly fast – they both inverted their DB3S coupes at White House – but referring to Eric's Lagonda incident, Wyer noted that 'a key locating one of the steering arms had sheared and there must be a strong suggestion that this and not an error of judgement was the cause of the accident.'

That crash was to have a variety of consequences for Eric. The French weekly colour magazine "Paris Match" featured a full-page sequence of twelve photographs of the crash and Eric's best efforts to extricate the Lagonda. "The facing page was a full-page photograph of Zsa Zsa Gabor which, when you closed the magazine was quite a nice experience, thinking I was so close to a beautiful movie star."

Thompson became something of a movie star himself. In the news. David Blakeley, the racing driver murdered by Ruth Ellis, the last woman to be hanged in Britain, was entered for Le Mans in 1954 as reserve driver for the Bristol team. In the film "Dance with a Stranger" the actress playing the part of Ruth Ellis is shown going to the cinema to see her boyfriend in the Pathe Newsreel. "Blakeley never actually got to drive that year but the movie shows Gonzales in the Ferrari leading in the rain...and then Thompson crashing the Lagonda. It's an old movie but it usually surfaces on some channel around Christmas..."

Pat Mennem and the Le Mans crash in '55

The horror of the accident when Pierre Levegh's Mercedes-Benz 300SLR swerved to dodge a slower car, somersaulted over the safety bank in front of the grandstand at Le Mans in 1955 and exploded in the crowd, has been told time and again but seldom with the personal impact that Pat Mennem manages when he recounted his memories over lunch at the Barley Mow. The enormity of the death toll (81 were killed, hundreds injured) almost brought a stop to motor racing in Europe and yet within an hour after the carnage had been cleared, the spectators were shoulder to shoulder at the fence again.

Pat was the motoring writer for "The Daily Mirror" and he saw the crash from the Girling hospitality bar above the pits. "It was obviously a catastrophe of enormous proportions, so I dashed down the stairs and ran across the track." In today's sanitised safety climate, it seems inconceivable that he could get access to the track, let alone run across it in the middle of a race under crash conditions, but this was the accident that brought motor racing safety measures to world attention. There was no barrier to the pitlane which was merely a widening of the track at that point, with only a white line separating the combatants from the pitcrews.

Pat entered the chaos of the crash scene and saw a photographer taking a reel of film from his camera. "I approached him, and in my inexorable French, I asked if we could perhaps come to some arrangement to buy his film, promising that *The Daily Mirror* would be a generous customer. He stared at me in blank incomprehension which made me think my French was even worse than I had imagined, and it was only then that he realised I was actually English -- he was *Welsh*!

"It was difficult enough to make a telephone call to England from France at the best of times in those days and it was simply *impossible* to get a line out of the circuit after that accident so I took a taxi into Le Mans. I wanted to contact the Mirror's office in Paris and arrange for the film to be rushed over to Fleet Street.

"We stopped at my hotel to pack a bag and I spotted Charles Fothergill from the *News Chronicle* at the bar. 'Where are you going, Pat? Over already, is it? Come in and have a drink.' In normal circumstances I would have been seriously tempted but the circumstances were anything but normal. I told him that there had been a huge accident at the track and that he should get out there as soon as he could. 'Oh don't worry about it, Old Boy...the Sundays (Sunday newspapers) will kill the story!'"

Pat took a taxi to Paris but by the time he arrived, the office manager with the money to pay for the film courier and the taxi, had gone home. "This put me in a rather embarrassing position because now I had scarcely enough francs to pay for the taxi back to Le Mans. Our trip had taken so long that I felt I should offer to buy dinner for the driver. He seemed like a good chap and I thought he would probably have a sandwich and a glass of wine...but the wretched fellow started to eat his way down the menu! By the time we eventually got back to Le Mans, I was seriously short of funds and I had yet to start on my report of the race and the accident."

After all that effort, *The Daily Mirror* used only one photograph with Pat's report. "They said the photographs were so horrific that they only used one. Today they would have used them all..."

Chris Amon remembers his Fire on Mulsanne

It was Chris Amon's first year with Ferrari in 1967 and he was sharing an open P4 4.2-litre V12 with Nino Vacarella at Le Mans. It was an open car that Lorenzo Bandini and Chris had shared to win at Daytona; they had driven a closed P4 to win the 1000km at Monza. "I elected to use the open car at Le Mans because it was more comfortable – fortunately I did because it was easier to get out of!" Amon had won at Le Mans driving a Ford with Bruce McLaren the previous year and he was really keen to do well with Ferrari. Bandini had been killed in the Monaco Grand Prix a few weeks before and the team were anxious to take the game to Ford. Do it for Lorenzo. That was Amon's ambition as he went back to Le Mans.

"We were hanging in there in second or third and the other Ferrari of Parkes and Scarfiotti was in there somewhere as well", Amon recalls. He was 23 and Ferrari team leader. "We were about seven hours into the race, just before midnight, and I'd come past the pits going into Dunlop Corner when I felt a bit of a twitch at the rear. It was a puncture and by the time I got on to the Mulsanne Straight the tyre was really flat and I could hear all sorts of graunching noises which meant that the suspension upright and the rim were starting to run on the road so I had no choice but to stop and change the wheel."

He pulled off to one side of the long straight and opened the engine cover to get at the spare, a get-you-home space-saver that only just scraped inside the letter of the regulations. Amon laughs as he describes the on-car tool-kit. "There was a sort of jack, a torch and a wheel-hammer to knock the centre-lock spinner off. The first thing I discovered was that the batteries in the torch were flat but there were plenty of cars coming past with their headlights blazing so I had light on and off – occasional illumination at 200mph!

"I got the jack out and proceeded to crank it up. It actually worked in a fashion and the next step was to get the wheel hammer, wait for a blaze of light and take a shot at the centre-lock wheelnut. I swung at it and the head flew off the hammer, disappearing into the night and the trackside ditch, never to be seen again." Amon laughs again at the recollection of the comic-opera situation he seemed to find himself in so often with Ferrari.

"I was obviously going to have to drive it back to the pits somehow, so I packed the kit away, got back in, fired up and drove away relatively slowly down the straight – but I was probably still doing 100mph and the tyre was disintegrating, flapping wildly. There were sparks showering back from the suspension upright and I assume what eventually happened was that a fuel line was knocked off one of the pannier-type fuel tanks just in front of the rear wheels. The whole car just went *BOOOF!*

"I had been tooling down the right-hand side of the track anyway and I aimed it for the ditch. It was getting bloody warm by that stage, so I jumped out, thinking I was almost stopped but I was probably still doing 50mph and I ended up som-ersaulting along in the ditch while the car rolled another 100 metres down the road before it came to a stop not far from a marshal's post.

"The marshals could see the flames from the car that was now well alight and they came running. There were four marshals and three Gendarmes and they soon had the fire out and were searching for the driver – me! They were looking around in the ditch, wondering where I was and I remember walking up the ditch, feeling a bit battered, and tapping a Gendarme on the shoulder, saying 'Here I am.' Poor guy. He bloody near died of fright..."

Steve McQueen making Movies

I spent some time at Le Mans while the McQueen movie *Le Mans* was being made and at one stage we were sitting on the safety bank opposite the pits, laughing at a 'rain scene' being shot where a car makes a pit stop and the photographers had to be drenched with a hose before they went into shot, to preserve authenticity. Nigel Snowden was getting fed up with wet photographers and dry journalists so he suggested to the Director that we should also be involved. He agreed and told us to get prepared for a wetting. At this point I explained that it wouldn't look real – who had ever seen a journalist in the rain with his notebook? He accepted this and we continued to sit on the bank and laugh while Nigel and his colleagues got soaked.

Steve McQueen strove to achieve reality when he took his Hollywood team to the Sarthe to make his box office movie "Le Mans" in 1970 and his cameras had shot hundreds of thousands of feet of high-speed action before the story-line was ever finalised. The financiers were anxious for more spectacular action and to this end, crashes were carefully planned and staged by a special effects team. But as in the very essence of the word *accident*, not everything went according to plan. In the book of the making of the movie "A French Kiss with Death" by Michael Keyser with former Ferrari racer Jonathan Williams, an ageing Lola T70 IIIB was decked out as a Ferrari 512 to be sacrificed in a staged crash. It was nicknamed 'Lolari' on set.

A special effects crew headed by Englishman Malcolm Smith, rigged up small servo motors that allowed him to steer and work the accelerator of the Lola with remote radio controls. Smith sat in a chair with a small joystick and a set of pedals in front of him, and when he steered or accelerated, radio signals were transmitted to the servo motors in the Lola. Once the radio controls were mounted, the car was taken to Le Mans airport adjacent to the circuit where test runs were made on the service roads to make sure everything was operating properly.

'A short time prior to the stunt, the section of the track around Indianapolis (corner) where the accident was to take place was doused with water by a tanker truck. (Ferrari team) driver Mike Parkes, playing the German Ferrari driver Erich Stahler, performed a spin in one of the 512s. Then while his car sat sideways in the road, skid specialist Rob Slotemaker, came through the right-hander before Indianapolis in another 512 and "lost control", performing a series of fishtails which set up the actual crash sequence.

'Slotemaker's expertise behind the wheel can be appreciated by viewing this sequence from the film. He "threads the needle" with the 512, sliding it between the guardrail and Mike Parkes's Ferrari which is sitting stationary across the road. The scene is a realistic depiction of what might well have happened in such a situation.'

Now Hollywood was to take over. Never mind the real thing – let's see the plastic action!

'When all was ready, the engine in the 'Lolari' was fired up and ten cameras set to record at slow, medium and regular speed – in front, behind and to the sides – began to roll. Seated at the controls in top of a 15-foot scaffold, Malcolm King brought the engine to 4000rpm and released the clutch. All proceeded according to plan for the first fifty yards or so. Then the car suddenly went out of control. It veered to the left and spun and, horror of all horrors, began charging back up the track toward the tower on which Malcolm Smith sat. There were controls for the steering and accelerator, but none for the brakes.

'"I can't control it! I can't control it!" Smith shouted over the loudspeaker mounted on the scaffold. "Get out of the way! Run for it!"

Film folk who had gathered to watch the staged crash, scattered, jumping the guardrails and running for the trees. Poor Smith was trapped on the scaffolding tower where he was trying to bring the rogue racing car to a halt. To Smith's relief the Ferrari-clad Lola went berserk again. 'The car began fishtailing on the wet track, then lurched to the right and smashed into the guardrail. Thankfully the engine died on impact.'

Derek Bell was on hand to watch the daily footage viewing the following evening and he recalled the manic excitement of the stunt-that –got-away.

171

"You saw the car heading toward the sandbank, then abruptly shoot off to the right and out of frame. A moment later one of the film crew appears on-screen with a shocked expression on his face and his hand to his head, looking off-screen to where the car had disappeared. I'm sure the people paying the bills weren't pleased but it got a good laugh from everyone in the audience…"

The Aviating Mr Percy

We were at dinner during a splendid weekend of classic racing in Adelaide, South Australia, when Win Percy told the most amazing story I ever heard of survival at Le Mans. Winston (Win) Percy lives up to his nick-name. He had won the British Touring Car championship three times, won the Spa 24-hour race twice, won the Bathurst enduro in Australia, won seven 500km touring car races in one season (1985) driving a Rover 3.5 Vitesse for Tom Walkinshaw – but he had never won at Le Mans. His after-dinner story was about the 1987 24-hour race on the Sarthe circuit when he went flying. Literally. Percy is so laid back, talking in that soft West Country burr that suddenly you catch on to what he is talking about and your toes start to curl. "We were using Dunlop Kevlar tyres on the Jaguar XJR8 and there were worries about tyre case fracture so we tested a system of sensors to warn the driver of a tyre problem. What we hadn't allowed for was that the rubber 'marbles' that you pick up had sealed-off the sensors. I just assumed that it was me reacting to the car because it was starting to buck on me."

The Jaguars that year were running 240mph down into the kink on the Mulsanne Straight. Win's car was up in second place after nine hours. It was one o'clock in the morning. "All of a sudden there was a mighty explosion! The left tyre had let go. It had taken the rear bodywork and wing off so the motorcar had no downforce at all on the back end. It just took off like a leaf tossed in the wind. It just flew. It went up backwards and I thought 'Winston. . .you ain't controlling this at all so you might just as well take your feet off the pedals and your hands off the wheel and think about yourself. I brought my legs up, brought my arms in and hunched up. You basically swell your body up against the belts so that you don't flail around too much."

All this description and philosophising in the middle of one of the biggest accidents ever survived at Le Mans. "I did open my eyes – God knows why I'd closed them! – and I saw that I was above the trees in the night sky. I remember that clearly. And I remember thinking 'My God. . .this is going to hurt.'

Incredibly these aerobatics were taking place above the track itself. The car had taken off 300 metres before the kink and eventually came to rest 300 metres after it. It took two hours to repair the damage to the barriers.

"Luckily we were still above the track. Not *off* the track. The first impact was before the kink and went it came down it just crashed and it bashed. It put Armco through the rear air jack which was a *huge* piece of almost solid material but it put a piece of Armco through that like a knife through butter. I've got it at home in my trophy cabinet. The car went along on its side but each time it hit there was a stunning impact. I could sense that it was slowing down and then it was skating along on its side. My head was getting hot. Later I found out why. My helmet was wearing away on the tarmac. When it eventually stopped there were no doors. . .no glass. . .the suspension was gone. . .the wheels were gone but it stopped the right way up and amazingly pointing in the right direction which was quite amazing.

"I undid the belts. I said 'Thank You' and I got out of the car and started to walk away when I suddenly remembered the bollicking Tom Walkinshaw had given us for forgetting the radio aerial leads and snapping them when we got out of the cockpit. They were a quid each. Like an idiot I stopped and stood in the middle of the Mulsanne and this thing is sat on the floor a total wreck and I carefully *unplugged* the aerial. I'd just written-off a

173

million quid's worth of motorcar and I was saving a quid. . .

I got over the Armco and it's funny how the brain keeps working the way it does because although it was horrendously quick and it was a crazy accident to have walked away from with just a little black mark on one knee of my white overalls and no bruising whatsoever. . .I suddenly heard this funny language in the night. I know it's daft, but at the time I remember thinking 'God, I've died and gone to heaven and they don't speak English there! That's absolutely true. It was the Japanese crew from the Toyota team. One of them knew me from the days when we were winning the British Touring Car title in a Celica and they gave me a lift back to the pits.

"I'm fortunate to have been a works driver for most major manufacturers in the world and I've been very, very fortunate. *Very* fortunate. I had a few accidents, obviously. I think we worked it out that I'd had 18 accidents. Two of them I will confess were total driver stupidity but usually it was tyres or brakes or a mechanical problem because they were mostly endurance races."

Intrigue and Grappa at Maranello

I lunched with Enzo Ferrari under unusual circumstances when John Surtees asked me to accompany him when he went down to Maranello to tell Enzo that he was leaving the team. I recorded the trip in my *Auto News* column in July 1966 headed **They Talked About Everything but Racing.**

'There's something about the Grappa that they serve in the little café across the road from the Ferrari factory in Maranello. It tastes like boiled willow wood! But it was the liqueur finish to a lunch that had lasted two hours. On my right was Enzo Ferrari and on his right, John Surtees. Dragoni, the Ferrari team manager, was also there and so were two other Italians, one from Ferrari's office, the other a friend of John's.

The conversation centred around just about everything but motor racing. That side had been talked about before the lunch started, when Surtees and Ferrari laid their cards on the big bare table in the Commendatore's office, and came to the agreement that John would part company with the prancing horse team. But it was all very friendly.

Their discussion had been quiet and very much to the point, and Ferrari was anxious to assure John that they would still be the best of friends.

While the two men were discussing their problems, I had a wander through the racing shop where all the grimy cars had just arrived back from Le Mans in various states of disrepair. The Formula 1 cars were all stripped down, but it would appear that Ferrari might be in a whole pile of trouble that could feasibly call a halt to his racing programme. At the moment Italy is in the crippling grip of a metal worker's strike. You could have fired a cannon down the assembly line of Ferrari GTs and not hit a

175

soul. Apparently they are striking three days a week now.

On the way back to Milan airport, John pointed out the Bianchi works with the gates guarded by armed police. They didn't have any coppers outside the steel railings at Ferrari...but then they didn't have any workers inside, either.

Modena is a mysterious town that seems to breathe motor racing – and with Ferrari, Maserati and a bunch of the smaller manufacturers all grouped around, curiosity runs riot when a scene like the Surtees v. Dragoni affair blows up. Everyone connected with motor racing stays or drinks at the Reale-Fini or the Palace Hotel, and five minutes at either bar can usually gen you up on the latest developments.

Chances are that Luciano behind the bar at the Palace knows more about the current Ferrari affairs than Ferrari does! Like the young lady who let it slip a couple of days before Le Mans practice that Surtees wouldn't be driving.

The big Ferrari badge on the back of the bar in the Palace bar was covered up by a Cobra sticker on the Sunday night after Le Mans, but it was hastily removed before heads started to roll!

I'm sure all Modena knew when Surtees was due on the Ferrari doorstep and the whole place was holding its breath. It was like a big football match – there were those pro and those against. Even the national newspapers were joining in, some siding with Surtees (presumably at the risk of never again being invited to Maranello) and some siding with the Scuderia.

What do I think about the breaking up of an anything but happy Ferrari home? The story is long and involved. Like Surtees being signalled to stay behind Bandini at Monaco last year; being refused the 2.4-litre car at Monaco this year; being refused permission to races in the 1000km at Monza by the Italian circuit doctor because he was unfit, not fully recovered from his Mosport CanAm injuries, but then having that opinion quashed when a specialist was called in by Surtees' lawyer. And finally the deal at Le Mans where Dragoni changed his mind overnight and went back on his word about the substitution of Scarfiotti as reserve driver in the Surtees/Parkes car, and his subsequent refusal to discuss the matter. I can't see that Surtees had any option but to see the boss and collect his cards...'

* * *

It may have been Franco Gozzi who was the Ferrari man who joined us at that final lunch and I am pretty sure that it was Gozzi who steered me around the silent factory while John and Enzo were agreeing to disagree. Franco speaks good English and when his plan to produce a final book (*Pilote Che Gente*) by Enzo lavishly illustrated with Ferrari art and images seemed to be stalling, he phoned me in England asking if I could provide any artwork. I knew that he was seeking artwork with a Ferrari link, but my offerings to Ferrari's sales office in the UK had been returned as unsuitable. After a long conversation on the phone we agreed that I would gather as many images as I could, including programme and magazine covers, paintings, cartoons, photographs – literally anything with a Ferrari or a Prancing Horse on it. Transparencies of the originals would be fine. It was understood that the purchase of the originals would be financially prohibitive but the copyright of the trannies would be covered by a swap for some early original Ferrari sales literature and the racing annuals.

I arranged about 125 transparencies and arranged to take them to Gozzi in Maranello on the way to the Grand Prix in Imola. The word had got around that I was doing a deal with Ferrari and the general consensus was that I would *never* leave Ferrari with either the swaps *or* the trannies.

Franco started looking through the transparencies and he was delighted. They were superb. They were *exactly* what he wanted. I was starting to get nervous. He was a little too grateful for my liking so I asked where his trades were, the yearbooks and the sales catalogues? Two secretaries, at this very moment, were going through the office in Mr Ferrari's old apartment seeking the items I had asked for. So when would they be back? Oh...to-morrow...next week... It was *not* looking good. Why didn't I come and meet Mr Ferrari? It was getting worse. I'd met Mr Ferrari before. I was more interested in not leaving Maranello empty handed. I left Maranello empty handed. I couldn't believe it. I'd been shafted. Shafted with smooth eloquence, certainly, but shafted nevertheless.

The arrangement was that Franco would bring the 'swaps' to Imola and we would arrange the handover during the weekend. I saw him on Friday in the pitlane and he said he was busy. I saw him on Saturday in the pitlane and he said he had 'an envelope' for me but it was late before he would be ready for me. I said I could wait. He had to pass the Elf hospitality motorhome on his way to the car-park so he would call there on his way out. Time fugited. It was gone 6pm when he finally appeared and said he would go immediately to his car and get my 'parcel'. I supposed it bode well that it had grown from an envelope to a parcel but I decided that I wouldn't risk him changing his mind and motoring straight home when he got to his car. We walked to the car park together. I was not at all comfortable. Then he opened the boot of his Fiat and there was a big carton with my name on it. Franco apologised about the delay and thanked me again for the quality of the transparencies. Then he drove away and left me in the Imola car park with a carton that I could barely lift.

I was sharing a room with Maurice Hamilton and he entertained our gang the next morning, recounting the way I had un-packed the contents of the carton on my bed, wide-eyed with each new item better than the one before. It was a veritable treasure trove of old sales catalogues that had never left the factory, stored long after the cars to which they referred had been superseded by new models. New old stock. There were

Sir Stirling Moss, Sir Jackie Stewart and Sir Jack Brabham.

Denny Hulme, Norah and Ken Tyrrell at Monaco.

Sir Jackie Stewart in his study, talking about the deal he did with Enzo Ferrari.

Lord March with the AC styled by his grandfather, after lunch at the Barley Mow.
L. to. R: Ken Tyrrell, John Cooper, Stirling Moss and John Surtees.

Cosworth designer, Keith Duckworth on his Yamaha GTS in 1995.

John Coombs with Stirling Moss at Monaco.

Ken Tyrrell with a 1952 Brands Hatch programme that lists him in his Cooper 500 in one of the races.

F1 paddock chat: Nigel Roebuck, Denis Jenkinson and Maurice Hamilton.

Eoin's partner, photographer
Gail Barwood in New Zealand.

Piers Courage in a Hispano Suiza.

Eoin Young with Citroen 2CV in New Zealand.

Eoin Young with Bruce McLaren at Monaco in 1966. (*Ferret Fotographics*)

The Bolster spirit lived at Prescott – Robin Harcourt-Smith's twin-engined Hornet special.

Eoin Young with the 1955 Mercedes 190SLR after the Austrian Alpenfahrt Classic rally in 2003.

The works Hawkins/Makinen Austin Healey 3000 in the Targa Florio pitlane in 1965. Eoin Young went for his UK driving test (unsuccessfully!) in this car.

John Andon, owner of the famed Barley Mow pub, with the Cobra he races in classic events, now with the provisional 'X' removed.

Gordon Murray and Ken Tyrrell at the Barley Mow before lunch. (*Peter Renn*).

Tony Brooks and Eoin Young at the Barley Mow pre-lunch. (*Peter Renn*)

Barley Mow lunch line-up with Gordon Murray's pink Thunderbird. Eoin Young, Eric Thompson, Dave Price, Gordon Murray, Tony Brooks and Ken Tyrrell. (*Peter Renn*)

Eoin Young and Jackie Stewart 'singing in the rain' after his win at Monaco in 1966. (*Peter Renn*)

Eoin Young with Lord March at Goodwood. (*Peter Renn*)

Eoin Young with the Peugeot 206 CC convertible coupe with the complicated front and rear opening boot lid. (*Peter Renn*)

Ted Walker and his autojumble offerings at Beaulieu.

Panoramic 1955 Monaco Grand Prix start photo over the fireplace at Englands House. (*Peter Renn*)

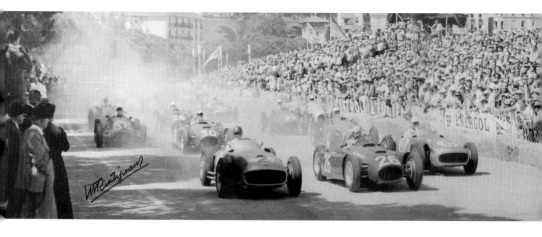

Eoin Young at Beaulieu with half of the Alfa Romeo 8C/35 Grand Prix inlet manifold on Ted Walker's stand.
(*Peter Renn*)

Eoin Young in action with Rob Walker's Delahaye at Ards for the 50th anniversary of the Tourist Trophy.
(*Peter Renn*)

Eoin Young and Franco Gozzi watch as Enzo Ferrari signs a copy of his memoirs at Maranello. (*Peter Renn*)

Jenks and I cresting the Test Hill at Brooklands in Rob Walker's Delahaye 135S

Eoin Young and Wally Willmott, Bruce McLaren's first Team employees, sharing a joke with Sir Jackie Stewart. (*Gail Barwood*)

Sharknose factory Ferraris smoking off the front row of the French Grand Prix grid in 1961 when rookie Giancarlo Baghetti scored a surprise win. (*Ferret Fotographics*)

Le Mans winner, Duncan Hamilton having dismissed the motorcycle traffic cop who had just chased me back to the showroom in the D-Type. (*Ferret Fotographics*)

A works DB2 Aston Martin at Le Mans for the first time when Eric Thompson and I took the gallant old charger back to the Sarthe for a retrospective run. (*Ferret Fotographics*)

Steve McQueen at Le Mans with Porsche team manager, Rico Steineman. (*Eoin Young*)

Paul Newman and Graham Hill. I had travelled 30 odd floors vertically in a Detroit hotel elevator with the movie star, desperately trying to stumble through conversation.

Harvey Postlethwaite in his clubmans racing days in a U2. (*Ferret Fotographics*)

pristine race programmes, team photographs, signed driver post-cards never sent after the driver had left the team, but never trashed. And a number of those oh-so-collectable Ferrari Year-books, the thick softbacks sent to customers and friends at the end of each season, packed with photographs of the races that season and the latest new Ferrari racing and road cars. Christmas arrived early that year.

* * *

Dr Gozzi featured again in another Ferrari happening when I bought a copy of the English edition of Ferrari's first auto-biography *My Terrible Joys* in an absolutely mint dustwrapper. I had been invited to a Ferrari press conference and I asked Gozzi if it would be possible to get my book signed by the Old Man. He said it would be absolutely no problem. I was in the body of the hall with journalists from all over Europe when Gozzi appeared on the stage and the conversation died. He said that Mr Ferrari would soon be arriving to address us, but he was in advanced years and his eyesight was failing and there would be no flash photographer allowed...and no autographs after the conference.

So much for my signature. Why had I bothered? Shafted again. With the press conference completed I caught up with Franco behind the stage and asked what the situation was with getting my book signed? No problem at all. I gave him the book and he took it up to Mr Ferrari who was still sitting at the table on the stage talking to journalists. Still marginally suspicious I climbed on to the stage too and watched over Enzo's shoulder as he carefully signed my book.

I was almost embarrassed at questioning Gozzi's promise and thanked him profusely. A few weeks later a photograph arrived, taken from the floor of the hall while the Old Man was signing my book and there I was, watching over his shoulder. In for a penny, in for a pound, I mailed the photograph to Franco and asked if he would get Enzo to sign the photograph and now I have a handsomely framed, signed photograph of Enzo Ferrari signing my copy of his autobiography.

Golden Oldies Race Again at Monaco

Martin Stretton stamped his command on the Monaco Historic weekend in 2002, winning in a C-Type high-tailed Connaught and the six-wheeled P34 Tyrrell that Patrick Depailler had driven to third place in the 'real' Grand Prix at Monaco in 1976. Frank Sytner won the pre-1966 race in a Brabham BT4 painted in the correct teal-green/blue from Thomas Bsher in a BRM P261.

There were golden oldies everywhere, cars as well as drivers. Phil Hill, 1961 World Champion for Ferrari, was elected President of the Ancien Pilotes Association, celebrating their 40th anniversary over the weekend, but was miffed when he was refused permission to race the shapely GT Alfa Romeo 6CM 3000 that Fangio had driven to second place in the 1953 Mille Miglia with a broken steering arm. A clutch problem in practice meant that Phil hadn't qualified but his team requested that he start from the back of the grid. Drivers and stewards all agreed that this was OK but Race Director, Jacky Ickx, vetoed the move, saying Phil was too old and if anything happened to him in the race, the organisers would be held responsible. Phil was allowed a disgruntled parade lap instead.

Maria Teresa de Filippis, who raced a 250F Maserati in the 1950s, is still Vice President and the prime mover behind the club, but she missed the anniversary meeting because she was recuperating from an operation.

It was like a Ferrari Old Boy's Club with Phil Hill, Dan Gurney, Cliff Allison and Tony Brooks together again and remembering their days in Enzo's scuderia.

I watched one race with Tony Gaze, 82, seven floors above the grid on the balcony of Roy Salvadori's apartment and he

181

wondered why Julian Bronson had painted his winning ERA green when he had watched Johnny Wakefield winning the 200 miles race at Brooklands in 1938 and the same car was blue. "Johnny stipulated blue when he bought the car new from ERA. The only thing blue on it now is the steering wheel centre..."

Everything about the weekend was larger than life including the wealthy Clark Gable clones with silver hair and moustaches to match the period of their Ferrari sports-racers. Bruce McCaw from Seattle was racing his BRM and a 450S Maserati and staying in some luxury on his brother's 360-foot boat which dominated the harbour. It had a 70-foot sloop as a tender, as well as a 50-foot powerboat. Indoors, visitors reported seven (count 'em!) working fireplaces, a pizza oven and a glass panel 18-inches thick in the hull to watch denizens of the deep. A landing craft that could have placed a Ranger Rover on the beach if necessary was also available.

There was a classic feel to the event with special touches like being able to reserve a lunch table by the paddock fence in the Stars & Bars restaurant and be serenaded by Chris Amon's Grand Prix Matra V12 being warmed up. There was a round of applause when it ended! I wasn't sure whether that was because of the quality of the wailing exhaust note...or the fact that it had stopped and we could get on with conversation around the lip of a glass of something red.

Kiwi Howden Ganley watched Flavien Marcais put his old BRM on pole, but a fuel pump drive belt broke after he had led the opening lap.

The Ancien Pilotes celebrated their club's 40th anniversary with a lunch at Mike Sparken's splendid home at Cap Ferrat. We went out by train with Cliff Allison and when we paused at the Eze-sur-Mer station, Cliff remembered driving the works Lotus F1 cars from their garage workshops there, to and from the track in Monaco. "That was great fun – you couldn't do it these days! We used to stay at a hotel called La Bananerie."

Belgian drivers Paul Frere and Jacques Swaters were sharing

memories of their first race together in a 1935 MG PB in the 1948 24-hour race at Spa. "It was 24 hours of fog and rain and we finished fourth," said Frere, the motoring journalist who had won at Le Mans for Ferrari in 1960. "The car was so slow up the hill from Eau Rouge that I could lean across and light a cigarette!" said Swaters. "It finished the race using more oil than petrol..." He laughed at the memory.

Jean Guichet and Nino Vacarella were remembering their Le Mans win in 1964. Giannino Marzotto, winner of the Mille Miglia in 1950 and 1953, wearing a collar and tie at the wheel of his Ferrari was also at the lunch, chatting with Gordini driver, Robert Manzon, now 85, and Maurice Trintignant, winner at Monaco in 1955 for Ferrari and in 1958 driving a Cooper for Rob Walker.

Sir Stirling Moss, 72, raced a Le Mans Replica Frazer Nash, similar to the car he drove to win the small-car section of the Monaco Grand Prix in 1952 when the race was run for sports cars. "It was misfiring all weekend. Too rich, I think."

I had brought along the copy of "Autosport" with a cover photograph of Bruce McLaren winning at Monaco in a Cooper in 1962. Phil Hill was looking over my shoulder and I mentioned that he had finished five seconds behind Bruce in second place. "It wasn't FIVE seconds...it was one point four!" he said with the emphasis of a crystal memory back over 40 years. When he double-checked the result he noted with some satisfaction that it was actually 1.3sec... That was the first Grand Prix I went to as the first McLaren employee and I was vastly impressed at the fact that my new boss had won the race.

Modern rookie F1 drivers Alex Yoong and Takuma Sato were driving a Lotus 72 and a Lotus 49 respectively to get some miles on a track they had never raced at, ahead of the 'real' Grand Prix the following weekend. Sato trashed the wingless Lotus 49 (the car Graham Hill had driven to win at Monaco in 1968 and 1969) in wet practice but Yoong was leading in the Lotus 72 in the main event when the appearance of a safety car coincided with his loss of all gears but top and he lost the race to Stretton in the Tyrrell six-wheeler. The safety car had picked up Yoong, but he said that with only fifth speed left, if the safety car had increased speed, he would have been unable to keep up!

It looked as though the mix of fragile old cars, the unforgiving street circuit and inexperienced, older (usually) wealthy (usually) drivers could be potentially dangerous but in fact there was only one injury. Julian Majub crashed out in his Bugatti while tilting for the lead and suffered a facial slash that needed nine stitches inside his mouth – but he was back in time for the black tie dinner that night!

The event was a time warp. All your heroes were there. At Nice airport on the way home, I had to point out to Stirling Moss that perhaps we should leave the toilet cubicle we were both in. I hasten to add that Stirling insisted on showing me the press-button controls for (a) lowering the seat and (b) working the flush. Phil Hill had replaced Toulo de Graffenried as President of what Dan Gurney called The Old Fart's Club. "The funny thing is that Toulo won the first Formula 1 race I ever saw. It was Goodwood on Easter Monday in 1949 or 1950 and he was driving a Maserati. And now I've taken over from him as President. An honour? Of course it is. . ."

The American old-car F1 people are encouraged to run in original livery, down to the old sponsor decals, driver names and helmet colours, thus we had John Dimmer with a tartan line to his helmet as Jackie

Stewart and John Delane as Francois Cevert. It was the first time both had driven at Monaco. Delane: "Our two Tyrrells were together on the last occasion at Monaco thirty years and five days ago. Cevert's 002 had more cockpit room for his long legs and Jackie had problems with his 003 regular car, so he raced the spare 004 that John is driving."

Gerhard Berger, former Ferrari driver and now BMW racing boss, visited the paddock on Saturday and said that he had absolutely no interest in racing again. . .but the idea of getting into one of these cars from his past had a certain appeal. He suggested a series of match races between Rosberg, Piquet, Mansell and himself in their original cars!

Neil Oatley, McLaren design engineer and soon to be made a director of the company, was visiting the historic Monaco races for the first time (this was the third staging of the event held every two years). "I'm among the cars of my youth," he said wistfully. Modern Formula 1 people are not encouraged to think about the past. Eamon ('Chalky') Fullalove was a former McLaren racing mechanic rather surprisingly visiting Monaco for the first time – for the past 40 years he has been at Indianapolis during the full month of May. In most paddock bays there were faces from the past as older Formula 1 mechanics were looking after their original steeds for modern owners.

A very good time was had by all.

The Total Enthusiasm of Dr Harvey Postlethwaite

To wonder why Harvey Postlethwaite didn't take his handsome share of the funds and retire when Ken Tyrrell sold his team to British American Racing, is to totally miss the point. It was a measure of Harvey's enthusiasm that he not only stayed on, but launched himself hugely into the Honda project. Mike Gascoyne acknowledges the enormous career boost he had working with Harvey at Tyrrell and Sauber and back at Tyrrell again, and he says "For Harvey it wasn't about having more money than the rest. It was all about trying to prove that motor racing was an intellectual exercise, it was about his love of engineering and his clever innovative solutions."

I always felt that Harvey became more Italian than the Ferrari mechanics during his two stints at Maranello. He liked a glass of red wine. He liked life. He could be serious and he could be angry but when he launched into a favourite story, he had an instant audience. He liked his classic Lusso and Daytona Ferrari road cars and the only outward sign of his profit from the sale of the Tyrrell team in which he had become a partner, was the purchase of a splendid red Maranello 550. He would wheel his new Ferrari into the car park at the Meridiana Italian restaurant in East Horsley and enjoy a burst of fluent Italian with owner Tony Orlando while he sipped a quick cappuccino before driving to a meeting.

The Meridiana is gone now and so is Harvey, who died in 1999.

He embraced Maranello and all things Ferrari, learning the language so that he could communicate his stream of ideas to the people he worked with. I remember him saying how one of

186

the older bodyworkers had been sitting at home one evening with his wife, watching Harvey being interviewed on television. "Listen to him," said the wife. "He speaks better Italian than you do..."

Racing with Ferrari and legends in the making like Gilles Villeneuve was what racing was all about before computers arrived. The drivers were the important component of the team then, not the designer or the ranks of computer-gazers who know high-tech but don't know much about racing. There was Harvey's story of leaving a restaurant in Modena with Villeneuve at the wheel of a 308 Ferrari. "There were 20 or 30 people waiting outside for him, as always. He had his 308 in the car park and as we climbed in, it was drizzling. He hauled it on to full lock, floored the throttle, wound the starter, the engine fired and went straight up almost to the limiter, lit the rear wheels up and spun three or four times without the front wheels moving. Then he flicked the steering straight and went off like a bullet with the wheels still spinning, up the ramp and out of the car park with the crowd applauding.

"He turned left into the traffic without worrying whether there was a gap and went straight down the outside of the traffic to Maranello, straight at anything that was oncoming, nipping into a gap and straight out again, talking the whole time." Harvey is re-living the escapade, accentuating every move Villeneuve made, laughing so much he can hardly continue. "There was a guy wearing a porkpie hat coming towards us on one of those Vespas with a tall windscreen, and turned left in front of us. Gilles, still talking, just did a big cadence brake, put it sideways to the right, put it sideways to the left and flicked it past the scooter. I don't think the guy on the scooter ever knew how close he'd come to an accident; any other driver would have killed him. As we were sliding towards him I remember thinking: 'My Italian isn't good enough to explain this to the police." Harvey lived for the moment.

He worked with Ferrari from 1980 to 1988. "Ferrari was a *super* team in the '80s when the Old Man was in charge. It was a *team*. Maybe I'm an old traditionalist, but motor racing to me is a *team* operation." When he went back to Maranello again it had all changed. "Ferrari without the Old Man simply wasn't Ferrari." And he was back to put his all into revitalising the Tyrrell team.

Bubbles Horsley, manager of the youthful Lord Hesketh's outrageous Formula 1 team in the 1970s, all champagne, Rolls-Royces and James Hunt, recounts how they went to March Engineering and came away with a car, a designer and a chief mechanic. "We went to hire a car, to do the deal with Max, and we left with the March, Harvey, and Nigel Stroud. To get Harvey we took him to the Carlton Tower, sat him down and forced alcohol down him until he said Yes. Which he duly did. It was fun with Harvey. He had a great sense of humour. He could be very mischievous but in a *nice* way. I have to say, though, that if you went back to 1973 and saw a photo of the four of us and wondered who would shuffle of this mortal coil first, you'd have to have put the Lord and myself in front of the Doc and James..."

Postlethwaite groomed Gascoyne, spiriting him away from Tyrrell when he left for what he thought was a back-door 'in' to a Mercedes Formula 1 project via Sauber but it didn't work out and Harvey was on the move again to Ferrari. But not before he had installed Gascoyne at Sauber. "He'd been gone from Tyrrell a month and I got the old secret telephone call. Come and meet him at a pub in Reading and next thing I was head of aerodynamics at Sauber. He didn't help much on aerodynamics but it was vintage Harvey when I was laying out this wind tunnel model and he walked in. He asked if the seat was going to be like that, what would the fuel volume be, and I suddenly realised that I was laying out the car, not just a wind tunnel model..."

Two years at Ferrari and Harvey was back at Tyrrell. "He wanted me to come back too, but as his technical deputy and that was a huge advance for me. I used to describe our relationship as one where he didn't want to run the hundred metres any more, he needed a younger guy to do it, but he'd be there to tap you on the shoulder and make sure you stayed in lane. He was a great innovator and a teacher. Things like the high nose and the fancy aerodynamics as Tyrrell – he wasn't the one who did them but he fostered the innovative environment where you had ideas. He was into good engineering. That's why all those who worked with him really enjoyed it."

Harvey was absorbed in all aspects of engineering. Journalist Denis Jenkinson arrived at Long beach after the long flight from London, saying how he had spent the whole trip sitting beside Harvey and working on the design of the ultimate motorcycle. "The only problem," said Jenks "was that it wouldn't work unless it had four wheels..."

If Gascoyne saw himself as Postlethwaite's younger shadow, Ken Tyrrell thought the same way, seeing Harvey as himself 20 years younger. Harvey even spoke like Ken, *emphasising* words in case you weren't paying sufficient attention. He felt the same way about racing. He lived it and *loved* it. "My hair stands on end at the start of a race. I get goosebumps. I love the tactics of a race. Ken does too."

Harvey had a way with words. When I asked him over lunch which driver had been his favourite, he thought a while and then said "Dull would he be of soul who could pass by a sight so touching in his majesty as Gilles Villeneuve." He laughed loudly at the memories. That was Harvey: a marvellous mix of the academic, a gifted engineer and one of motor racing's real characters. Sadly, we are running out of them.

The Ultimate Bangers & Mash Lunch
at the Barley Mow

It was one of those perfect motor racing lunches at the Barley Mow, my favourite pub, in July 2001 when everything gelled. Ken Tyrrell was there, weak now from prolonged chemotherapy treatment for cancer, Tony Brooks still looking more like a dentist than the driver Sir Stirling Moss says he would include in his all-time Grand Prix team, Gordon Murray, the laid-back free-thinking free-wheeler who has designed some of the most exciting cars of all time for road and track, Dave Price who helped put the Panoz team together for Le Mans, Eric Thompson, who raced works Aston Martins and Lagondas at Le Mans in the 'fifties and now a dealer in rare motor racing books and Rob Widdows, PR man for the mercurial Lord March who has re-created Goodwood as a motor racing Mecca. In fact it was Ken Tyrrell's last appearance in public before his untimely death and he was on great form.

The Barley Mow is one of those unique British institutions, a traditional village pub. When I wrote the first volume of my autobiography in 1996, I made what I reckoned to be a considered observation: "Bricks and mortar don't make a pub. People make a pub. That quirky mix of personalities and prejudice, friendships and feuds, gossip and intrigue, together with the smell of beer and smoke that blends in the curious ambience of an English country pub, is found nowhere else in the world. The Barley Mow in West Horsley, Surrey, is like no other English pub in England, never mind the world..." The low-beamed pub dates from the 1500s and the traditional Bangers & Mash features high on the pub food menu.

There was a *pink* 1950s Ford Thunderbird in the car park as we wheeled in. It *had* to be one of my lunch guests and if I'd given it a moment's thought it had to be Gordon Murray's. He was sitting outside at a table in the sunshine in a patterned Hawaiian shirt, long-haired and relaxed, halfway through a pint. Hardly the image of modern charcoal-grey McLaren Man. "I've *always* wanted a Thunderbird but only three were any good – 1955, 1956 or 1957 – and it *had* to be pink or turquoise with white trim and the big engine…and no power-assisted any-thing." This from the South African who came up with the centre-seat F1 McLaren road car and now head of the project designing and building the new Mercedes SLR – the first car Mercedes ever allowed to be created outside their factory in Germany.

"We were in California racing the GT McLaren and I had a call from a dealer who said an old boy out at Pebble Beach was selling off a collection that included a T-Bird and he would bring it over to show me. I waited and waited at the motel but practice was about to start and I was driving out when this pink Thunderbird drove in. It was as though I'd written the spec myself. It was ideal. I asked him how much he wanted for it, he told me and I said I'd take it. He said 'Don't you want to drive it?' and I told him it would be just fine. I shipped it straight back to England!

"Touch wood, the T-Bird is fairly bullet-proof. It's so simple. With a distributor and carburettor you can't go wrong. The total count on the wiring loom from the dashboard through the grommet into the engine bay is just *six* wires. The wiring harness on the new Mercedes SLR McLaren is 190 pounds of wire – something like five or six *kilometres* of wire."

Murray is immersed in cars and racing and pop music. It's said that he sits in a darkened room on the anniversary of John Lennon's death and I find this easy to believe. He was born in South Africa and he designed and made his own sports car to race. And engine. "I designed my own engine when I was 19. It was based on a 105E Anglia block and crank but with my own pistons, gudgeon pins, those sort of things."

Dave Price interrupted "But Gordon, you could *buy* those bits then."

"Not on my money, you couldn't," Murray shot back and the table laughed. "Two hundred quid, that car cost me. In total. It was front-mid engined..."

"A bit like the Panoz then?" asked Price.

"Sort of. The flywheel was beside my hip because the engine was so far back in the chassis for weight distribution. I sent across to England for all the books on Cosworth, Holbay and How to Design Your Own Camshaft. They all said not to reduce the weight of the standard 105E flywheel which weighed 15 pounds, below 10 pounds because it was a grey cast-iron flywheel and it would explode at 8000rpm. I'd got mine down to *seven* pounds by machining it at work, getting it down, getting it down, getting it down. And I had 18-gauge aluminium between me and it and I kept thinking about this..." More laughter around the table. "Every time I got on the straight I kept thinking about this flywheel an inch from my hipbone doing eight grand and about to explode like a grenade. But it never did. I did burst my elbow though. Most of my shunts were caused by my welding breaking on the chassis. I learned to weld on that car and learned the hard way from my mistakes. I had a short prop shaft and the welding broke on the rear UJ and the prop-shaft came through the tunnel like a windmill in the middle of the straight and smashed my elbow."

Price brought the prop-shaft story up to date saying they had carbon fibre prop-shafts on the Panoz, replacing the earlier aluminium shafts, which had a tendency to bend under torque. "We had one come through the floor. Now the carbon ones just go to dust..."

"And I suppose they cost £100,000 each?" asked Goodwood PR man Widdows. "No. They cost eight grand each," replied Price, as if that made them a bargain.

The table had firm opinions about the Le Mans 24-hour race the previous weekend. "Bentley? Bentley!" spluttered Price. "The green Audi, d'you mean? And the thing is they put it in a Toyota chassis as well. That's all it was." Ken Tyrrell agreed. "It's all bullshit, isn't it? It's got nothing to do with Bentley, that car." Murray agreed. "I'm old-fashioned but I'd like Le Mans to go back to cars that people can recognise as an MG or a Bentley. Or a car that you actually buy a version of, for yourself. It's been pushed too far down the order since we won with the McLaren. If a Corvette wins its class, big deal. Publicity-wise it's nowhere. Bentley and MG – what do those cars have to do with their manufacturers?"

Tony Brooks raced at Le Mans with Aston Martin in the 1950s but when he signed with Ferrari, he had the 24-hour race specifically excluded from his contract. "To me, Le Mans was a high-speed tour, it wasn't a motor race. If you went round Le Mans at a competitive speed, your car wouldn't last and driving around for 24 hours at 15sec a lap slower than you and your car were capable of was an absolute bore. And there was a tremendous speed differential in those days. You could be passing an Austin Healey on the straight with a speed difference of 70-80mph. In the early morning mist and rain it could be quite difficult trying to overtake cars because you'd be on them before you could see their red tail-lights."

Eric Thompson gathered the table's attention with his description of Le Mans in 1954 when he was racing a bloated version of the DB3S Aston Martin fitted with a 4.5-litre V12 Lagonda engine that David Brown hope would match the Ferraris. "It was an absolute pig to drive. It understeered horribly but it was very fast down the straights, I'll give it that. I'd passed Peter Collins on the 6th lap and the Parnell/Salvadori supercharged DB3S on the 15th. I was on the tail of a Talbot going down into the Esses and thinking about how and where I'd pass him rather than what I was actually doing and I got on the white line and spun. It went backwards into the wattle fence on the inside and bounced across the track into the bank on the outside of the circuit, pointing the wrong way.

193

"I had a hammer for the wheel hub spinner and a sort of mini hacksaw and I was banging and cutting away at the bodywork that was graunched on to the tyre. This meant I was standing on the circuit at the apex of the left-hander and every time Duncan Hamilton came through in the leading D-Type, he swerved closer and closer to me, blasting the horn! Which was more than a little disconcerting at the time but he thought it was enormously funny. To make the situation even more embarrassing, a Gendarme on the safety banking was telling me I was wanted on a field telephone. It was our team manager, John Wyer! Somehow he had found the number of the telephone at the flag marshal's post and I was in a lather trying to explain to him what I'd done to the chairman's favourite Lagonda!

"I eventually got the car back to the pits and got the Death-Ray treatment from Wyer but they decided to withdraw it because the rear lights were damaged, but I think it was because the chassis was bent. Years later I had a letter from the chap who had been chief mechanic at Le Mans that year. He said 'I don't know why you looked so worried when you got back to the pits in '54. You'd only written off the Chairman's dream car!' He also told me that it was his private conviction that all the oil in France wouldn't have got the big V12 to the end of the race..."

The talk switched to favourite cars. Murray again: "I've got a 12-month rule with my cars. If a year goes by and I haven't used one of the cars, I sell it. My 1968 Lotus Elan came desperately close last year. I did only 150 miles in it because it just will not start. I used to have an Elan thirty years ago, they didn't start then...and they *still* don't start." More table laughter. "But it's the best sports car I've ever driven. On a good day on an A-road with a couple of roundabouts, you can forgive it all it's problems because it's such a beautifully balanced car."

Then they were talking about fuel mileage in Formula 1. "That first Alfa Romeo engine we had at Brabham in 1976 did *half* the fuel mileage of the Cosworth DFV, for just an extra 20 horsepower. We would *never* have finished a race on fuel, but I never told the drivers because I didn't want to de-motivate them.

"Nelson (Piquet) got injured in the big shunt in Argentina when Jody Scheckter went off in the opening lap, hit the barrier and bounced back in to the track and there was a huge cloud of dust covering the circuit. It was a fifth gear right-left with an awesome 180-degree corner at the end which was basically flat. He said to me afterwards that the circuit was just a dust cloud and at first he thought he would lift or brake, but it was his first race with the team and he thought he could come out the other side in the lead because he'd started well back. He didn't. Scheckter had come back on to the circuit and stopped and Nelson went into him at 150mph. We got to the crash scene and Nelson was still trapped in the car with his knees up by his ears. And all he'd done was dislocate his toe but he said it hurt like hell. The car just folded. It was just the fuel tank and 18-inches of cockpit. That was it. We gave him the monocoque when we got back to the factory.

"We had a new car for Nelson going to the next round, his home race in Brazil, but he said he didn't think he could last the race from the pain of his foot. So to make it look good, we put in ten gallons and I think he went from last to third pla-ce...and then stopped in the pits."

The following weekend, the famous Brabham 'fan car' designed by Murray and driven by Niki Lauda to win the Swedish Grand Prix in 1978, was to be demonstrated at the Goodwood Festival of Speed.

Murray shook his head in disbelief at the situation in Formula 1 when he designed the car with a fan to create downforce. "It'll be good to see it running again. I can't believe I chopped up one of those. We made three. We didn't quite finish the third car so we took it to Sweden in parts to use as spares, but it meant we didn't have a T-car. We had no yard at Brabham in those days, no space for storage. I was so pissed off with Bernie for withdrawing the car that when the mechanics asked what to do with it, I told them to chop it up. Which they did."

195

Tyrrell raised a laugh when he said "Now Bernie's got plenty of space!" referring to Ecclestone's ownership of the Biggin Hill war-time fighter airfield and all its hangars where his fabulous collection of old racing cars are stored. Michael Schumacher had tried a 1951 Tipo 375GP 4.5-litre Ferrari before the Grand Prix at Silverstone, similar to the car Froilan Gonzales drove to win Ferrari's first Grand Prix at Silverstone half a century earlier. It was from Ecclestone's collection, as was the pre-war Grand Prix Mercedes John Surtees drove at Goodwood.

I asked whether it was true that the fan car was banned because it threw rocks at following cars. "That's all bullshit," said Murray, still smarting after all these years. "For a start it was a radial fan so if it did anything it was going to be tangential, not rearwards and the fan e-flux was geared down. When the engine was doing 12,000rpm the fan was doing 7,900rpm and the e-flux was only 55mph so if the car was going down the straight at 150mph, the e-flux was 100mph slower than the car speed. So it wasn't going to thrown anything out the back. You would see a lot of dust coming out but it did *not* throw stones."

I wondered how much downforce the fan-car generated compared to other cars.

"It wasn't a lot more than a good wing car. Only about a ton, if I remember correctly. But you could generate a ton in first gear, that was the difference. We could do – and *did* – a 2G start. I was terrified about the drive-shafts and the CV joints. I remember standing behind Lauda at the Balocco test track in Italy. I'd told him that we had to do loads of starts because I was worried about the drive-shafts. When you dropped the clutch, the car had something like three times its own weight already, so there was no wheelspin. The tyres just went *CHIRP!* And you were doing 40mph instantly. There wasn't any lag with the big tyres. We never did break a drive-shaft. It was like a cartoon, standing behind the car with the engine doing 10-11,000rpm. It just *went!* It went from three feet in front of you to a dot in the distance in about a fifth of a second!"

Murray explained that the suction from the fan demanded a totally different approach from the driver. "You had to brake and then accelerate into the corner as fast as you could go and the higher you got the revs, the quicker you went round the corner. Niki said it really took a while to get your head round it. At Paddock Bend at Brands Hatch you could have a confidence lift and then 100 yards before the corner you floored the throttle and you could go round the corner *flat*. You had to have confidence to do it and you had to have the revs high. If you were in a gear too high, it wouldn't go round the corner. It was down to drivers, really. Most of them are fairly thick – they've got loads of natural ability, these guys, but trying to think about the mechanicals and the gearbox and tyres and *then* say to yourself 'Well, I can go quicker if I'm in a lower gear and revving higher...and *then* race someone as well.' It was too much to ask most of them, to be honest. But Niki (Lauda) could actually cope very well."

Someone mentioned that, while Michael Schumacher was romping away with another world championship for Ferrari, it was 40 years since Phil Hill had won the title for Ferrari in one of the sharknose cars. Was Phil really as nervous as legend had it? "I remember he used to polish his goggles relentlessly before a race," said Tony Brooks. "If I say ten times, it was only a very slight exaggeration. There was going to be no glass left in the lenses. It was just a nervous twitch and I was always pulling his leg about it. He was a nice guy but I didn't really get to know him properly until we drove together in 1959." That was the season when Brooks should have won the championship himself, as he revealed to the lunch table.

"We should have won the manufacturers championship and the driver's championship in 1959. The car was front engined but it was capable of it. That would have been the last year. Cooper was putting the writing on the wall for rear-engined cars. Ferrari didn't go to the British Grand Prix at Aintree because they had a strike at the factory. We had been first and second there in the '200' a few weeks before so we would have had points there for sure. Then they cancelled the Belgian Grand Prix on the superbly fast Spa circuit which would have favoured Ferrari because on the slow to medium-speed circuits the rear-engined cars like the Cooper, were much better. And they cancelled the race. I'd won the three times I'd been raced there – including the 1958 Grand Prix in a Vanwall. It was a Ferrari sort of circuit and we had a car that was fast and basically reliable. At Monza they changed the clutch the night before the race and I did just 100 metres off the grid. At Sebring for the final Grand Prix, I was still in with a chance of the championship but Taffy von Trips shunted me up the backside off the start and I stopped at the pits to check for damage. I know it sounds like another if-only story but you have to admit it's a longer story than usual. Jack (Brabham) won the title for Cooper by just four points – and even then he ran out of fuel and had to push over the finishing line.

"We had a wonderful team relationship at Ferrari that summer. It was an Anglo-American team with Phil, Dan Gurney, Cliff Allison and myself. The only oddball was Frenchman, Jean Behra and he had a punch-up with team manager Tavoni – literally – in the pitlane at Reims, and quit. Enzo Ferrari didn't try to set us against each other. We were competitive, sure, but we didn't have this enmity almost verging on hatred that existed between some Ferrari drivers in those days."

Sir Stirling Moss rates Brooks as one of the top six drivers of all time, up there with Fangio, Clark and Senna, but the man himself is wonderfully unassuming and great company. He left Ferrari in 1960 because he had been promised a rear-engined Vanwall but it didn't eventuate. "For some reason that I never had explained to me Tony Vandervell decided he wasn't going racing when it was too late for me to get another drive and I was left high and dry..."

Then they talked about Juan Pablo Montoya, the Colombian who had started ruffling feathers with the Williams-BMW that season, after success in the CART series. Gordon Murray reckoned him. "He will be good. I promise you. I came back from Monaco three years ago when he had run in the F3000 race. He didn't win but I was watching from a balcony and his car control was...*phewwww*...I came back to Ron (Dennis) and I said, whatever it takes, get hold of that guy. He's got heaps of natural ability"

"He seems to have lots of problems in practice," said Brooks. "I'm sure he's going to be good but he seems to be having a bit of a problem getting used to Formula 1 cars after the CART cars in the States."

Rob Widdows wondered whether young Finn, Kimi Raikkonen might not have been even more impressive because he hadn't seen any of the tracks. Ken Tyrrell agreed.

"He's certainly promising," said Brooks, warming to the relaxed atmosphere of the lunch. "He's only had about 23 car races before he came into Formula 1. Everybody seems amazed but these guys start racing karts as kids – 6-7-8-9 years of age and there's nothing more cut and thrust than karts. Formula 1 cars these days are just large karts so I don't see why people are so astonished that these guys like Raikkonen and Button can come from karts and go quickly."

Widdows put a lot of it down to the media. "It's all press hype, isn't it? New kid on the block is always a good story."

Murray despaired of the modern generation of Formula 1 drivers. "I know we have to move on and the industry has to become more professional but the most disappointing thing to me is the drivers. They so soon forget why they're there and why they started and what they want to do and they become superstars. You look at motorcycle racing. Take a guy like Valentino Rossi. He just wants to go racing. He's won something like 80% of the races this year and when he's interviewed all he says is he wants to be there and ride bikes fast and beat everybody. They don't forget what they're there for. These Formula 1 drivers who become superstars in two seasons...they drive me nuts.

199

"In the Japanese Grand Prix, Rossi passed Biaggi and Biaggi put him in the dirt half-way down the straight at Suzuka. They must have been doing 170-180mph and Biaggi gave him the elbow, gave him the knee, flick...into the dirt. They interviewed the little guy after the race and he said, well, in Italy there was a big rivalry between them, but it was OK... And he'd just elbowed the guy into the dirt! That was it. End of story. If it had happened in Formula 1, it would have been headlining the next ten issues of "Autosport"...What Does Ron Think? What does Todt think? What Does Bernie Think?"

Ken Tyrrell supposed it was due to the money today. "It must be partly about the huge amount of money they're getting. That must be a factor. Look at Jenson Button. He's bought a million pound house, bought a big powerboat in Monaco. And what's he done this year? He's been out-qualified by his team-mate, Fisichella at every race."

Nelson Piquet was obviously one of Gordon Murray's favourite drivers and I recalled talking with the Brazilian driver in the hotel lobby in Adelaide some years ago while we waited for the shuttle to catch an early flight out. Nelson was talking about making a move to reduce speeds in the pitlane. "The mechanics have got to have total trust in you. I'm coming in at 100mph and I've got to stop right on that spot," He said pointing to a mark on the lobby floor. I asked where he had been doing 100mph and he said "By that tree." I looked out the window for a tree, but he was indicating a tall shrub in a pot about ten feet away in the lobby!

"Yeah, that's how it was then." Gordon Murray had fond memories of racing before it became sanitised with more and more regulations to save the young men from their own excesses. "Piquet. Now there's a chap who was in it just for the racing. That's all he wanted to be there for. People thought he was a bit basic, a bit crude and I suppose he was. We used to call him the Indian from the Amazon forest, but he was a super guy. He just wanted to go racing..."

Tyrrell remembered talking to Piquet in Adelaide airport. "He'd finished with Formula 1 and he was going to go to CART. I said he didn't ought to go to CART because he'd have an accident and hurt himself. And he did. I asked him why he didn't stay in Formula 1and he said he couldn't get a winning car. He told me he'd earned $30-million in Formula 1 and he didn't want to do it any more. He's got a son, hasn't he?"

Murray: "Several!" Laughter.

Tyrrell: "All over the place."

Price: "And not with the same name." More laughter.

Tony Brooks asked about the background to Montoya and Jacques Villeneuve having a pitlane punch-up. "Didn't I read that they got each other by the throat?" Tyrrell reminded Murray about Nelson throwing a punch after he retired from a race at Hockenheim. "With Salazar, wasn't it? More of a kick than a punch. They both had their helmets on and they looked ridiculous."

"What was really embarrassing about that race was that it was one of the few that I took my son to," Murray recalled. "He was quite young and we were hanging around waiting for the charter flight with the drivers as we did in those days. Salazar was sitting there and my son went up to him – he was only four or five years old – and started having a go at him!"

Dave Price mentioned that Jack Sears had bought his old racing Galaxy back from South Africa a couple of years ago, and restored it. "They were Holman & Moody cars on drum brakes. That was when I was a lad. The first job I had was at Willments. They had Galaxys and Lotus Cortinas. Jack wrote his Galaxy off at Brands, didn't he? Ran out of brakes."

"I remember Charlie Cooper, John's father, buying a Galaxy from Alan Brown," said Tyrrell with a big grin. "John was livid! Charlie had gone down to pay Alan a visit at his place at Send and have a cuppa with him...and Alan tucked him up with this huge Galaxy!"

"We didn't have enough cars when I raced in South Africa,"

said Murray. "I used to compete in my sports car against Lotus Cortinas, Galaxys, Lolas, Mini Coopers and an Elfin which was an Australian sports racing car like a Lotus 23. I really fancied my chances as a racing driver and I wrote to Colin Chapman at Lotus. Cheeky 19-year-old kid. Told him I'd designed my own car, designed my own engine, coming to England, wanted to be a racing driver, wanted to get into motor racing design..."

"You mean you haven't heard from Bobby Rahal, yet?" asked Brooks to a gust of laughter. Rahal at Jaguar and Ron Dennis had just been battling over designer Adrian Newey's contract.

"I've still got the letter from Chapman," Murray continued. "Thank God I kept it, because he was my hero. He said to speak to Brian Lough, head of vehicle engineering at Lotus. I wrote to him and he suggested that I came over for an interview. It was the end of 1969. The second day I was in Britain, I was up to Norfolk and Lotus but what I didn't realise at the time was that Lotus had 1100 unsold cars at Hethel, they'd just laid 60 people off the month before, and the company was going through a really big dip. No vacancies for racing drivers. Or designers..."

It had just been announced that Jackie Stewart had received a Knighthood in the Queen's Birthday honours list. Brooks wondered if Ken had put in a word for the Scot who had won three world titles in Tyrrell's cars. "I didn't actually," said Ken. "Well, they wouldn't take any notice of me, anyway, but I'm pleased he got it. It's good for motor racing."

Brooks pointed out that it was unbelievable that there had been two knighthoods in motor racing in two months, with Jackie's title following close behind Stirling Moss's award.

Ken recalled a royal occasion when Jackie was shooting at Sandringham with the Queen. "I was shooting with Jackie and the Head Keeper from Sandringham was also shooting. There was another guy who was always invited at the same time as Jackie; they were good friends but they took the piss out of each other all day long. They went on and on and on. Apparently the Queen said to the Head Keeper one day 'What will we do

202

with those two?' and he said 'There's only one thing to do, Ma'am -- we've got to put them down...!'"

Eric Thompson said it was a good thing that Sir Jackie had been able to take over from Ken as President of the British Racing Drivers' Club. "I couldn't do it now," said Ken, as the lunch party broke up to have a group photo taken with Gordon's pink Thunderbird. "I'm not well enough now, but Jackie's doing a great job."

Dave Price recalled his first event as a team manager in 1974 when he was looking after Jody Scheckter and me on the Tour of Britain Rally. We were in a pretty awful 3-litre Adlards Capri and I was supposed to be navigator. Jody had rallied at home in South Africa and as, always, he was super-competitive. The rally visited various race circuits and special stages around Britain and the arrangement was that navigators rode as passenger in the rally stages but the drivers were on their own in the races. Which suited me fine. I clearly remember (clearly remember? It's engraved on my mind!) the special stage at Knebworth Park at *midnight* and Jody is hurling the big Capri in clouds of dust between huge brick gateposts and nearly shaving bark from big oak trees. He was just a tenth of a second slower than Roger Clark in the works rally Escort, which I felt rather said it all. Jody was full of himself, as always in those days, and the rally drivers were predicting a huge accident for us when we reached the Welsh forest stages. Mercifully Jody had our accident all on his own at Oulton Park, right in front of me where I was watching at the first corner. He was unscathed but the Capri was beyond help, so we left it with Pricey and his crew and went back to London on the train. That was the beginning and the end of my rally career, and Dave Price remembered it well!

It was one of those lunches when the group just clicked with stories sparking from one to the other around the table punctuated by spontaneous laughter. Next time I'll sell tickets to it!

Writer's Block

You are the final judge on this, but I find that writing comes so easily to me that it's just like written-down talking. Our journalistic lunch-table conversations at Grand Prix paddocks around the world have always considered that if you could write the way you spoke you would be a very readable writer. It was not always thus with me. The first piece I ever wrote for publication was a report on a beach race north of Christchurch, won by my Timaru hometown mate, David Young, in his XK120 Jaguar. It must have been in 1957 and it took me literally *hours* to write and it was only six inches long in *The Timaru Herald* the next morning. This may have been less than I expected for the effort involved and I may have started my hatred of sub-editors on the morning of that first day (even though I would later admit that this was the baptism by fire that every young writer needs – you're never as good as you imagine yourself to be in those early days of wordsmithery!) In those days your name never appeared as penman, and I was awarded the title of *Dipstick* which I probably wouldn't have picked, given a choice. Which I wasn't. My very first article started out:

'At the New Zealand beach racing championship last Sunday, an 18-year-old Timaru driver, D. Young, in his Jaguar XK120C drop-head coupe, won the saloon race by a mile and a half from B. Kinzett (Vanguard), and E. Sprague, another local driver in a Zephyr, who was third.'

I like writing and I like reading good writing. Denis Jenkinson rode as sidecar passenger with Eric Oliver when he was winning motorcycle championships in the late1940s but his most famous feat as a combatant was to ride with Stirling Moss when they won the Mille Miglia, the 1000-mile race round Italy, at record speed in 1955. Jenks, the D.S.J. in *Motor Sport*, could be a curmudgeon, a difficult little bearded man (we called him the gnome when he wasn't within earshot) who lived by his own rules. He wrote with his own style, always longhand, never a typewriter of any kind in the days long before laptops. Jenks was a loner through the 1950s, a friend of the drivers, fascinated by their different personalities and performances and writing his book *The Racing Driver* which was accepted as the bible of motor sport for generations of budding racers. This was in the days when there were writers as opposed to journalists, predating the modern 'media'.

You could not accuse Jenks of a flowing style. As with all things it was his own crafted manner of getting it down on paper. If we were brave when the wine had flowed well into a convivial dinner, we would say that he finished a page in his easily legible longhand...and then shook a pepper-pot full of full stops and commas over it.

It was a badge of some courage as much as a mark of having made it, if you could count Jenks as a friend.

I remember one lunchtime at The Barley Mow when my New Zealand photographer mate, Euan Sarginson, was visiting and Jenks had joined us for lunch. Both bearded, they looked like bookends side-by-side at the table and suddenly Euan turned and said "F**k you, Jenks!" Jenks looked suitably startled and said "What did you say that for?" Sarge gave a big smile and said "Jenks, I've *always* wanted to say that to you." Another mark of bravery from a guy who had until then only known Jenks as DSJ at the foot of his reports and columns in a magazine that arrived in New Zealand maybe two months after the events he was writing about. But every issue was devoured word by word, and Jenks to his followers was up there somewhere just to the left of God. I may not have captured the moment as I meant to, but you have to confess it was a difficult moment. For Euan it was a sort of colonial compliment...as I explained to Jenks a year or two later when he raised the subject after a dinner somewhere in Europe over a Grand Prix weekend.

My supreme advantage in this area was that I just sort of dropped into the European racing scene as a mate of Denny Hulme in 1961. Of course I knew of Jenks by reputation, but I wasn't aware of his prickly reputation, especially with other journalists. He preferred the company of the drivers, and mostly he preferred his own company. He regarded *Motor Sport* as a privileged domain and when the weekly *Motoring News* newspaper joined the Teesdale Publications group, Jenks simply refused to register its existence. But nobody had told me that. I had been covering the international pre-Tasman races in New Zealand for *Motoring News* and before I left to travel around the European Formula Junior races with Denny in 1961, I signed on to cover the events for 'MN'. I wrote my report on the Formula Junior race at Rouen and as Denny had introduced me to Jenks earlier in the weekend, I asked if he'd mind taking my report back for 'MN'. No problem, he said. The guys at 'MN' couldn't believe it when my copy was delivered to their office by the little man who refused to acknowledge the very existence of their publication.

He had been round the race tracks long enough that his word was lore. I remember once arriving late for qualifying at a Belgian Grand Prix on the Zolder circuit, and meeting up with Jenks in the pitlane. "Who's quick?" I asked. He gave one of those quizzical looks and said sagely "They're *all* quick...even the slow ones are quick..." And if you digested that throw-away comment, of course he was right. And he still is. Even the poor wretch condemned by talent or machinery or misfortune to the back of the grid in a Grand Prix could still drive hugely faster than any of us in the Press Room (now the Media Centre, of course...) who were writing how slow they were when compared with the man on pole position.

After Jenks' death in 1996, John Blunsden, coincidentally editor of *Motoring News* when I first started writing for it in New Zealand, now the owner of the Motor Racing Publications publishing company, had commissioned a book (*Jenks – A Passion for Motor Sport*) as a tribute to the little man and had asked for memories from his friends.

I tried to isolate a piece of Jenks' writing that would mark his talent and then I remembered his report from the 1968 Belgian Grand Prix. He had written it as though you, the reader, was sitting beside him at the circuit and he was confiding snippets to you during the race, chatting while he was keeping his lap-chart. It was compelling reading and I asked if he planned to write all his reports like this. No. He was never going to write like that again. But why? Hadn't there been letters from readers who, like me, had thoroughly enjoyed his new-style story on the Grand Prix. Yes, there had. So? There had been *one letter* from a reader who didn't like it, and he maintained that he wrote for *all* his readers and he would be going back to his old style. Which was pretty much a measure of the man.

The '68 Belgian was the race which saw the first use of wings in Formula 1. Jenks was sceptical and in that whimsical one-off report he wrote "Ferrari came out with an elaborate aerofoil mounted high above

the gearbox like a miniature Chaparral. Whether any of these devices has any real effect is debatable, for the results depended entirely on the psychological effect on the drivers. Like contented cows, contented drivers drive well, and a driver convinced of the improved stability of his car would take the fast corners just that bit faster."

Although the wings would soon gather height and take control of Formula 1 pace to the point where they were declared dangerous and eventually banned, Jenks was close to the truth with his opinion at Spa that day. Chris Amon was comfortably on pole with the winged Ferrari but what only his team knew was that he had set an identical time *without* using the wing and team-mate Jacky Ickx would ask for all the wings and fins to be removed from his car before the start. Amon would say later when we were working on his biography *Forza Amon!* that he wishes he had raced without the wing as well, because his perceived winged speed prompted Lotus to launch into a programme of wing development with their Type 49 which to date had not been a match for the Ferrari.

Jenks wrote a 'straight' précis of the race and then followed with what he called his Francorchamps Monologue which I have used in the Spa-Francorchamps chapter because I feel it is an important part of the history of the old Spa circuit, like a memorable painting by a famous artist.

Autosport seems to have nurtured Formula 1 writers with style over the years starting, I suppose, with founding editor, Gregor Grant when the first issue appeared in 1950. His editorial started "In presenting the new weekly, AUTOSPORT, we feel confident that we shall give readers a service which cannot be surpassed, or even equalled, by any journal other than one devoted entirely to motor sporting affairs. A monthly periodical can only hope to achieve topicality, as and when press arrangements permit. Events which take place one week-end are apt to make stale reading unless reported before the following week-end. It will be our aim to publish details of every event and item of news that is bang up-to-the-minute."

John Bolster was Technical Editor and Swiss-born French-domiciled Jabby Crombac was listed as French Editor in that first issue. Most of the correspondents seemed to sport a moustache as Gregor did, judging by their photographs. He and Bolster were great travelling companions, both enjoying the liquid issue of the barley and the grape.

Jabby and I are members of the British Racing Drivers' Club and we always have lunch together at the BRDC over the weekend of the British Grand Prix. One year we were about to sit down when I had a tap on the shoulder and turned to see Geoff Duke. We greeted each other and I introduced him to Jabby, feeling they must have met before, but Jabby didn't seem to evince any recognition. When Geoff had gone to his table and we sat, I said a tad impatiently "You *do* know who that was, don't you?" Jabby looked blank. "It was Geoff Duke, the motorcycle champion." Jabby beamed. "Oh," he said in his clipped accent, "You mean Geoff Duke, the *Aston Martin* driver!" Poor Geoff. His car racing record had lived on a good longer than he'd hoped it might have. In his autobiography (*The Certain Sound*), Aston Martin team manager John Wyer recalled the fateful incident in the 1952 Sebring 12-hour race when Geoff and Peter Collins were paired for the first – and last! – time: "In the race Collins made a very good start and for the first two hours had a battle with Walters in which the honours were at first even but then Peter pulled away and when he came in to refuel had a lead of more than half a minute. But soon after Duke took over he crashed, hitting a marker barrel and another car. The De Dion tube was fractured and the car was withdrawn. Peter Collins was understandably furious and complained bitterly at having been partnered with an inexperienced driver. I was sorry for Duke but a good deal more sorry for Peter, for the team and for myself..."

In 2003 Geoff was at Silverstone for the Grand Prix with his son and I asked him if he knew he had become a figure of rhyming slang in Ireland. He didn't so I explained that when I was over there to cover the Ards TT 75th anniversary, I heard a girl say "Have a Geoff Duke at that..." You have to know that with an Irish accent, 'look' becomes 'luke'. Geoff was amused.

BRDC lunch with Jabby at Silverstone in 2003 and he was sitting, staring quietly at the menu with the club shield featuring a head-on view of a racing car below a Union Jack flag. "That car," Jabby said carefully, "is the Razor Blade Aston Martin." I asked him how he could possibly have known that and he replied "It is not for discussion, it just *is*..." I marvelled at his depth of motor-sporting knowledge, knowing that the slim-line 1920s Aston was the model for the badge I was honoured to wear. Then, while researching notes for this book, I was reading a 1980s Diary column relating to a visit to the Harrah Museum in Reno, hosted by then-curator Joel Finn. One of the cars on display was the Razor Blade Aston Martin, which Finn explained was the car on the BRDC badge. So I had known about it for twenty years...and forgotten it!

In the recent past Pete Lyons, son of the American motor racing writer, Ozzie Lyons, wrote in *Autosport* with a flowing style and an understanding of the men and the machinery that was always a joy to read. And when the drivers made comment on what he had written or the way he had written it, he could know that his work was appreciated which is always so important in a world where a journalist lives for his work and necessarily lives *by* his work.

Nigel Roebuck then took over the Formula 1 coverage for *Autosport* when Pete went back to write about the CanAm sports car races and the Indy-car races in North America. I am pleased to count Nigel – somehow I've always known him in paddock-talk just as Roebuck, which is certainly not a disparagement – as a good friend so fulsome praise may by judged as self-serving but it is definitely not. A large amount of credit where it is due. Like Alan Henry, Roebuck has written several books, and my favourite is *Chasing the Title* covering fifty years of Formula 1. Sir Frank Williams wrote the foreword and closed saying "I have known Nigel Roebuck for a long time; we met at Monaco in 1971, when my team was called 'Frank Williams Racing Cars', running a March for Henri Pescarolo. We got along famously from the beginning and I identified him almost instantly as one of that small group of people who live and die for motor racing, and particularly in Formula 1.

This group, whether they be team principals, engineers, drivers or journalists, are the fundamental core of Formula 1 – the engine house that has driven the sport from success to further success. Nigel occupies a special place in this core, not least because of his defiant approach to the sport he loves. He writes exactly what he thinks, and that I have always much admired. Of his desire to recount events as he sees them, and to reproduce them accurately, there has never been any doubt."

Defiant. I like that. Rather sums up Roebuck, I feel.

We all pen a piece that stands out now and then and as this book was going together, Roebuck was at Indianapolis for the 2003 Grand Prix and went to Mo Nunn's 65th birthday. Mo was christened Morris Nuffield Nunn so, one way or another, he was committed from birth to be involved in the automobile business. He raced in Formula 3 and then designed and built his own Ensign cars which eventually ran in Formula 1 with Clay Regazzoni and Chris Amon included in his driver lineup. He had more enthusiasm than budget and eventually packed up and went to the U.S. where he engineered success for several Indy-car drivers. You have to appreciate that Roebuck regards Indianapolis and the '500' on a par with Monza and Formula 1 so when the U.S. Grand Prix moved to Indianapolis it was some sort of motor sporting marriage made in heaven as far as NSR was concerned. He also joins me in being a fan of Juan Pablo Montoya and the way he goes about being a racing driver so I much enjoyed what he wrote in his *Autosport* column: 'On the Thursday evening before the race, I went to the 65th birthday of my old pal Morris Nunn – appropriately held at Mo's Place, the best steakhouse in Indianapolis – and JPM, who is very fond of his former engineer at Ganassi Racing, showed up, apologising that he could only stay for a few minutes. Two hours later after enjoying himself hugely, he grabbed Connie's hand and finally disappeared into the night.

'Nunn was touched that Montoya had found the time to drop by. "He might be a superstar these days, but I don't think he's changed at all. Really hope he wins on Sunday..."

'A great many people felt the same way, not least because they believed Montoya as world champion would be the best possible thing for the sport as a whole. He is an engaging fellow, after all, very quick with the witty rejoinder, and thus rather unlike many of his fellows. As with Tiger Woods, Michael Schumacher's endless successes have almost ceased to register any more, and Kimi Raikkonen, for all his incredible flair in a racing car, is hardly a man for the public stage, even by comparison with his countryman Mika Hakkinen. "Kimi," Flavio Briatore recently said to me, "makes Mika sound like Jerry Lewis."

Jenks used to refer to himself, Alan Henry, Maurice Hamilton, Roebuck and me, as the 'Famous Five', a group description sometimes sourly received by those not included, but I suppose 'twas ever thus. Given the choice, I guess I would prefer to be, as the saying goes, on the inside pissing out than on the outside pissing in.

We always used to eat together on Grand Prix weekends and in Montreal for several years we dined in a sort of upmarket hamburger place while the rest of the visiting cognoscenti ate in the expensive restaurants of the Old Town. It was Jackie Stewart's birthday and we invited him to join us, not expecting that he would arrive. He did, apologising that he could only stay a few minutes – and left hours later when the dinner ended. Only then did we realise that he had a chauffeur waiting in a Ford limo ticking over outside! So I'd like to think that great drivers operate alike...

Maurice Hamilton started out in motor racing journalism working for and travelling with me to the races and we formed a strong friendship in those early days when I hosted the Elf hospitality motorhome at tracks around the world and worked closely with Ken Tyrrell and the team. I was in New Zealand when Maurice's excellent biography of Ken was published in 2002 and I was later to learn that he had dedicated the book to me: 'For Eoin, who introduced me to Ken and all the good times that followed.' Thanks mate.

Roebuck fiercely defends (there it goes again, defiant and defending...) his right to smoke whenever and wherever he can and to this end he has cancelled his desire to go on long-haul flights, so he has agreed an arrangement with *Autosport* whereby he still pens his weekly column but new-man Mark Hughes takes over the Grand Prix reports. This seems to suit both men admirably. Roebuck gets relieved of the day-to-day detail of

Formula 1 to concentrate on crafting his columns, while Hughes is gifted the opportunity to perform on centre stage. He is a new talent with an amazing three-dimensional ability to describe the world of racing as he sees it. They said of Ernest Hemingway that he described the world around him literally with devastating simplicity and Hughes does this for Formula 1. Join him at Imola on the morning of the first practice session in 2003. It's as good as being there. "The morning haze is just beginning to lift. I'm starting to feel the power of the sun. There are 30 minutes to go before Saturday morning's practice session begins. Birdsong, Italian chatter from the grandstand, the babbling brook. These are the sounds from *Acque Minerale* at the bottom of the gorgeously contoured green valley. A deep V8 growl, sounding like an old Mercedes W196 racer, echoes off the trees and the barriers between the gravel trap and the parkland. That and the crowd's chatter which, with 15 minutes to go, has risen noticeably in pitch." The session hasn't started yet, but already Hughes has painted in the background of suppressed excitement...

George Begg is another writer who I think excels in capturing the mood. In fact he is a man in his 70s who started out in engineering in the deep south of New Zealand's South Island, and would race motorcycles on the Isle of Man, build his own racing cars in New Zealand and work for a season at the McLaren factory in the late1960s when Bruce was still heading his team. Begg's ability is his bald honesty, writing what he sees as opposed to what he would have liked to see. He wrote his autobiography *A Classic World and When the Engine Roars*, a sort of updated sequel with the first book blending into the second. It was a different world when the McLaren team was based at Colnbrook on the Heathrow flight-path. I had still been with the team then, but I had forgotten much of the way of life that to George was new and interesting. "One of the first things any newcomer at McLaren had to get used to was the aircraft noise. At times it sounded like huge jets were trying to land on the factory roof. Newcomers would at first try to shout through the noise, but soon they learned to stop talking for about 30 seconds until the noise abated. It became so normal that people didn't realise they were doing it."

George had built his own racing cars in New Zealand but in 1968 he moved to McLaren's fabrication shop. "Bruce was great," he said at the launch of his book. "There are lateral thinkers and there are upward thinkers but Bruce didn't know the meaning of any of it. He'd just say: 'Let's bloody well work it out, glue it together and make it go.'

"When we put the seven-litre all-alloy V8 engine in the back of an M6 CanAm chassis as a prototype for the first M8, they pushed the starter button in the workshop and it just ate the starter gears. The car was up on trestles and Bruce slid in underneath, where he just stared at the problem for half an hour. Not saying anything, just looking up and thinking it out. Then he jumped out, grabbed a sheet of paper, sketched up his ideas and shot off to the machine shop. They made up a compound gear-train arrangement and the whole thing went together and it worked.

"Bruce loved racing for the sake of creating something. He loved the engineering challenge as well as the driving. He certainly didn't do it for the money because there was practically no money in it then. He loved to be the force behind the creation of a new car. I don't think fame and fortune were very high on his list of priorities. When we finished the first M8 CanAm car and lifted it down off the build-up trestles and sat it on the floor there was a look of pride in Bruce's face. You could just see him thinking 'Yeah, I made it all happen together with these other fellas.' But he never hogged the whole thing to himself. He wasn't an egotist; he was remarkably candid in his praise for everyone."

Begg has an amazing ability to read a personality: "We've all got good and bad sides but Bruce was a remarkably kind, generous and considerate person. He could suffer fools gladly, too. People just burbled on to him but Bruce would listen. He would never destroy that person. He would give him his attention and would never reveal his private thoughts."

Begg went down to Goodwood on CanAm test sessions early in that summer of '68 but his favourite tale came when the car had yet to leave the factory. It was before they had implemented Bruce's starter gear cure, and at 2 o'clock on a Sunday morning, he asked the crew to push-start the prototype in the factory; he planned a trial run up the 35 metre- long workshop. Six of them, including Begg, were pushing the length of the factory but the engine kept stalling. "On what seemed like the umpteenth time, the engine fired and roared into life. The noise of that fearsome motor was deafening inside a confined space.

"But the exercise wasn't over yet. 'Back we go,' Bruce indicated over the roaring engine, and once more we pulled him to the other end of the workshop. I will never forget the look of sheer glee on Bruce's face as he dropped the clutch and laid two tracks of black rubber the entire length of the workshop before jamming on the brakes."

George lives in restless retirement in Queensland these days, working on a book of his memories of Bruce and the McLaren days. One of my favourite George Begg stories was when he appeared on a viewing bank at a small race meeting at Timaru in New Zealand. We were chatting and he asked who the driver was in one of his early Formula Ford Beggs. I told him that it was Robin Judkins, the bearded totally enthusiastic entrepreneur who promotes the Coast-to-Coast foot race in the South Island. He also races in Formula Ford because he enjoys it, but he has no allusions towards laurels. George thought he was slow. In the paddock after the race, I introduced 'Juddy' to his car-maker and the two men chatted for a while before George asked Robin if he had any tank tape in his toolbox. What do you want it for? asked Juddy. "To put over my name on the nose!" said George, with a big grin...

POSSUM BOURNE – RALLY ARTIST AND ARTISTE

"Possum" Bourne was a folklore figure in New Zealand motorsport, a rally driver with impeccable international credentials as a works driver with Subaru and his death stunned a country that had come to accept him and Scott Dixon as their icons to replace Bruce and Denny and Chris on the world motorsport stage.

Possum died twelve days after his freak accident on the Cardrona hillclimb course on Good Friday, 2003, the day *before* the Race to the Sky started. As fate would have it, he was driving *down* the hill in a road car when he collided with a Jeep Cherokee driven by another competitor coming up the hill in a controlled convoy of entrants in the rally class with their co-drivers checking pace notes. Possum received severe head injuries and broken legs and was in a drug induced coma on life support. The tragedy was compounded by the fact that if he had been in his rally car with full roll cage, safety harness and crash helmet he would probably have survived unscathed.

Possum always reminded me of Bruce McLaren, with that ever- present grin, and his way of making life look easy. Until he got behind the wheel of his Subaru rally car. Then he was a bespectacled Clark Kent turning into a Kiwi Superman. Like Bruce he regarded his team as his mates. They worked together more as a family than a team. Possum's way of running his business made it not seem like work. They were doing it for Possum, and like Bruce McLaren his team would have worked all the hours God made available, if it meant success for their mate.

He always had time or *made* time for his fans. There was the lad he wrote to after he had been expelled from school. Imagine what a character re-vamp that would have meant for a young guy who must have imagined that society had abandoned him and was ready to rebel? There is more to success than the money. It was a measure of the man.

Of course he wasn't christened 'Possum' but that was fine with his fans. Probably few of them knew that it was a family nickname bestowed after he had wrecked his mother's car, dodging a possum on the road at night when he was 15. His name was Peter but the world knew it was really Possum.

His wife Peggy wrote after the news that they must have all been dreading while we had been hoping against hope that somehow, because he was Possum he would win through: "To say the children and I will miss him is a vast understatement. He was the love of my life and the greatest loving father to our children. We had great adventures and it has been the time of my life and an honour to have shared 16 years with the most loving, genuine, fair, down to earth competitive and amazing man. He was our world. He was our hero."

Mine too. These days I can do without the political pressures of a Grand Prix paddock but I always looked forward to the Race to the Sky because it was my one chance in the year to have a chat with Possum. He really was a breath of fresh air. You felt better for being able to spend some time with him. I knew zilch about rallying, but he always had the patience to explain whatever it was I didn't understand this time...

That doyen of motor sporting writers, Denis Jenkinson, always used to say that we should be able to read our obituaries before we departed so that we would know what people really felt about us. Possum would have been hugely impressed at the headlines day after day in the national and international newspapers and on television and radio while his life was on hold. He had built a proud following in New Zealand and Australia and if, as a Kiwi, he could become regarded as a sporting icon in Australia, he had *really* achieved another of his goals.

In Christchurch, "The Press", ran Tremain's cartoon after the news of Possum's death, showing a couple standing on the footpath listening as cars come revving towards them and then storming past at speed. The man looks to his companion and simply says "Possum's cortege." It could have been in the worst possible taste, but New Zealand read it and laughed about it in the pub that night, almost relieved that they could. Somehow you had the feeling that he would have been laughing too. Another measure of the man.

Possum was aware of his place in things but he was also aware of the help he had on his way to the top. He appreciated his friends and after that crash in the Australian rally that killed his co-driver and close mate, Rodger Freeth, Possum's rally cars always carried a special tribute on his number plate. It just read ROJ. He never forgot.

He effortlessly combined the roles of the artist and the artiste. My mini Oxford dictionary says an artist is *one who does something with exceptional skill* and an artiste is *a professional entertainer.*

Possum regarded the Cardrona hillclimb as a favourite event and he squeezed it into his crammed schedule this season, jetting the world as a bona fide member of the Subaru factory rally team in World Championship events after 20 years carrying the colours of the Japanese car maker as a privateer. He had won the Australian Rally Championship seven times in his own Subaru, and had at last scored a works drive in a Group N car. On the 15-kilometre Cardrona shingle climb, Possum performed with his usual finesse behind the wheel, winning overall in 2001. He used to say of the Cardrona climb that it was the most fun he'd had in a car with his pants on. And then the damned hill killed him.

The crash was a total freak, one of those things that just *couldn't* have happened. But it did. The stretch of the hill where the accident happened was ironically the longest, widest, straightest part of the climb just a kilometre and a half from the start. What set the stage for the crash was a blind brow with a left kink after it on the way up the hill. A convoy of eleven rally cars with drivers and co-drivers, were driving up the hill with official cars front and back to keep speeds down as the competitors checked their pace notes. Mike Barltrop was two cars from the end of the convoy in blinding dust and this was probably a contributory factor.

While our sympathies go out to Peggy and the extended Bourne family, I really feel for Mike Barltrop and what he must have been going through since the accident. Because it really was an *accident*, a tragic happening that he wouldn't have been part of for the world, because Possum was his hero too. He had bought a rally Subaru from Possum a few years ago, and Possum had always kept in touch with his progress. Possum has gone, but Mike will have to live with the memory of that fatal Good Friday for too long to come.

Bruce McLaren put it for us all in times like this when he wrote, after his team-mate Tim Mayer had been killed in Tasmania. "It would be a waste of life to do nothing with one's ability, for I feel that life is measured in achievement, not in years alone."

Sir Stirling & Sir Jackie – and the Commendatore!

Grand Prix history could have been changed forever if Stirling Moss or Jackie Stewart had teamed with Ferrari. Both drivers were courted by the Commendatore, and both agreed to drive for the Italian team – but history records that neither did.

Pride kept Moss and Ferrari apart until 1961 and Stirling's Goodwood crash on Easter Monday 1962 cancelled the deal that had been agreed for Moss to race a Ferrari in the 1962 World Championship!

"At the end of the 1961 season I had a call from Enzo Ferrari asking if I would go to Maranello and discuss a contract to lead his team in 1962," Sir Stirling told me. "I asked Fangio what he thought about me driving for Ferrari and he said 'Drive for him, but don't *sign* with him.' That was Fangio's suggestion."

It was an unusual period for Ferrari in Formula 1. The elegant 'sharknose' cars had dominated the 1961 season, beaten only twice on tracks where driver skill counted for more than horsepower. That driver was Stirling Moss and his victories were at Monaco and the Nurburgring.

The '61 season opened at Monaco in May and Moss won from the Ferraris of Richie Ginther, Phil Hill and Wolfgang von Trips. At Zandvoort it was a Ferrari 1-2, Trips and Hill. At Spa it was a Ferrari clean sweep with Hill, Trips, Ginther and Olivier Gendebien, first through fourth. The French GP at Reims was a surprise when rookie Giancarlo Baghetti in a Ferrari *muletta* outlasted the works cars and the rest of the field to win his maiden world championship GP at his first start. Aintree for the British GP it was the red-car roller-coaster with Trips winning in the rain from Hill and Ginther. On the 14.2-mile Nurburgring, however, Moss was master in the Rob Walker Lotus, winning from Trips and Hill.

There was shared frustration that summer. The Ferraris were seen to be over-powering the rest of the field but Phil Hill, for one, said he would trade any of his supposedly surplus horsepower for the handling of Stirling's Lotus.

At Monza it all came unstuck when Trips came off pole position and tangled with Jim Clark's Lotus slipstreaming on the opening lap, somersaulting into the crowd and killing himself and 14 spectators. Hill won the race and clinched the title. Enzo Ferrari cancelled his team entry in the final race at Watkins Glen citing respect for von Trips, but it meant that Phil Hill was robbed of his chance to race in front of his home crowd as the new champion.

The British teams paid the price of protest having refused to accept what they saw as down-grading the world championship from 2.5-litres to 1.5-litres in 1961. There was a move to a breakaway 'Intercontinental' formula keeping the trusty, lusty 2.5-litre 4-cylinder Coventry Climax engines but this served only to delay the inevitable and for 1961 the British teams started the season with outclassed 4-cylinder engines against the Ferrari V6s which had been raced as Formula 2 in the latter seasons of the 1950s.

Coventry Climax produced a 1.5-litre V8 and it would eventually dominate but it was too new and too late for 1961.

Stirling Moss was about to switch sides. He was the best driver and he was about to get the best car and yet he had misgivings. Enzo Ferrari was not an easy man to work with. He had crossed Moss ten years before, offering the British youngster a Grand Prix drive at Bari. "When he asked me to go down and drive his new 4-cylinder Ferrari at Bari, I said 'OK...fabulous!' and I crossed myself and faced Modena, that sort of thing. I went down to Bari, found where the team was based and climbed into the car to try the cockpit for size. A mechanic asked what I thought I was doing and I said 'I think you'll find this is my car,' but he said 'Oh no, it isn't – it's for Mr Taruffi!' Now Taruffi was a bloody good driver and I had no problem with that, if only Ferrari had phoned me and told me he had changed his mind. But he hadn't and he didn't have the courtesy to call me. I just wouldn't take that sort of treatment. I vowed to myself then that I would *never* drive for Ferrari."

Stirling kept his word. He never drove *for* Ferrari but he did race Ferraris. In fact he drove a Ferrari on that Bari weekend when David Murray, the Scot who would found Ecurie Ecosse, loaned him his elderly privately-entered short-wheelbase, swing-axle car with a supercharged 2-litre V12 engine and a central accelerator which Stirling had never experienced before. "It wasn't a major problem, just that it was confusing and I had to consciously remember it. When something happened suddenly in front of me, I had to back off. I hit the wrong pedal, and shunted it into the hay-bales. That put me off cars with central throttles for good.

"In fact I drove Ferraris on 13 occasions according to my diaries. Graham (Hill) and I were leading the GT class at Le Mans and lying third overall in 1961 when the fan blade came off. It wasn't supposed to have one. It should have been removed but Chinetti hadn't done it. Then there was the time I came into the pits at Sebring to change brake pads, one of the mechanics automatically added fuel and we were disqualified. I won the other 10. . ." After a Tourist Trophy win at Goodwood in a short-wheelbase Ferrari 250GT, Stirling told journalists he had been listening to the commentary on the car radio in the closing laps.

In 1961 rapprochement was looking like a good move for Moss. "I went down to Maranello and I must say that Ferrari was extremely hospitable. I knew his reputation of keeping people waiting just because he was Enzo Ferrari and he could do it. But he came straight out and we kissed both cheeks and he asked if I would like to drive for his team. I said no. I said what I would like to do was drive his car if he would paint it in Rob Walker's dark blue livery, the Walker team would look after it at the circuits, and Ferrari would maintain it. Alf Francis would be responsible for the car at the races. It would be entirely a factory car for me, left with us in England, financed by Ferrari. I remember the principle was that we looked after the car at the track and I presume we would have transported it. There was also to be a sports car for me, which would be prepared by the UDT/Laystall team. I wasn't going to pay for this project, I'll tell you that!"

Ferrari told Moss that he would build a car to his personal specification. "I said the current Type 156, which had just won the championship and been dominant through the season, would be just the job and he agreed it would be Walker blue and brought to England for me. Ferrari had been keen to get me and I was now happy to join him because that Ferrari was a damn good car and I would enjoy doing it with Rob and Alf. Then I had the Goodwood crash and never drove it."

Racing history switched that Easter Monday afternoon when Stirling's Lotus plunged into the bank at St Mary's in an accident that remains a mystery. Moss was unconscious for a month and was paralysed for six months.

Ken Gregory, Moss's manager from 1952 to 1966, recalls the meeting with Ferrari at the end of the 1961 season and how Moss was adamant that he would *not* sign to drive for Ferrari. "The only way for Stirling to drive a Ferrari was for them to send the car to Rob (Walker). He wouldn't drive for the works. There was another problem to be overcome. Stirling wouldn't drive a car with a central accelerator. That was a feature on the 250F Maserati I had bought for him in 1954. We worked until nearly midnight on that Maserati contract. The sticking point was where the accelerator was going to be. I insisted that it should be on the right and they had never even *heard* of a car with a right-hand accelerator. Nevertheless we won the day. Alf Francis would have changed the accelerator layout if the Ferrari deal had eventuated with Rob."

Rob Walker told me that he didn't know much about the

Ferrari Formula 1 project until the deal was done. "And after Stirling's crash, I wasn't interested. I was only interested in Stirling. After the accident, Ken Gregory took over the project and got Innes to drive it."

Innes Ireland was a driver a generation adrift. Only Innes, a Scot as fiercely loyal to his nation and its liquid products, could survive named Ireland. He was a hell-raiser who loved racing for the thrill of it and was still despising moves to make racing safer, five years later when Jackie Stewart was leading a safety crusade. Safety was for sissies, Innes maintained. In his firm opinion, motor racing was *meant* to be dangerous; that was one of the sport's essential dimensions as far as he was concerned.

It was Ireland who won the first Grand Prix for Team Lotus at Watkins Glen at the end of the 1961 season, when Ferrari elected not to send cars after Trips' fatal crash at Monza. Moss had won GPs for Lotus in the privately-entered Walker car, but Innes was the first to win for the works team. Colin Chapman's surprise response was to sack him so that he could concentrate his efforts on Ireland's young fellow-countryman, Jimmy Clark. History would prove Chapman right, but at the time Ireland felt his trust had been betrayed by the Lotus chief, and also by Clark, a fellow-countryman and at that time a junior driver. No matter that Clark's only crime was being there, Innes was happy and eager to blame everyone within range. Furious didn't make a start on it.

Innes had been driving for the UDT/Laystall team and with Moss still hospitalised, Ken Gregory put Ireland's name in the Ferrari frame. "On the Wednesday after the Aintree 200 Ken and I met at Linate airport in Italy and whistled down to Maranello where we lunched with the Commendatore. What a character he was. With very little in the way of preliminaries he said he would like to make available one of his Formula 1 cars for me to drive in the International Trophy race at Silverstone on May 12. This was a real bolt from the blue. I nearly fell off my seat and thought for the moment that one of us had gone mad! It was obvious, though, that he was deadly serious and, of course, I was absolutely delighted. In my ears the mere name Ferrari was fabulous. I'm quite sure that had he asked any other driver the same question, they would have jumped at the chance as I did that day."

Ferrari explained that he was making the offer because of his tremendous admiration for Stirling Moss with whom Innes had been signed to drive the Ferrari V6 sports-racer being made available to the UDT/Laystall team by the factory.

Writing in the monthly magazine, *Motor Racing*, of his drive in 1962, Innes's style is stiff and period, by comparison with his acquired skill as a writer when he became Sports Editor of *Autocar* after his retirement from racing in 1966. "That was, of course, before Stirling's prang, and Enzo Ferrari said he wanted to show his appreciation of the world's greatest driver by sending the car for me at Silverstone. The whole thing was settled over that very agreeable lunch. We didn't discuss the actual car I was to drive, but one of his chaps took us into the factory where the Commendatore asked 'Which is the Silverstone car?' So it looked as though he was pretty certain I couldn't resist the invitation!"

The modern comparison, forty years on, is David Coulthard being offered Michael Schumacher's Ferrari.

Ironically, Innes presents a different view of this drive when he wrote his best-selling autobiography "All Arms and Elbows" in 1967. "I became, I think, the only person to be given a full-prepared works Ferrari Formula 1 car to drive while not a member of the Ferrari works team. This was a total surprise and quite inexplicable. Indeed, I still don't know why it happened since there was no suggestion, as far as I ever knew, of my being put on trial as a possible Ferrari works driver." No mention that Enzo was 'doing it for Stirling' or even that Innes was well aware that he was 'standing in' because Stirling was still hospitalised.

The Ferrari was flown over to Heathrow, on loan to UK Ferrari agents, Maranello Concessionaires, with two mechanics and four engineers. A light green stripe ran the length of the car in

225

honour of the UDT/Laystall team entry. In fact Ireland knew this Ferrari quite well – from a distance. It had been raced at Aintree by junior driver, Giancarlo Baghetti (surprise winner at Reims) and Innes had kept its pace with his 4-cylinder Lotus-Climax. "It was slightly quicker on the straight but not by any great margin, and I found my old Lotus was considerably quicker through the corners."

Ireland was the first British driver to be given the chance to race these first rear-engined Ferrari Formula 1 cars. His initial impression was the performance of the V6 engine that revved to 10,000rpm, where Innes had been used to the 4-cylinder Coventry-Climax that couldn't be taken beyond 7,800rpm. "The gearbox was a dream. I honestly think that car had the best gearbox I have ever experienced in a racing machine. It was extremely easy to change from cog to cog, and terribly quick; there was no roughness, grinding or groaning. The change was absolutely positive."

Reading between the careful Ireland prose and his undoubted delight at being chosen for the Ferrari drive, it seemed that Phil Hill had been right and the Tipo 156 was not all that it had appeared to be, just that the British competition in 1961 had been below par waiting for the 1500cc V8s from Coventry Climax and BRM. In practice Innes ran with Trevor Taylor in the second works Lotus 4-cylinder and found that his Ferrari was only a shade quicker on the straight and something of a handful in the corners, flicking between understeer and over-steer. "Certainly I formed the opinion that the Ferrari did not corner as well as a Lotus." Taylor was also out-braking him. "I found that he was leaving his braking a good 25 yards later than I was at almost every corner. Frankly, I never used the brakes to the maximum, because somehow I was not confident about them. They seemed to do funny things; now and again one wheel would lock up, and occasionally the rear end would twitch as though they were about to lock. For reasons which you can well imagine, I didn't feel inclined to experiment too much with the brake pedal. I ask you, would you want to bend a Ferrari you had been loaned by the boss?"

The new British V8s had found form in the opening races of 1962 and in the International Trophy race at Silverstone on May 12, they filled the four-car front row with Graham Hill on pole with the BRM at 1min 34.6sec. Clark (Lotus) was second fastest, Surtees (Lola) third and Ginther fourth on the outside in the second BRM. Innes was in the middle of the second row at 1min 37.4sec in the Ferrari. Clark grabbed the lead from the start on a damp track, and Innes was starring in second place but first Hill came through and then Surtees in the Lola. It started raining again and Innes, no hero in the wet as he readily admitted, was holding station in fourth. The action was up front. Clark had a 19sec lead after 40 laps with 12 laps left and on lap 45 he lapped the Ferrari. "...something that would have been thought impossible last season" as the *Motor Sport* reporter noted. For reasons not immediately apparent, Clark was easing off and Hill was speeding up. As they set off on the last lap the lead gap was down to 3sec and half way round the lap, Clark came up behind a meandering Masten Gregory in a Lotus, unaware of the drama behind. Hill was now right with Clark and going into the final corner at Woodcote, he threw the BRM wide, both cars sliding wildly under heavy acceleration as the race telescoped down to the final yards – and Hill won by a nose!

Would the matching of Stirling Moss's cockpit talent and Enzo Ferrari's sharknose Ferrari have been a winning combination in 1962? History suggests probably not. Stirling's Goodwood crash may have saved him from making a major career mistake. As World Champion, Phil Hill led the Ferrari team into the 1962 season but it was a summer of despair for the Californian. His best finish was second to Bruce McLaren's Cooper at Monaco and there were thirds at Zandvoort and Spa but that was the end of it. The Ferraris that had steamrollered the season in 1961, never came close to winning in 1962. Graham Hill won four GPs and the championship in a

227

BRM V8 and Jim Clark won three GPs in the Lotus-Climax V8. Ferrari was in disarray and at the end of the season, team chief Carlo Chiti split with Enzo and led a breakaway group away from Ferrari to set up the A.T.S. team, an F1 challenge that also foundered. Moss may have been able to match the new generation of British V8s from Coventry Climax and BRM with his sheer talent in a dark blue Ferrari tended by Alf Francis for the Rob Walker team, but it seems more likely that Stirling would have gone down with the Ferrari ship in that summer of '62.

We will never know...

Sir Jackie Stewart tells a similar tale of what might have been if Enzo Ferrari had not gone back on a deal they agreed in his Maranello office late in 1967.

Racing history could have been written differently if Enzo Ferrari had signed Jackie Stewart to join Chris Amon in the Formula 1 team for 1968. Stewart had shaken hands on a deal with Enzo Ferrari only to discover within days that Ferrari wanted out of the arrangement and was telling his aides that the Scot had asked for too large a retainer. Rumour suggests that it was £20,000 – a huge retainer at the time, F1 pocket-money now. "Stewart wants *Maranello*!" Ferrari told Franco Lini, and sent the journalist-turned-team-manager down to the Formula 2 race at Enna to offer the Grand Prix drive to Jacky Ickx – Stewart's F2 team-mate!

Stewart was remembering how close he came to being a Ferrari works driver, relaxing in a huge armchair in the study of his magnificent country home not far from Silverstone, surrounded by trophies from his career as a three-time world champion.

"I had raced an LM and P1 and P2 Ferraris for Maranello Concessionaires but I had never driven a Ferrari works car until Mauro Forghieri phoned to ask if I would drive the works P4 with Chris in the 1967 BOAC 500 race at Brands Hatch. They needed extra drivers and cars to try and clinch the championship in this final round. At Porsche, Huschke von Hanstein was doing the same thing and his secretary had asked me earlier. I asked how much they were paying and she said "Money? It is an *honour* to drive for Porsche!" I explained that I was Scottish and I didn't come for free.

"When Mauro phoned and offered the P4 drive, I was delighted to accept because I honestly thought the P4 was the most beautiful racing car that had ever been built. I know the 250F Maserati is fantastic as a single-seater, but the lines of the P4 were impeccable. And I have to say that it was the *only* racing car I ever drove that felt good on the bumps at Brands Hatch!

"Chris was ill before the race started and he was ill in the car during the race which was fairly unpleasant and it meant that I had to drive a very large percentage of the race. That Ferrari felt fantastic at Brands. It was a lot to do with the damping and rebound control. We couldn't match the pace of the Chaparrals with their high wings, but it drove well and I really enjoyed working with Forghieri. If you think how much racing has changed today, Mauro was definitely of the 'old school' before telemetry when you couldn't download – you had to talk to the engineers. Mauro was very good at understanding dynamic movement if you could colour the picture for him. We finished second and that secured the championship for Ferrari which was a big deal for them.

"One of the reasons I was interested in a Ferrari Formula 1 deal was the chance to work with Forghieri. I was really in a difficult position at that time because I was with BRM, the H16 simply wasn't competitive and when the Ford engine came out, Colin Chapman and Walter Hayes signed Jimmy Clark and Graham Hill so my options were to go to Brabham or Cooper or stay with BRM...or go to Ferrari. Remember Ken Tyrrell didn't have a Formula 1 team at that point. I had made up my mind earlier that it was *not* the right thing for me to drive with Jimmy at Lotus because I had had that chance. He and I were the best of friends and we shared an apartment in London, but I decided that there weren't any other number two drivers at Lotus who were getting to do a good job. All the effort went into Jimmy.

"It was much more logical for me to go to Ferrari, or at least talk to them. Keith Ballisat at Shell had put the wheels in motion and Franco Gozzi did the interpreting. They had laid on the red carpet treatment at Maranello and the Old Man was at the gate to meet me which was pretty amazing. I never knew how he managed to do that, because that was in the days before mobile phones. I was impressed! It was an intoxicating thing to see the whole Ferrari operation at work. Remember that at that stage Ken was still working out of his timber shed at Ockham and although BRM had a good facility at Bourne, it was nowhere near the scale of Ferrari with their dynos and all the engineering equipment."

Keith Ballisat from Shell had made the contractual arrangements and Jackie and Enzo Ferrari agreed terms and shook hands on a deal for the 1968 season that would include a special arrangement for Formula 2 where the car would be painted Stewart's 'Scottish blue' on the bottom half and 'Ferrari red' on top. Ken Tyrrell would run the car in Formula 2 as a works-backed private entry, similar to the arrangement Stirling Moss had worked out to drive a privately-entered Ferrari for Rob Walker in Formula 1 in 1962.

"The instruction to Lini obviously came from Ferrari. Franco wouldn't have been 'winging it' – working on his own volition. He told Jacky Ickx that I had asked Ferrari to for too much money – 'Stewart's asked for Maranello' was the term he used – and he said that if Ickx agreed to the deal that weekend, he would drive for Ferrari in 1968. Jacky came to me and asked if I had been talking to Ferrari about next season. I told him I had and that we had a deal in principle and it was a case of having a contract drawn up. Ickx said Lini had told him if he made a quick decision, the drive was his.

"It wasn't a case of me saying 'Let me think about it and I'll get back to you.' I told Jacky to take the deal. I said I'd changed my mind and I wasn't going to drive for them. It was an easy decision for me and it was a good decision for Jacky as well. If they had told him he could have the drive, it meant they were going against what they had said to me.

"Jimmy and I were flying to Indianapolis after the race at Enna, so I had to phone Franco Gozzi at Ferrari and tell him that the deal was off. He was *really* upset.

"I suppose one of my fears about Ferrari was that I considered their record with drivers was poor, the way they always put one team driver against the other and so-and-so was favourite, but really who *was* the favourite?

"I think Chris and I would have combined well if I had driven for Ferrari in 1968. You could never have said that Chris was under-rated, it's just that somehow or other he always failed to close the loop. It's not a totally unusual thing with racing drivers. When Chris was at Ferrari, he had Forghieri to work with but I don't think Chris had what was needed in the way of all the Ferrari resources behind him, to be able to hit the nail on the head on a consistent basis. Chris had an abundance of natural talent, a God given gift of being able to drive a car in a very smooth and unspectacular way, unlike a lot of other drivers who have buckets of ability but over-drive all the time. Somehow or other throughout his career, Chris just missed out. While his driving ability would have taken him wherever he wanted to go, he never had the package.

"That's the secret of Schumacher's success at Ferrari today. He *knew* when he went to Ferrari that it wasn't what he needed so he brought the group he had experienced success with at Benetton and he added to that even more. They were getting better and learning more and were more sound, so for the past several seasons now this team is not only the top group of people but it has been lubricated properly and Schumacher has the skill level to call the tune all the time."

The End of the Beginning – 100 Years on from Paris-Madrid

It was the end of the beginning. The last of the great city to city races across Europe. Almost the end of motor racing. It was the ultimate motoring classic in a century only three years old with automobiles still a noisy novelty but growing fast. Eight hundred miles flat out on the roads of the day, from Paris to Madrid, in 1903. It beggars belief even now, a century on. There would be high-speed crashes, driver deaths and spectator fatalities in an event that could not be contemplated now, even with the latest competition cars and the best efforts at crowd control.

Gabriel's winning average in the 11.6-litre 4-cylinder Mors revving to 1100rpm, was a flicker short of 60mph – 59.9mph – which must have meant fighting speeds up to 90mph all the way through the blinding dust from his mid-field starting position, to the first and what would turn out to be the final stop at Bordeaux. The Mors looked more like an upturned boat with a wind-splitting nose pre-dating conventional aerodynamics.

There had been a race from Paris to Rouen in 1894 but this was more of a challenge to the reliability of the new-fangled automobile than any contest of speed. Continuation of forward motion was the target in those early days, never mind pace. There would be later races radiating from Paris to Bordeaux, Marseilles, Dieppe, Amsterdam, Berlin and in 1902 to Vienna. For 1903 the ultimate road race was to be run from Paris to Madrid, 800 miles over dusty roads designed for horses not horsepower. The French authorities were becoming nervously wary of the dangers of these races over public roads, but the Spanish King Alphonse XIII was eager to share the technological

232

excitement of the new century. The competitors were aware of the horrors of Spanish roads and were reckoning to make up speed on the French stages, and reduce pace over the Spanish unknowns.

The race was scheduled to start in the pre-dawn of Sunday, May 24, 1903 with an entry of 314 competitors in cars and motorcycles flagged away at 60sec intervals. There were only 13,000 cars registered in France then, so the automobile was still an object of curiosity, and a *speed contest* was guaranteed to draw huge crowds. These enthusiastic and largely uncontrolled crowds would contribute to the demise of the European road races.

There were three categories with maximum weight limits of 400kg for the voiturettes, 650kg for light cars and 1000kg for the biggest contenders.

Charles Rolls was entered in a French Panhard, or more properly *on* a Panhard as the driver sat high above his machine with no concession to the elements or stones thrown high by other cars. Charles Jarrott, the British champion had drawn number one in the ballot for starting position in the long lineup. His huge De Dietrich had finned gill radiator tubes stacked squarely at the front of the car. The riding mechanic, Bianchi, who would help with tyre changes and engine-tending as well as warning of faster cars endeavouring to pass, usually sat lower to the side of his driver. Neither had any form of safety restraint and loss of control meant the luckless *mechanician* was flung out. The driver could at least cling on to the steering wheel.

Vincenzo Florio, later to father the Targa Florio race in Sicily, was a keen entrant in the Paris-Madrid classic in a new 90hp Panhard but his elder brother and guardian, Ignazio, effectively marooned him on the Mediterranean family-owned island of Favignano by sending him on a tunny fishing expedition and giving orders for no boat to return to the mainland without his written consent. Vincenzo was allowed to nominate Teste in his place with Felice Nazzarro. They finished 18th.

Jarrott wrote a book on his racing career in 1906, titled *Ten Years of Motors and Motor Racing.* Phil Hill, 1961 World Champion for Ferrari, himself a polished penman today, rates this early tome as one of his favourite books on motor sport. A second edition was published in 1912, a third in 1928 and, amazingly, a fourth edition in 1956. Jarrott died in 1944 and he notes in an introduction to the 1928 edition that the publisher suggested he update his original manuscript but he boldly refused, preferring to leave his original writings, opinions and descriptions unchanged.

Jarrott might have been sitting lower behind his motorcar but this advanced design for De Dietrich by the talented young Ettore Bugatti had been rejected by the Department of Mining Engineers, the government agency charged with control of the engineering standards of these complicated new automobiles. Bugatti was reportedly furious.

Louis Renault was starting behind Jarrott in a car built by the company he shared with his brothers, Marcel and Ferdinand. Chains and belts were the transmissions of the day, but the Renault brothers had pioneered direct drive by a pair of pinions. The Renaults flaunted an early form of streamlining with a swooping nose, afforded by surface-cooling radiators along either side of the engine and contrasting with the square fronts of most cars of the day. Louis's riding mechanic was a young Hungarian, Ferenc (Franz or Francois) Szisz, who would win the 1906 Grand Prix for Renault as a driver in his own right. Marcel Renault's draw for the start placed him as 63rd starter.

Herbert Austin was another who would soon build a car carrying his own name but on the race to Spain, he was driving one of three Wolseley 'Beetles', so called because of their low bonnet line allowed by the horizontal arrangement of the cylinders. As a young man, Austin had worked for the Wolseley Sheep Shearing Machinery company in Australia, returning to Birmingham to persuade the company to branch into the automobile business. Sidney Girling drove a second Wolseley and

234

the third was driven by an Irishman, Leslie Porter.

Brakes on these early cars offered little more than a steadying form of slowing rather than any suggestion of stopping, which added a further dimension of danger to the excitement of conducting these antiques at speeds up to 90mph. Girling would become a pioneer in the development of braking systems.

Crowds were estimated at 20,000 crammed into the Tuileries Gardens at Versailles for the start. The day before, the cars had been scrutineered, weighed and fixed with seals for customs identification when they crossed the border into Spain. Each car was fitted with a small, sealed metal box with a slot on the top to accept a card noting times of arrival and starting at each control to speed the results count at the end of the run. Each car also received the attention of a gentleman with a die and hammer, who made 'indelible marks on the axles and other parts capable of being surreptitiously replaced.' The engine number was also noted.

Each entrant was handed two elegantly hard-bound fold-out maps of the route, one from Paris to the border, and the other from the border across Spain to Madrid. The second book was fated never be used.

Jarrott wrote in his memoirs that he had dined the night before the with English De Dietrich team-mates Stead, a Yorkshireman living in France and Claude Lorraine Barrow, who lived in Biarritz.

"Barrow and I had lived together, worked together, and waited together during that wretched week (before the race) in Paris, when it seemed impossible for human hands to overcome the troubles which cropped up at every turn in preparing our cars. My one great consolation lay in the fact that Stead's and Barrow's machines were giving as much or nearly as much trouble as mine."

After scrutineering the De Dietrichs were rushed back to the workshops and frantic preparation work continued. Stead's car was finished first on the night before the race, then Barrow's.

"He shook hands and said he would keep dinner for me at the hotel. I was left disconsolate, realising that even if my car went at all, I had no chance of doing anything with it, as I had never had it on the road."

Jarrott's main problem was a slipping clutch and they had fitted a lever to force the clutch in if problems continued. When he was finally cleared to leave for his hotel, he was amazed to find that the car was running cleanly. "Untried as it was, I nevertheless quickly realised that it was capable of travelling quite fast, but as for Madrid, why of course it was an impossibility..."

Barrow and Stead had waited for Jarrott until the dining room was closing and they were eating when he eventually arrived. Let Jarrott tell the incredible situation as he arrived at the restaurant. "There occurred one of those tragic little prophecies which are met with sometimes through that strange law which seems in some manner to give an inkling to mankind of the dark and misty future. The incident is as clearly defined in my memory now as when it occurred. As I approached, Barrow was raising a glass to his lips, and seeing me walking towards him he set it down, and expressed his delight that I had at last got to the start safely, and then, seeing me still lugubrious and unhappy, he slapped me on the back, and again raising his glass exclaimed: 'Whatever is the matter with you! Are we not all here? Let us eat, drink and be merry, for tomorrow we die!' – words spoken in jest, but (which would be) fulfilled to the bitter end."

At 2 a.m. Barrow woke Jarrott, they had a hurried cup of hot chocolate and started their cars in darkness. Perversely, Jarrott's car which had given so much trouble the previous day, fired up immediately and it was Stead's De Dietrich that refused to start. Jarrott had to rush to take his 'pole position' and he bade Barrow farewell.

"Never did I wish a friend good luck more sincerely than I did Lorraine Barrow on that eventful morning, and never did a wish go more awry. It was the last time I ever saw him, and the memory of that hand- grip in the darkness in the hotel yard at Versailles is one of my few sad recollections in connection with motor-racing."

The Autocar reported that 'The morning now quickened every minute and at five and twenty minutes to four the loud report of a bomb intimated that the officials were about to take the start. The engines of the first half dozen were now running, and while the din of the buzzing monsters was almost deafening. The blue haze of burnt lubricating oil rose up in huge volumes, poisoning the morning air. One of the officials scribbled something on a card, and, lifting the lid of the tea-caddy shaped metal box affixed to the side of the De Dietrich, asked Jarrott to get ready. The cool hand settled himself, his *mechanician* (Bianchi) took his seat, and the first speed was slipped in..."

The start of the last Great Race had all the crowded excitement of an event of Homeric proportions. "On with the switch and away went the motor," Jarrott wrote. It was his car that would cut the first swathe through the surging crowds. "It seemed impossible that my swaying, bounding car could miss the reckless spectators. A wedge-shaped space opened out in the crowd as I approached and so fine was the calculation made that at times it seemed impossible for the car not to overtake the apex of the human triangle and deal with death and destruction. I tried slowing down, but quickly realised that the danger was as great at forty miles an hour as at eighty..."

The last of the motorcycles was flagged away at 6.45am and race officials and members of the Automobile Club were already on their way to Bordeaux by a special train with saloon cars well supplied with champagne and food. A total of 215 cars and 57 motorcycles were away down a dusty ribbon of tree-lined highway on the 350 miles south-east route to Bordeaux and the oblivion that would threaten the very future of the new sport of racing with automobiles.

The front runners enjoyed the open road, denied those late starters who were forced to race through slower traffic in the

237

blinding dust. Louis Renault went through to the front, passing Jarrott and later De Knyff came past Jarrott as well but soon the old-car problems of punctures and fuel blockages caused roadside repairs while Marcel Renault in a family entry and Gabriel in the Mors battled past car after car, more by luck than skill and often guided only by the tops of the trees to judge the curves and corners.

The incidents on the long run from Paris to Bordeaux could only be covered retrospectively as reports of accidents and incidents brought in by finishing drivers reflecting glanced observations in passing or roadside rumours. The road was supposedly free of traffic for the race but in fact it seemed like just another day for French country folk. Serpollet on his steam car reported a long line of wagons piled with wood, some of them 30-40 yards in length, crawling along the race route oblivious to regulations...

Louis Renault made the pace out front and led into most of the 'neutralised' towns en route through Tours, Poitiers and Angouleme where vintage racing is now staged on course around the historic city ramparts.

W.F. Bradley recorded that Vanderbilt's Mercedes was out with a cracked cylinder while Baron de Caters 90hp Mercedes had hit a tree in a blind overtaking manoeuvre. A young woman had been killed, running across the road in Ablis soon after the start. Leslie Porter arrived at speed at a closed railway crossing, swerved into a ploughed field avoiding a house in his Wolseley and somersaulted. When Porter regained consciousness he realised his mechanic had been trapped under the blazing car and had been burned to death. "I felt this race might be dangerous," Porter told Bradley. "Just before the start I gave my mechanic all the cash I had, about 7000 francs to be used, 'just in case'..."

Jarrott was getting into his stride running second or third on the road when he was passed by Werner's Mercedes as they left Tours. "Five kilometres farther on, with a wrench of the wheel I just missed the fragments of his car in the road, smashed to bits and in the same second I saw both Werner and his man standing by the car, obviously unhurt and the corner sufficiently unconcerned as to be occupied in lighting a cigarette before even he could have known the cause of the accident."

The contemporary mention of Werner's riding mechanic as 'his man' makes him sound like a rider's groom, which, in the context of the day when more gentlemen had horses than automobiles, I suppose he was regarded as such.

Fifty miles from Bordeaux, Delaney in a De Dietrich missed a corner completely and plunged off the road, mounting a high banking. Contemporary accounts argue whether the car was on its wheels or upside down, but agree that Delaney and his mechanic escaped from the wreck and then Delaney ran back to rescue his camera and take a photograph of his amazing escape. His grandson, Tom Delaney, following the family racing trait and still competes in the Lea Francis he bought to race in the Ards TT races in the 1930s!

C.S. Rolls gave up near this incident in his Panhard & Levassor, Mark Mayhew retired the sole Napier entry with broken steering and Austin and Girling had retired their Wolseleys.

Stead was hounding Salleron's Mors. "They were racing side by side at probably 70mph, the drivers and mechanics yelling excitedly," reported Bradley. "Salleron swerved slightly, his car striking the De Dietrich and throwing it out of control across the road into a ditch, where it overturned, pinning the driver to the ground." The Mors continued but Stead was seriously hurt and Madame du Gast, the only lady driver in the event, also in a De Dietrich, abandoned the race and spent three hours attending to Stead's injuries.

Marcel Renault had been storming alongside Thery's Decauville in the dust, missed a yellow flag warning a dangerous corner and despite Thery's shouted warning, Renault plunged past going far too fast to make the bend. Marcel spun, overturned, and suffered severe injuries. Maurice Farman, stopped and like Madame du Gast, abandoned the race to get help for his friend.

The three Farman brothers were Renault agents in Paris and close friends of the three Renault brothers. Farman borrowed a farmer's bicycle and went in search of a doctor but Renault died of his injuries. He was 32.

The final stages of the run to from Angouleme to Bordeaux saw the worst of the crashes but for Jarrott with a clear road, it was heady run to the finish and in those 90 kilometres he had averaged over 60mph and halved Louis Renault's lead to fifteen minutes.

As other cars arrived they brought the stories of crashes and injuries and Jarrott wrote "Every driver had a different story, until at last it seemed as if the road of passage must have been bestrewn with dead and dying. Who was killed? Who was hurt? What had happened?"

Lorraine Barrow had hit a dog and jammed his steering, slamming head-on into a tree and his mechanic was killed instantly. Barrow received injuries that would prove fatal 18 days later. Stead also succumbed to his injuries, both in the same hospital in Libourne, leaving a shocked Jarrott to dwell on their 'Eat drink and be merry,' toast of the previous evening...

The tragic chaos of the event had reinforced the original opinion of the French authorities and they cancelled the remainder of the race, taking possession of the cars in Bordeaux. Special trains were arranged and the cars were hauled to the railway station by horses. Motors were not allowed to be started. The internal combustion engine was receiving its share of the blame for the carnage.

Gabriel's Mors was adjudged the winner on elapsed time, having driven a truly heroic race, starting 168th and fighting his way past every car and driver in the towering dust clouds. His time was 5hrs 14min at an average of 59.9mph and Salleron on another Mors was second. Jarrott was classified third in the De Dietrich in the big car class, although Louis Renault had won the Light Car class and finished ahead of Jarrott on the road.

Marcel Renault's death prompted Louis to withdraw from

racing, although Renault would return to win the Grand Prix in 1906 (with Louis's Paris-Madrid *mechanician*, Szisz at the wheel) at which point the company withdrew again, not returning to Grand Prix racing until 1977! As well as being one of the top French racing drivers, Marcel was an astute businessman and something of a ladies' man with a mistress, Suzanne Davenay, who inherited a one-third share of the Renault car company. She insisted on a cash payment which would have brought the fledgling company to the point of failure, but Louis persuaded her to take a substantial annuity and a new Renault car every year in full and final settlement. Suzanne died half a century later, in 1953...

Two days after the race had been terminated, Jarrott drove back to Paris with Madame du Gast and Baron de Turckheim. "The number of cars left upon the road was extraordinary. The most fearsome and terrible sight was the fragments which remained of Lorraine Barrow's car. His *mechanician*, Pierre, a Spaniard and an old servant of Barrow's, was shot out of the car, head-on into the tree and killed instantly. Barrow himself had been flung out of the car, clearing the tree and pitching over twenty yards away into the ditch on the side of the road, sustaining terrible and, as it eventually proved, fatal injuries.

"I have in many races seen many cars wrecked, but never could I have conceived it possible for any car to be so completely broken up as was Barrow's. One of the front spring hangers was driven up to the hilt and broken off short in the tree, the force of the impact being so great that the strap holding the starting handle and the string and leaden customs seal were also driven right into the solid wood. The car, as a car, did not exist. The shock had torn the motor out of the frame and hurled it yards away, and even the pistons themselves in the motor, were in fragments, scattered in the road; frame, gearbox and road wheels were all in small pieces.

"As I stood and gazed on the ghastly evidence of this tragedy I thought how quickly had come the end to my cheery and

241

good-natured friend. At one moment slipping along on the road, all well, driving a fine race and rejoicing in the knowledge that Bordeaux was but thirty kilometres away, and then the fearful crash, the momentary realisation of disaster, oblivion, and eventually – death.

"And thus ended the most dramatic race in the history of automobilism..."